Lenin, Trotsky
and the
Theory of Permanent Revolution

John Peter Roberts

well red
books

Lenin, Trotsky, and the Theory of Permanent Revolution
By John Peter Roberts

First published by Wellred December 2007
Foreword by Alan Woods
Copyright © Wellred Publications

UK distribution: Wellred Books, PO Box 50525
London E14 6WG, England
Tel: +44 (0) 207 515 7675

USA distribution: Wellred books, PO Box 1331
Fargo, ND, 58103, USA. wellredusa.com

Wellred on-line bookshop sales: wellred.marxist.com

Typeset by Wellred
Printed by intypelibra, London, England

British Library cataloguing in Publication Data
A catalogue record for this book is available from the British Library

ISBN-13 9781 900007 32 0
ISBN- 1 900007 32 0

Cover design by Espe Espigares

CONTENTS

FOREWORD

The publication of *Lenin, Trotsky and the Theory of Permanent Revolution* comes at an appropriate moment. 2007 is the 90th anniversary of the October Revolution, an event which, whatever you may think of it, undoubtedly represents one of the turning points in world history.

In the past one and a half decades since the fall of the Soviet Union there has been an avalanche of books which claim to represent a "startling new appraisal" of the Russian Revolution and its principal leaders, Lenin and Trotsky. The purpose of this new literary genre is quite clear: to discredit the Bolshevik revolution in the eyes of the new generation.

It is therefore refreshing to read a book which, with a wealth of interesting material based upon an exhaustive research of the subject, develops new insights into the history of Bolshevism and the Russian Revolution. This book is well written and logically structured, each part being related to what has gone before and what follows. A wide range of authorities are quoted, providing a comprehensive bibliography on the subject. Above all, the author allows Lenin and Trotsky to speak for themselves. The numerous quotes from these outstanding revolutionaries allows the unprejudiced reader to form his or her own judgement on their ideas and their place in history.

Particularly interesting is the detailed account of the way in which Lenin's position on the nature of the Russian Revolution evolved from his original theory of the democratic dictatorship of the proletariat and peasantry to his final position in 1917. The author provides a wealth of quotes of Lenin and Trotsky which conclusively show how the two men, proceeding by different routes, eventually arrived at the same conclusions.

This book includes a lively and accurate account of the events of 1917. It details the inner-party struggle by means of which Lenin achieved the ideological rearming of the Bolshevik Party after his return to Russia in April 1917. The author shows clearly that the intention of the Bolsheviks was not to achieve a "Russian road to socialism" but to ignite the flame of international revolution.

Of particular interest to present-day students of Marxism is the author's polemic against revisionist writers such as Doug Lorimer, who has attempted to revive the old discredited formula of the democratic dictatorship of the proletariat and peasantry and the Menshevik-Stalinist theory of two stages. Where ever this theory has been put into practice it has led to bloody defeats. The most terrible example was the massacre of one and a half million Communists in Indonesia in 1965-66.

The experience of the Venezuelan revolution is a living proof of the impossibility of limiting the revolution in Third World countries to the tasks of the bourgeois democratic revolution. Through his own experience, Hugo Chávez has drawn the conclusion that the Bolivarian revolution, if it is to succeed must go beyond the limits of capitalism and carry out the socialist transformation of society. What is this, if not the permanent revolution?

One could make criticisms (what book cannot be criticised?), but these criticisms are of a secondary character, and do not affect the overall positive impression this book makes. The Russian Revolution had an enormous impact on the European working class. It led immediately to the November revolution in Germany in 1918, which was followed by a series of revolutionary upheavals in that country which only terminated in 1923. One year later, in 1919, there was a revolution in Hungary. In the same year a Soviet Republic was briefly declared in Bavaria. There were also revolutionary upheavals in Britain, France, Italy, Bulgaria, Estonia and other countries. These events demonstrated the essential correctness of Lenin's (and Trotsky's) perspective that the Russian Revolution could be the start of the European socialist revolution.

The reason why these revolutionary movements did not lead to the working class taking power was the absence of mass revolutionary parties and the betrayal of the leaders of Social Democracy. The revolutionary movement of the European working class was strong enough to prevent military intervention against Soviet Russia (in 1920 the leaders of the British Trade Unions threatened the government with a general strike over this) but was paralysed by the leadership of the labour movement.

The book quotes the words of the English historian E.H. Carr: "... The innumerable economic conflicts that had gone on before October now multiplied, and indeed became more serious as the combativity of the contestants was everywhere greater. The initiative for acts of expropriation, undertaken as necessities of struggle rather than according to any design for socialism, came from the masses rather than the government. It was only eight months later, in June 1918, that the government adopted the great decrees of nationalisation, under the pressure of foreign intervention. Even in April 1918 it was envisaging the formation of mixed companies which would have been floated jointly by the state and by Russian and foreign capital.

"The liquidation of the political defences of their capitalist exploiters launched a spontaneous movement among the workers to take over the means of production. Since they were perfectly able to take control of the factories and workshops, why should they abstain? The employers sabotage of production entailed expropriation as an act of reprisal. When the boss brought work to a halt, the workers themselves, on their own responsibility, got the establishment going again. [Council of Peoples' Commissars had to decree the nationalisation of Russo-Belgian Metal Company's factories, the Putilov works, the Smirnov spinning-mills and the power station belonging to the 1886 Electrical Company.]".

These words could have been written today in relation to the situation that is developing in Venezuela. Of course, the destiny of the Venezuelan revolution has still not been decided by history. However, it shows that the theoretical controversies that formed an essential part of the history of Bolshevism are not only of academic interest. They have a direct bearing on the events of our own times, and it is quite impossible to understand these events without having made a careful study of the history and ideas of Bolshevism. In this respect John Roberts' book represents a most valuable contribution.

Alan Woods. London. 2nd December 2007.

8

ABBREVIATIONS AND EXPLANATORY NOTES

CI   Communist International
Imperialism   Imperialism, the Highest Stage of Capitalism
RDDPP   Revolutionary Democratic Dictatorship of the Proletariat
                      and Peasantry
RSDLP   Russian Social-Democratic Labour Party
RSDLP(B)   Russian Social-Democratic Labour Party (Bolsheviks)
SD   Social Democracy or Social Democrat, as determined by
                      the context
SDs   Social Democrats
SR   Socialist Revolutionary
SRs   Socialist Revolutionaries
The ... Renegade Kautsky The Proletariat Revolution and the Renegade
                      Kautsky
ToPR   Theory of Permanent Revolution
Two Tactics   The Two Tactics of Social Democracy in the Democratic
                      Revolution

St Petersburg
St Petersburg, capital of the Tsarist empire, had its name changed to
Petrograd in 1914.

Dates
All dates before 1 February 1918 are given according to the old Russian,
Julian calendar which was 13 days behind that used in the West. To change
to a modern calendar add 13 days.

Emphasis
Within quotations the author's original emphasis is indicated by *italic script*.
Added emphasis is in **bold script**.

Within quotations, explanatory notes are contained within square brackets,
[...]

INTRODUCTION

The collapse of the Soviet Union and the so-called socialist states of Eastern Europe, followed by the transition of China to a capitalist economy, confirm the essential correctness of both Lenin's and Trotsky's appraisal that the Russian Soviet state they established would inevitably be defeated if there were no socialist revolution in the advanced capitalist countries. These world-changing events also validate Trotskyist claims that the Soviet bureaucracy not only failed to produce socialism in Russia, but also to ensure its own continued existence.

Trotsky and Lenin were the acknowledged leaders of the world's first socialist revolution in October 1917. This book seeks to show, by studying Lenin's own writings, that the October Revolution followed the trajectory predicted by Trotsky's Theory of Permanent Revolution (*ToPR*), and argues that in early 1917 Lenin broke with his previous goal of a revolutionary bourgeois Russian state, and from April onwards adopted a permanentist policy that was, to all intents and purposes, identical with Trotsky's.

Amazingly, the author has found no systematic analysis of Lenin's published writings that attempts to show the transition of his ideas to congruence with the *ToPR*. This analysis limits itself to texts available in English, so that each and every reference can be checked for authenticity by the reader. This is considered legitimate and desirable; the belief that a researcher can produce a more accurate translation of the original than those available smacks of arrogance, while references to one or other of the various editions of Lenin's Collected Works in Russian appears 'academic' in the worst sense since most of the editions referred to were edited and produced after the bitter faction fights of the 1920s and 30s were over, and the Stalinist wing of the bureaucracy was in control. The more recent access to secret archives of the CPSU after the fall of the Soviet Union has contributed nothing qualitatively new to our knowledge of the development of Lenin's ideas in the period up to 1921 because Stalin and the future rulers of the USSR added little or nothing to the discussions at the time.

While this book is based on events in Russia that took place before 1921, the author considers the *ToPR* to remain highly relevant today, and that any serious attempt to revive consideration of it is worthwhile. In a great many of the countries in the Middle East, in Asia, in Africa and in Latin America, the essential tasks of the bourgeois revolution - democratisation, secularisation, and the solution of the agrarian question, have not been accomplished, and will not be accomplished without a permanentist perspective. Nevertheless, it is not within the scope of this book to examine whether the *ToPR* has been further verified by the history of the 20th century, positively as in the revolutions in, say, Cuba (1959) and China (1949), and negatively by the demise of the Soviet Union (1991). Nor does the book attempt to discuss any limitations of Trotsky's analysis, but instead restricts itself to the one revolution which Trotsky most definitely led to victory - the Russian Revolution.

The Russian, Eastern European and Chinese bureaucracies are no longer an ideological and financial prop for a tirade of lies against Trotsky, Trotskyists, and the *ToPR*. This makes it much easier to have an objective discussion and reach a new audience for the proposition that Lenin adopted a permanentist orientation in 1917. However, for two generations the Soviet bureaucracy, founded on the basis of opposition to the Theory of Permanent Revolution, held state power in its hands, meaning that its class collaborationist ideas have been long and widely promoted on a world scale by the various national Communist Parties, and have entered the consciousness of many revolutionaries. Most recently, the failure, so far, of President Chàvez in Venezuela to take power through a popular, socialist revolution, is a consequence of this non-Leninist tradition. It is thus, timely to re-investigate and re-discover Lenin's actual politics in 1917 and, hopefully, participate in their re-invigoration.

This book demonstrates that Lenin, in 1917, threw aside his stagist approach to the Russian revolution, as expressed in the Revolutionary Democratic Dictatorship of the Proletariat and Peasantry *(RDDPP)*, and adopted a more permanentist approach; that the agrarian problem in semi-feudal Russia could only be solved by a revolution that placed all state power in the hands of the proletariat. In particular it shows that:

- in April 1917 Lenin replaced his perspective that the Russian socialist Revolution would follow the socialist revolution in western Europe, with the core concept of the *ToPR*, that the international socialist revolution could begin in semi-feudal Russia before it began in the west,
- during 1917, Lenin replaced the Constituent Assembly as the governmental goal of the Russian Revolution with Commune-type Soviets that would immediately take the first steps towards socialism,
- from August 1917 Lenin explicitly argued that the Russian Revolution could solve the land question only if all state power were in the hands of the proletariat,
- in October Lenin demanded that the Bolsheviks alone lead the armed uprising and, in direct contrast to his previous perspective in which a revolutionary government with a majority of SDs was not only undesirable but 'impossible', justified a Bolshevik-**only** government as the legitimate expression of Soviet rule.

- after October 1917 Lenin consistently presented the October Revolution as a socialist revolution, and the regime that resulted from it the dictatorship of the proletariat,

and by reviewing and criticising alternative interpretations the book demonstrates that the arguments underpinning the claim that the post-October 1917 regime in Russia was the *RDDPP* until at least the summer of 1918, are fatally flawed on a number of levels.

The first chapter introduces the two main protagonists, Lenin and Trotsky, briefly gives their backgrounds, and outlines their interaction from the 1903 Second Congress of the Russian Social Democratic Labour Party (RSDLP) to the outbreak of the 1905 Revolution.

Chapter 2 charts the experiences of the two men during the first Russian Revolution, and explores how those experiences influenced the development of the two theories: the *RDDPP*, and the *ToPR*.

Chapter 3 further investigates the origins and content of the Bolshevik programmatic slogan of the *RDDPP*. The chapter discusses the slogan itself, attempts to identify what was new in it and what elements Lenin retained in common with his Menshevik opponents. Importantly, the outcomes Lenin expected from the implementation of the slogan are given. Chapter 4 does the same for Trotsky's *ToPR*.

Chapter 5 argues that in the period February to October 1917, Lenin's strategy for the Russian Revolution passed from the stagist position of 1905, to a position that was, in all essence, identical to the *ToPR*.

Chapter 6 reviews Lenin's writings from October 1917 through to the summer of 1918, and searches for any indications that he was not working consciously and deliberately towards a proletarian revolution that would transfer all state power to the proletariat and initiate the first steps towards socialism. It shows that in the nine months from the October Revolution to the summer of 1918, Lenin consistently described that revolution as a socialist, proletarian revolution with a Workers' and Peasants' Government resting on the dictatorship of the proletariat.

Chapter 7 examines the demand for a Constituent Assembly - one of the 'three pillars of Bolshevism' - in the context of the October Revolution, and compares the scenario envisaged by Lenin for the *RDDPP* with actual events.

Chapter 8 concludes that Lenin, as much as Trotsky, is the author of the proposition that in the epoch of imperialism, in a backward, semi-feudal economy, the agrarian problem can be solved only after the proletarian revolution and the beginning of the dictatorship of the proletariat.

Chapter 1
LENIN, TROTSKY, AND THE REVOLUTIONARY PARTY (1903)

1.1   Introduction
1.2   Lenin
1.3   Lenin's Conception of the Party
1.4   Trotsky Arrives
1.5   The 1903 Second Congress of the *RSDLP*
1.6   References

1.1 Introduction

Lenin considered Trotsky as one of his main opponents for most of his political life. This hostility was largely determined by the disagreements between the two men on the nature of the political party required for a successful revolution in Russia. Because the disagreements between Lenin and Trotsky were such an important element in the way Trotsky's theory of Permanent Revolution (*ToPR*) was first received, and largely ignored, it is necessary to give some relevant background. Especially as, in later years, these disagreements would provide the Soviet bureaucracy with a smoke-screen behind which to hide their slide into class collaboration.

The differences over the nature of the party first showed themselves in the divisions that occurred during, and after, the 1903 Second Congress of the Russian Social Democratic Labour Party (*RSDLP*). Lenin's goal for the Congress was the creation of a disciplined, centralised Marxist party of professional revolutionaries but, at that time, so new was the concept that even his closest co-workers failed to appreciate the absolute necessity of such an organisation for the success of the Russian Revolution.

The divide in the *RSDLP* took place in the context of a new, organisationally immature party whose leaders, while of the first order politically and personally, did not have the experience to place personal considerations second to political. Consequently, even amongst the *RSDLP* leaders, opposition to Lenin's idea, at least initially, tended to be expressed in terms of personalities. Indeed, it was Lenin's attempt to remove the veteran Social Democrat (*SD*) Vera Zasulich, from the editorial board of *Iskra (The Spark)*, that initiated the rupture in relations between himself and Trotsky that lasted some fourteen years, until the spring of 1917. The young Trotsky did not have the experience or political maturity to recognise that the differences over the composition of the editorial board were political, not personal.

1.2 Lenin

Vladimir Ilyich Lenin's elder brother Alexander, was hanged for an attempt on the life of Tsar Alexander III in March 1887 when Lenin was just seventeen and this, combined with political activity by Lenin himself, meant he was excluded from all Russian universities. Lenin's intellect, his single-mindedness and determination were made clear when, in 1891, after a period of respectability, the Tsarist police agreed to his request to take the final law examinations at an imperial university (St Petersburg). Normal preparation for these examinations was four-years' full-time study. Lenin's situation meant he had just eleven months to prepare and had to study alone at home. Lenin took his examinations during the illness and final days of his younger sister, Olga, who died of typhoid on the very day that four years earlier Alexander had been executed. Lenin passed each of the thirteen examinations with the highest grade, and achieved the highest aggregate mark in a class of 134[1].

By 1895, Lenin was living in St Petersburg, a full-time revolutionary leading a group of about a dozen (including his future wife, Nazdezhda Krupskaya), which had established links with militants in many of the workers' districts[2]. In the November of that year, a newly-established group of *SD*s led by Julius Martov fused with the so-called 'veterans'. Martov, three years Lenin's junior, a gifted writer and dedicated socialist, was to be Lenin's closest collaborator for the next seven years[3].

On 19 December, a meeting of Lenin and others to discuss the first issue of a Marxist newspaper, *Rabocheye Dyelo (The Workers' Cause),* was raided by the police who found the material written for the journal. The participants were arrested for possession of illegal literature. By early January, Martov and the other members of the St Petersburg group had also been rounded up. All were held in prison over a year for interrogation, and in January 1897, Lenin, Martov and the other members of the group were sentenced to three years exile in Siberia[4].

It took nearly eight weeks to reach the village of exile, Shushenskoye, but, despite the physical isolation, Lenin's day-to-day conditions allowed him to write a number of important works including *The Tasks of the Russian Social Democrats*[5] (Autumn 1898) and *A Draft Programme of Our Party*[6] (end of 1899). Lenin was able to keep abreast of events in Russian Social Democracy (*SD*), and communicate his opinions to its leaders, including those outside Russia. He also wrote and prepared for publication, a major book, *The Development of Capitalism in Russia*[7] (1899), probably the best analysis of capitalism emerging from feudalism in the literature of Marxism. Lenin emphasised Russian internal economic development to the virtual exclusion of foreign investment, whether industrial or finance capital because, at that time, he was seeking to show that capitalism would inevitably arise in Russia as part of the natural economic processes in the countryside[8,9]. This was in marked contrast to Trotsky who, as will be shown, emphasised the relative importance of foreign investment in the growth of modern industry in Russia, and made it a key feature of his analysis.

At this stage of his development, Lenin was already an important figure in the internal life of Russian *SD* as an exponent of the orthodox, or "classical", Marxism of the pre-1917 leaders of European *SD*, such as Kautsky. Just how important was demonstrated during the period of his arrest and exile when a reformist current (Economism), supported by Russian *SD*s, who believed their main activities should be organising strike support funds and workers' self-help circles, began to crystallise around the newspaper *Workers' Thought* which promoted economic activity as an end in itself. With Lenin in Siberia, the fight against Economism was left to Georgy Valentinovitch Plekhanov, a brilliant Marxist theoretician with a European-wide reputation, who had made Marxism intellectually respectable in Russia, and who, through his writings, was the acknowledged teacher of all the leaders of the new generation of Marxists now coming to the fore in Russia. However, on its own, the Emancipation of Labour Group singularly failed to halt the new reformist current, and it was not until the re-entry into the struggle of Lenin and Martov, that the balance was tipped decisively against reformism.

During Lenin's exile, the First Congress of Russian *SD*s was held in Minsk in March 1898, attended by nine delegates representing groups from Moscow, Kiev, St Petersburg and Yekaterinoslav, as well as *The Workers' Journal* group and a Jewish Social Democratic organisation, the Bund. Within weeks, five of the nine delegates and some 500 *SD*s nationally had been arrested[10]. To Lenin, the outcomes of the Congress demonstrated the impossibility of having the Social Democratic organisational centre inside Russia, and he called for this to be located abroad, in a country where conditions permitted continuity of leadership and relative freedom of the press.

1.3 Lenin's Conception of the Party

It was during his exile, that Lenin devised his plan for the unification of Russian Marxists into a national party. The key to this was the production of a widely distributed national newspaper, *Iskra*, to be produced fortnightly, to become the champion of revolutionary Marxism. However, since police persecution made the regular publication of a revolutionary newspaper in Russia impossible, Lenin planned to publish the paper abroad, using a chain of agents to smuggle it into Russia and distribute it.

Repression by the Tsarist authorities, and the arrest and exile of militants as soon as they came to police attention, meant a lack of continuity in leadership; the resulting political and organisational inexperience meant that *SD* in Russia was fragmented and immersed in local work which, in turn, led to a bending to local pressures with the consequent spontaneous generation of reformist tendencies. Lenin saw that a necessary step towards eliminating such shortcomings and welding the diverse local currents into a single, All-Russian Social Democratic movement, was the creation of an All-Russian political newspaper. Without such a newspaper the party could neither effectively communicate its propaganda and agitation, even to its own members, nor focus its activities. The role of a newspaper had also to be as a collective organiser; likened by Lenin to the scaffolding round a building under construction, "which marks the contours of the structure and facilitates communication between the builders, enabling them to distribute the work and to view the common results achieved by their organised labour"[11]. He posed the simple question, if Russian *SD*s were unable to organise their own paper, how on earth could they organise to overthrow the Tsar?

The technical tasks of supplying the newspaper with copy, and of regularly distributing it, required an organised, disciplined network of party agents. To be successful, these agents would have to work in close and regular contact with the local party organisations and have their active support. For Lenin, this had the hugely important consequence of unifying the disparate elements that then formed *SD* in Russia. The Central Committee was to be the brains of the organisation, the agents the skeleton, and the local organisation, the eyes, ears and muscles.

Because of Plekhanov's eminence, the strategy of building a revolutionary party around a Marxist newspaper could only succeed if the paper were associated with him, and its editorial board included leading members of the Emancipation of Labour Group (founded in 1883 and led by Plekhanov, Zasulich, and another prominent Marxist, Pavel Axelrod)[12]. With fellow exile Arsenyev Potresov (who had inherited some money which he used to finance the publication of Marxist works), Lenin and Martov determined on joining forces with their co-thinkers in the Emancipation of Labour Group. By the time of his release from exile on 29 January 1900, Lenin's life-goal - the building of the Russian revolutionary Marxist Party - was decided. He began to put this plan into effect immediately his term of exile ended.

For six months Lenin criss-crossed European Russia illegally, visiting Social Democratic groups in Ufa (February), Moscow (February, where he heard of preparations for the Second Congress of the *RSDLP*, which given the thrust of his activities, it is likely that he welcomed), St Petersburg (February, in May when he and Martov were arrested and detained for ten days, and again in June), Pskov (March), Riga (March), Podolsk (June), Nizhni-Novgorod (June) and Samara (July)[13]. He also established written contact with Social Democratic groups and individuals in various other Russian towns, invariably gaining their support for *Iskra*. By the summer, Lenin, aided by Martov and Potresov, had established a network of individuals, groups and agents who were committed to supporting both *Iskra* as a publication, and the concept of a centralised party composed of professional revolutionaries organised around, and by the paper.

In St Petersburg (June), Lenin met Zasulich who had been sent by the Group to establish contacts with the interior, and, together, they negotiated its participation in the publication of an All-Russian Marxist newspaper. Zasulich was one of the most popular individuals amongst Russian Marxists. As a young girl she had (in the year before Trotsky was born) attempted to shoot General Trepov, the police chief of St Petersburg, in protest at his torture of political prisoners. She had an exceedingly sharp mind and rare personal insight, affectionately known as "auntie" to a generation of Russian Marxists because so many had turned up on her doorstep to be fed and housed. It was through Zasulich that the Group could claim a direct link to Marx and Engels[14].

On 16 July 1900, Lenin and Potresov left Russia for Zurich to meet the Emancipation of Labour Group which, in fact, was a small propaganda circle, relatively few in number and poorly organised. On the other hand, when Lenin went abroad he stood in first place amongst the internal, Russian, *SD*s; he was one of the few people to have met most of the important Social Democratic groups, he had shown an excellent grasp of Marxist theory in his debates with the Economists, he had a solid store of practical revolutionary experience and, most importantly, he had a vision of a practical programme that would unify the movement and give it direction[15]. Lenin was important to the émigré group because it was not until they met him, that they had any regular links with *SD*s inside Russia[16].

Whilst the initial discussions between Plekhanov, Axelrod and Zasulich on the one side, and Lenin and Potresov on the other, were extremely tense, working relations were established, meaning that *Iskra* had an editorial board of six, consisting of Lenin, Martov and Potresov, and Plekhanov, Axelrod and Zasulich, with Plekhanov having two votes. The tone of the meeting in which this last point was agreed, was so bad that Lenin said later that he felt he "had been fooled and utterly defeated" since the voting system would give Plekhanov "complete domination" over *Iskra*[17]. It is clear from Lenin's report of the discussions with the Group that he saw the arrangement for the editorial board as a purely temporary measure, and it was necessary to determine a plan by which the *Iskraists* would take editorial control.

In the next twelve months Lenin cemented the foundations of a national newspaper as organiser of a revolutionary Social Democratic party. In September 1900, the *Declaration of the Editorial Board of Iskra*[18] was published, aggressively attacking all the reformist and non-Marxist currents within Russian *SD*. In December the first issue of *Iskra* was printed in Leipzig, and in February 1901, the second issue was published in Munich, both on secret presses supplied by the German Social Democratic Party. That Lenin made Leipzig and then Munich, rather than Zurich, the city in which *Iskra* was published, could be ascribed to his intent to minimise the influence of the members of the Group. In the late spring of 1901, Lenin proposed a detailed and concrete plan for the unification of Russian revolutionary Social Democratic organisations, to be grouped around *Iskra*. In April 1901, the third issue of *Iskra* was published and Krupskaya became secretary to *Iskra's* editorial board. By this time Lenin was, *de-facto*, editor-in-chief, *Iskra* was becoming identified with him, and the organisation was commonly known as the *Iskra* organisation[19]. In May 1901, the fourth issue of *Iskra* carried Lenin's *Where to Begin*[20], which was spontaneously re-issued by local Social Democratic organisations in Russia as a separate pamphlet.

The editorial board gave Plekhanov the task of producing a draft programme for the *RSDLP*, but in the early part of 1902, Lenin submitted a counter-proposal which could only be seen as a challenge to Plekhanov's authority. This caused considerable difficulties in the relations between the two men[21], and the discussions on drafting the party programme led to such bitter exchanges that it was necessary for Zasulich and Martov to act as peacemakers and intermediaries, for Plekhanov and Lenin, respectively. Fortunately, both were naturally conciliatory, and were friends who shared lodgings. However, as these dealings proceeded, Martov and Potresov increasingly came under the influence of Zasulich[22]. After nearly a year of each man nit-picking over the others draft, Plekhanov's programme was submitted to the 1903 Congress with only one real change - the addition of a short section by Lenin on the agrarian question[23].

In March 1902, *What Is To Be Done?*[24] was published in Stuttgart and Krupskaya recorded that its publication was greeted enthusiastically by "everyone" including Plekhanov and Martov, and especially those who understood the practicalities of work inside Russia[25]. In this, one of his most influential works, Lenin elaborated the ideological foundations of a new type of party - the Revolutionary Marxist Party. It was a summary of *Iskra* tactics and *Iskra* organisational policy.

Iskra was becoming, as Lenin had hoped and planned, a rallying centre for Russian *SD*s, a mechanism for training, educating and informing party workers, and it had a decisive role in unifying the dispersed Social-Democratic circles. In a number of Russian cities (St Petersburg, Moscow, Samara, and others), groups and committees of the *RSDLP* were organised along the *Iskra* line. The agents of the editorial board - nine in number at the end of 1901 - travelled secretly all over European Russia contacting local groups, welding these into compact groups of professional revolutionaries, establishing groups where none existed, and co-ordinating their work. They delivered party literature, helped to establish illegal print shops, and collected the information needed by *Iskra*. Moreover, they fought ideologically to win the groups to a Leninist position against the Economists and other non-*Iskra* groupings[26].

In April 1902, the owner of the Munich printing press decided to cease printing *Iskra* and the editorial board agreed to transfer to London rather than Zurich. Lenin and Krupskaya left Munich for London and on 1 June 1902, *Iskra* No 21 which carried the draft programme of the party, was published there. From mid-1902 onwards, Lenin's major activity was preparing for the forthcoming Second Congress of the *RSDLP* (travelling, meeting, speaking, writing, forming an organising committee, making conference arrangements, delegates' arrangements, etc.).

1.4 Trotsky Arrives

In October 1902, Trotsky, only recently escaped from exile in Irkutsk, Siberia, had made his way to London via Samara, Kiev, Kharkov, Vienna and Zurich, and arrived at dawn at Lenin's and Krupskaya's lodgings. Nicknamed "the young eagle", party name "the Pen", Trotsky is described in the first volume of Deutscher's biography[27] as having joined a revolutionary group in Odessa at the age of 20, been banished to Siberia, but escaped at the end of three years. While in exile he became acquainted with smuggled copies of *Iskra*, circulated from London and Geneva, and read Lenin's *What Is To Be Done?*[28]. After his escape he worked secretly in Russia for a short time, eluding the police, and forming circles for aiding the distribution of *Iskra*.

It was no coincidence that Trotsky had made a bee-line for Lenin since Lenin concentrated all connections with Russia in his own hands. As secretary of the editorial board, Krupskaya received comrades when they arrived and instructed them when they left. She found Trotsky lodgings with Zasulich and Martov[29].

Only four months after Trotsky's arrival, Lenin wrote to Plekhanov suggesting he be co-opted as a member of the board on the same basis as other members. That Lenin was using Trotsky against Plekhanov is clear, since he argued that the editorial board needed a seventh member as a balance in voting, conveniently forgetting that Plekhanov had two votes. Lenin proposed two specific tasks for Trotsky; formulation of the rules of voting on the editorial board, and the drafting of a precise constitution[30]. As might have been expected, Lenin's proposal was vetoed by Plekhanov, who subsequently maintained a lifelong hostility towards Trotsky. Nevertheless, with the support of Zasulich, Trotsky was subsequently invited to editorial meetings in an advisory capacity, although any reorganisation of the editorial board was deferred until the forthcoming Congress.

1.5 The 1903 Second Congress of the *RSDLP*

By the time the Congress was convened, the overwhelming majority of the local Social Democratic organisations in Russia had agreed to support *Iskra*, approved its programme, organisational plan, and tactical line, and accepted it as their directing organ. It looked as though Lenin's goal of a centralised *RSDLP* comprised of professional revolutionaries, with its guiding light a regular newspaper, was being achieved and close to formal endorsement. The years 1900-03, during which Lenin was building *Iskra* and creating a national network of professional revolutionaries as the backbone of the future party, coincided with a massive upsurge in revolutionary feeling in Russia. In a sense, Lenin was pushing on an open door since his natural constituency - the workers - were, year on year, an increasing proportion of the revolutionary movement until, in about 1903, they became the largest single grouping, replacing intellectuals and students[31]. Railway strikes, factory strikes, mass demonstrations of workers in St Petersburg, street barricades in Moscow, political strikes in Baku - for the first time workers became the main active political opponents of Tsarism.

The Second Congress of the *RSDLP* was held from 17 July to 10 August, 1903. Rarely can there have been any party Congress that began with such high hopes and ended in such acrimony. Lenin was the motor force driving the Congress, he played the key role, drew up the outline of the report on the work of the *Iskra* organisation, composed the draft party rules, the agenda and the standing orders of the Congress, and drafted a number of resolutions. He was elected to the Bureau of the Congress and was a member of the three main committees: Programme, Rules and Credentials. He took the foremost part in a number of debates and spoke on almost all the subjects on the agenda. Given his input to, and expectations of, the Congress, the outcomes can be seen as a personal and political disaster for him.

In his *Account of the Second Congress of the RSDLP*[32], Lenin reports that there were thirty-three delegates with one vote each, nine delegates with two votes each, and ten delegates who could not vote but could contribute to the discussions. Lenin undertook considerable preparatory work among the delegates, determining the general situation and state of organisation in various parts of the country, and discussing many of the problems confronting the Congress. This made it possible for him to ascertain the political stance of each delegate prior to the opening of the Congress. Present were:

- The Bund, a movement of Jewish workers that could be described as more akin to a trade union than a revolutionary party. The Bund was politically nearer the reformist Economists than *Iskra*, but the First Congress had constituted it a section of the party so it had to be to invited to the Second, 5 votes.

- The paper *Workers Cause* delegates. These were strongly inclined towards Economism, definitely cuckoos in the nest of the Congress, 3 votes.

- The paper *Southern Worker* delegates. This paper, based in the Ukraine, tended to be 'soft' on the liberals and intended to continue as a separate publication no matter what the outcome of the Congress. Plekhanov, in particular, wanted this paper represented at the Congress against the opposition of Lenin, Martov and Trotsky, 4 votes.

- The "Marsh". This was the name given by Lenin to the indecisive and wavering elements, 6 votes. Predominantly *SDs* from outside Russia.

- *Iskra* supporters, 33 votes. Largely representatives from *SD* groups within Russia.

The first thirteen sessions of the Congress were held in Brussels, but owing to difficulties created by the Belgian police, the Congress moved to London. The most important sessions for the future of the *RSDLP* were: the party programme, party organisation (confirmation of the party rules), elections to the Central Committee, and elections to the editorial board.

Lenin wrote a long and detailed report of the Congress in *One Step Forward, Two Steps Back*[33], in which he describes the disruptive tactics used knowingly from the start by the Bund and *Workers Cause* delegates, and possibly unwittingly by the *Southern Worker* delegates - the former because of their reformist politics and opposition in principle to the kind of party Lenin was working towards, the latter to preserve its independence, individualism and parochial interests and to prevent it from being swallowed up in a disciplined party. There was no suggestion that the early sessions, held in Brussels, indicated any serious differences between Lenin, Martov and Trotsky. This was confirmed by Krupskaya who said that, at that time, Lenin and Trotsky were considered so close that Trotsky was commonly known as Lenin's cudgel. "Indeed, Lenin himself, at that time least of all thought Trotsky would waver"[34]. Trotsky in *My Life* says that "Lenin's schemes of organisation aroused certain doubts in me. But nothing was farther from my mind than the thought that the Congress would blow up on those very questions"[35].

Just over two weeks into the Congress, a number of minor differences among the *Iskraists* had emerged on secondary issues. Then on 2 August, at the 22nd session, the discussion and vote on Paragraph 1 of the party rules, which defined the conditions of membership, took place. Here, for the first time, a rift appeared between Lenin and Martov. Martov wanted to dilute, in an individualistic way, Lenin's proposal that a member of the *RSDLP* was a person who not only accepted its programme and supported the party financially, but participated personally in one of the party organisations under its discipline. Martov's alternative tended to blur the differences between members and sympathisers, defining participation as regular personal co-operation under the direction of one of the party organisations. Lenin wanted clear-cut, definite relationships within the party. Martov tended toward more diffuse forms. With the support of 14 votes from the Bund, the *Workers Cause*, the *Southern Worker,* and the 'Marsh', Martov's proposal gained an overall majority. Those *Iskraists* who remained loyal to Lenin's view of how revolutionary *SD* should be structured found themselves in the minority.

On the day after the vote on Paragraph 1 of the rules, the 'hard' *Iskraists* held a meeting, with Trotsky in the chair, to determine their position on the editorial board elections. It could be argued that it was at this meeting that the coming split between the Bolsheviks and the Mensheviks first took shape. By a substantial majority, the meeting decided to support Lenin's proposal to reduce the membership of the editorial board to three - Lenin, Martov and Plekhanov. Thus, Martov was *de facto* elected to the editorial board at a meeting, to which he had demanded entry but from which he had been excluded for being too 'soft'!

Before it devoted itself to organisational matters, the Congress voted for the dissolution of all independent party organisations and their fusion into a single party; seven of the eight delegates from the Bund and the *Workers Cause* withdrew. The issues implicit in the vote on Paragraph 1 of the rules now came to the fore in a much more developed form on the question of membership of the editorial board. Through a special resolution the Congress adopted the newspaper as the central organ of the *RSDLP* and approved an editorial board consisting of Lenin, Plekhanov and Martov.

Lenin believed he had the support of Martov and Plekhanov that the editorial board be reduced from six to three. He argued that in the three years of its operation, 99% of all political decisions had been made by himself, Martov and Plekhanov[36]; and that in the literary work the same three had predominated; in 45 issues of *Iskra,* Martov had written 39 articles, Lenin - 32, Plekhanov - 24, and between them Zasulich, Axelrod and Potresov had written only 18[37]. To move towards a more professional organisation, and away from personality politics, it was sensible to recognise these facts and re-constitute the editorial board accordingly.

Frantic pressure from Zasulich persuaded Martov, Potresov and Trotsky to change their minds[38]. Trotsky moved a counter resolution, based not on the needs of the party but to protect the feelings of Zasulich, that the original editorial board be retained. Before the London Congress in 1903, Lenin's centralism had been theoretical, and many, Trotsky included, had failed to draw the necessary practical conclusions. But now the *Iskra* 'hards' were in the majority and the new editorial board consisting of Lenin, Martov and Plekhanov was approved on 7 August. It is from this vote that the Bolsheviks (majority) and the Mensheviks (minority), derived their names. Despite the decision of the Congress, Martov refused to participate in the editorial board, and Nos. 46 to 51 of *Iskra* were edited by Lenin and Plekhanov.

The split within the *RSDLP* came unexpectedly. Lenin did not foresee it, and certainly did not want it. The vote on Plekhanov's programme, which Lenin defended, was passed with only one vote against. Apart from subsequent changes by Lenin to the section on the agrarian question, which he had written, this remained the *RSDLP* programme until after October 1917, both Mensheviks and Bolsheviks agreed with its basic formulations. Of particular importance for us, is that the programme clearly separated the bourgeois and the socialist revolutions[39].

Trotsky had attended the *RSDLP* Second Congress as a delegate from Siberia, his place of exile and from which he had recently escaped. Almost immediately after the Congress he wrote his *Report of the Siberian Delegation*[40] in which he characterised Lenin as the "party dis-organiser" who would "mercilessly tramp over *Iskra*'s editorial board" using his "iron fist" to impose a "state of siege" on the party[41]. Trotsky placed personal feelings before politics[42] and failed to appreciate the necessity of an organised, disciplined, centralised cadre party for the success of an armed uprising against the autocracy. What the young Trotsky saw was two groups professing the same principles and policy, separated only by Lenin's apparent ruthlessness in dealing with such dear comrades as Vera Zasulich. He expressed this new hostility to Lenin in his report of the Congress with his usual flair and style. Trotsky ceased to contribute to *Iskra* and became a member of the Menshevik shadow Central Committee and, with Martov, drew up the resolution expressing the Menshevik boycott of *Iskra*[43].

Lenin had attended the Second Congress as a representative of the League of Russian Revolutionary Social Democrats Abroad and gave his report on the Congress to a meeting held in Geneva in October. The Mensheviks held a majority in the League and considerable time was taken up with a reply from the floor by Martov, in which he made a scathing attack on Lenin. Martov flatly rejected Bolshevik statements that he had been party to Lenin's 'intrigues' against Axelrod, Potresov and Zasulich, giving his own version of private conversations with Lenin. His speech further personalised the discussion. Getzler says "Martov's indictment of Lenin was greeted by calls of 'Bravo!' and 'Shame!' from the party elite, sitting almost as a court of honour. Lenin had no answer but to walk out from one of the great humiliations of his life"[44].

Trotsky was a leading figure in all of this, co-authoring with Martov, the resolution passed at the meeting. Alongside Axelrod, Dan, Martov and Potresov, he was elected a member of the Menshevik 'bureau', a body that was clearly intended to be the core of any leading committee of a new party if the split led to formal separation of the two factions[45]. Trotsky was identified as a leading anti-Bolshevik.

Martov's boycott was soon successful. Plekhanov proved unable to make the transition to the new historical period, one of active preparation for revolution, which demanded a new 'Leninist' type of party and leadership. The evening of 18 October saw Plekhanov's break with Lenin and the majority of the party. He presented an ultimatum to Lenin, that the old editors be reinstated or he would resign from the editorial board. Plekhanov's decision was a heavy blow. By 13 November, Plekhanov had co-opted the old editorial board, and Lenin resigned shortly afterwards, after the publication of issue No 51 of *Iskra,* in order not to stand in the way of possible peace in the party[46]. However, his supporters immediately co-opted him onto the Central Committee which he then used as a base to conduct a campaign to win back *Iskra*.

However, the co-option of the old editors onto the editorial board gave the minority control of the new *Iskra*. The central organ and public face of the *RSDLP* was now a Menshevik paper with Martov the de-facto editor. The Central Committee was Bolshevik, but it was deprived of a public voice. Gradually, the new *Iskra* ceased to publish the copy sent in by the supporters of the majority, and the position of Lenin looked extremely bleak.

At this point Trotsky wrote a series of articles for the new *Iskra* on Menshevik policy towards the Russian liberal bourgeoisie, his analysis was a penetrating condemnation of Menshevik strategy. Plekhanov, to whom support for the liberal bourgeoisie was the key to the success of the Russian Revolution, threatened to resign from the editorial board in protest when *Iskra* continued to publish articles by Trotsky[47]. Rather than lose their most important ally the editorial board attempted, unsuccessfully, to persuade Trotsky to agree to tone down his views and, gradually, Trotsky's articles ceased to appear.

Yet, even as he was leaving the Menshevik ranks, in August 1904, Trotsky published *Our Political Tasks*, in which he reviled Lenin's brochure *One Step Forward Two Steps Back*, and made reconciliation between them virtually impossible[48]. Deutscher described the pamphlet as the "pent-up emotion of the romantic revolutionary ... (Trotsky's) inclination, his tastes, his temperament revolted against the prosaic and business-like determination with which Lenin was setting out to bring the party down from the clouds of abstraction to the firm ground of organisation"[49]. A more experienced revolutionary would not have been so publicly venomous or personally hurtful. Through his youth and inexperience, Trotsky made a serious enemy of Lenin, who for the next thirteen years considered him one of the most vicious of the Mensheviks. The resulting mutual hostility helped block any possible collaboration between the two men for well over a decade, and required the momentous events of 1917 to overcome it.

In later years Trotsky accepted that his 1904 disagreement with Lenin was, at root, concerned with differences over a "philosophy of history and political conception", while its form took the appearance of differences over the roles and qualities of individuals - which, due to the inexperience of many of those involved, tended to make the discussion over-heated and personal[50].

By the end of 1904, and the start of 1905, Trotsky was more or less on his own, at loggerheads with virtually everybody, politically isolated. Whatever his intentions, Trotsky was now outside the two major groupings within the *RSDLP* and, while a brilliant journalist and great speaker, had not shown any significantly greater political insight than his contemporaries.

For Lenin the situation seemed grim. Everything which had been expected of the Second Congress was in ruins. With the capture of *Iskra*, the Mensheviks had achieved a substantial victory. The great majority of the party activists understood that there had been significant differences over the composition of the editorial board of the party's paper, but didn't accept that they were serious enough to justify the split, and so rejected it. Even leading Bolsheviks close to Lenin did not fully understand the differences and tended to play them down which made the split look even less justified. Indeed,

Lenin, himself, later confirmed that the political differences between the Bolsheviks and Mensheviks only emerged clearly well after the Second Congress[51], and explained the forces which lay behind the split as due to the opposition of, primarily, intellectuals whose conditions of life and work naturally inclined them against the necessary discipline of a revolutionary party[52]. Plekhanov's defection made things appear even more complicated, but at grass roots level increasing numbers of local Social Democratic committees were expressing support for Lenin's call for a new Congress as the only way of resolving the crisis.

By the autumn, the prospects for the Bolsheviks were looking brighter. Lenin put together a new leading team, encouraging reports received from Russia, where Lenin's agents had managed to distribute *To the Party* to many local *RSDLP* committees. By the end of 1904 a Bolshevik Organising Centre had been established in Russia, with the backing of thirteen party committees. Despite their lack of resources, the Bolsheviks had managed to launch a new paper, *Vperyod* (*Forward*), and at a meeting in Geneva on 3 December, an editorial board was elected with Krupskaya as secretary:

"The first issue of the first truly Bolshevik newspaper duly rolled off the press on 22 December 1904. Just over a fortnight later, the Russian émigrés were amazed to hear the newspaper boys on the streets of Geneva: 'Revolution in Russia! Revolution in Russia!'"[53].

1.6 References

1. Trotsky, *On Lenin,* George Harrap and Co., London, 1971, p167-169.
2. Cliff, 1975 *Lenin, Building the Party,* Pluto Press, London, 1975, p52
3. Woods, A., *Bolshevism the Road to Revolution*, Wellred Publications, London, 1999, p80
4. Woods, A., *op cit,* p90
5. Lenin, V.I., *The Tasks of the Russian Social Democrats,* 1897, CW 2:323 - 347
6. Lenin, V.I., *A Draft Programme of Our Party*, 1899, CW 4:227 - 254
7. Lenin, V.I., *The Development of Capitalism in Russia*, 1899, CW 3:21-607
8. White, J.D. *Lenin, The Practice and Theory of Revolution*, Palgrave, 2001, p43
9. Harding, N., *Lenin's Political Thought, Vol 1 Theory and Practice of the Democratic Revolutio),* Macmillan Press, London, 1977, p87
10. Harding, N., *op cit,* p139
11. Lenin, V.I., *Where to Begin,* 1901, CW 5:19
12. Woods, A., *op cit,* p113
13. Krupskaya, N., *Memories of Lenin*, Panther History, 1970, p33-34
14. Sennett, A., *Permanent Revolution in Spain* PhD Thesis University of Manchester, 1992, p37. Not to be confused with long-time friend of Krupskaya and fund-raiser for *Iskra*, the feminist Mrs A. M. Kalmykova who used 'Auntie' as an alias. See Wolfe B.D., *Three Who Made a Revolution*, Penguin, London 1984, p123
15. Trotsky, L.D., *On Lenin,* George Harrap and Co., London, 1971, p39
16. Harding, N., *op cit,* p31
17. Lenin, V.I., *How the Spark was Nearly Extinguished*, 1900, CW 4:333-349
18. Lenin, V.I., *Declaration of the Editorial Board of Iskra,* 1900, CW 4:351-356
19. Woods, A., *op cit,* p113-124
20. Lenin, V.I., *Where to Begin*, May 1901, CW 5:13-24
21. Krupskaya, N., *op cit,* p61
22. Trotsky, L.D., *On Lenin,* George Harrap and Co., London, 1971, p35
23. Wolfe, B.D., *Three Who Made a Revolution*, Pelican, London, 1984, p256-7
24. Lenin, V.I., *What Is To Be Done?*, March 1902, CW 5:347-529
25. Krupskaya, N., *op cit,* p60
26. Cliff, 1975 *op cit,* p100-102
27. Deutscher, I., *The Prophet Armed*, Oxford Paperbacks, 1954, p30-6

28. Trotsky, *On Lenin,* George Harrap and Co., London, 1971, p40
29. Trotsky, L.D., *My Life,* Penguin Books, 1984, p159
30. Trotsky, L.D., *Ibid,* p158
31. Cliff, T., *op cit,* p98
32. Lenin, V.I., *Account of the Second Congress of the RSDLP*, Sept 1903, CW 7:19-34
33. Lenin, V.I., *One Step Forward, Two Steps Back*, May 1904, CW 7:201 - 423
34. Krupskaya, N., *op cit,* p86
35. Trotsky, L.D., *My Life,* Penguin Books, 1984, p162
36. Lenin, V.I., *Letter to Alexandra Kalmykova,* Sept 1903, CW 34:162
37. Lenin, V.I., *Account of the Second Congress of the RSDLP*, Sept 1903, , CW 7:19-34
38. Woods, A., *op cit,* p145
39. Wolfe, B.D., *Ibid,* p272
40. Trotsky, L.D., *Report of the Siberian Delegation*, New Park Publications, London, 1979
41. Deutscher, I., *op cit,* p86
42. Trotsky, L.D., *My Life,* Penguin Books, 1984, p167
43. Deutscher, I., *op cit,* p84 - 85
44. Getzler, I., *Martov,* Cambridge University Press, 1967, p84
45. Deutscher, I., *op cit,* p85
46. Lenin, V.I., *Why I Resigned From Iskra Editorial Board,* Dec 1903, CW 7:118-124
47. Deutscher, I., *op cit,* p86-87
48. Thatcher, I. D., *Trotsky,* Routledge, London and New York, 2003, p32
49. Deutscher, I., *op cit,* p88-97
50. Trotsky, L.D., *Stalin,* Hollis and Carter, London, 1947, p50
51. Lenin, V.I., *Historical Meaning of the Inner Party Struggle in Russia*, April 1911, CW 16:380
52. Lenin, V.I., *To the Party*, Aug 1904, CW 7:452-459
53. Woods, A., *op cit,* p166

Chapter 2
LENIN AND TROTSKY IN THE FIRST
RUSSIAN REVOLUTION (1905)

2.1   Introduction
2.2   Bloody Sunday to the General Strike
2.3   The October Strike and Formation of the St Petersburg Soviet
2.4   The Bolsheviks and the Soviet
2.5   The Struggle for the 8-hour Day
2.6   The Moscow Uprising
2.7   Summary
2.8   References

2.1 Introduction

The events of the First 1905 Revolution, are given only in enough detail to show the very different experiences of Lenin and Trotsky; differences which played a major role in the subsequent development of the conflicting theories of Permanent Revolution *(ToPR)* and the Revolutionary Democratic Dictatorship of the Proletariat and Peasantry (*RDDPP*).

Trotsky returned to Russia early, in February, and was at the very heart of the St Petersburg Soviet from its inception, gaining a unique insight into working class psychology and the dynamics of proletarian struggle. Due to a conjunction of circumstances, Trotsky played a much greater role in determining the course of the 1905 Revolution than any other member of the *RSDLP,* specifically: the absence from Russia of other leading figures in the *RSDLP*; Trotsky's exceptional all-round leadership abilities; the split in the *RSDLP* which allowed considerable scope for personal and independent activity separate from, and outside, party discipline; the relatively short duration of the St Petersburg Soviet (the 'Fifty Days') which meant that there was little time for either the Bolshevik or Menshevik faction to come to dominate it; and the conservatism of the Bolshevik "committee-men" (both in not opening the party to young workers, and their subsequent opposition to participation in the St Petersburg Soviet), which allowed others to take the lead in core working class activities.

Trotsky's experience as a leader of the day-to-day struggle of the workers gave him a deep understanding of just how much the workers would sacrifice for their class aims, and how determined they would be to retain leadership of the struggle once they embarked on the path of direct action, and confirmed unambiguously in his mind that:

"the proletariat, once having power in its hands, would not be able to remain confined within the bourgeois framework of the revolution. On the contrary, precisely in order to guarantee its victory, the proletarian vanguard in the very earliest stages of its rule would have to make extremely deep inroads not only into feudal but also into bourgeois property relations"[1].

At the start of 1905, the workers' response was largely spontaneous, with neither Bolsheviks nor Mensheviks having any substantial weight in the workers' movement[2]. The beginning of the revolution found the *RSDLP* seriously weakened both by the split in the leadership and by arrests inside Russia (including nine of the original eleven members of the CC)[3] which had left the organisation confused and disorientated. The emphasis on internal party discussions after the Second Congress had paralysed public activity for many months and, until *Vperyod* appeared in January 1905, the Bolsheviks were without a public face, with a consequent lack of focus and organisation[4]. Lenin, for much of 1905, concentrated his attention on Bolshevik membership and structure, launching a new weekly paper, *Proletarii,* organising a Bolshevik-only Congress in London from 12-26 April, and working towards healing the split in the *RSDLP*.

Immediately, Lenin had to correct the errors and mistakes of the Bolshevik committee-men: he had to persuade them to increase the recruitment of young workers, and to place these new recruits in local leadership roles. During this period, at the Third (Bolshevik-only) Congress, on the basis of actual events, he redefined the main ally of the proletariat in the Russian bourgeois-democratic revolution as the peasantry as a whole. This proposed class alliance was the basis on which he developed, over 1905, the slogan that would be at the core of Bolshevik governmental policy until 1917, the *RDDPP*. As the proposed key for a successful revolution, this perspective was at the heart of Bolshevik strategy and, in the summer of 1905, in a key text, *The Two Tactics of Social Democracy in the Democratic Revolution*[5] (hereinafter referred to as *Two Tactics*), Lenin described how the strategy and tactics for a successful bourgeois-democratic revolution flowed from this central concept.

Then, in November, he had to persuade the committee-men to participate in the activities of the Soviet as loyal members. Simultaneously he had to publicly campaign and argue that a principled unification of Mensheviks and Bolsheviks was possible and necessary. This required organising a preparatory Bolshevik Conference in December 1905 in Finland, and then preparing for, and participating in, the Unity Congress, April 1906, in Stockholm.

It can be seen that while Trotsky was more directly engaged with the workers themselves, Lenin's activity in 1905 was overwhelmingly concerned with working to re-orient and re-group the party to meet new events.

2.2 Bloody Sunday to the General Strike

On 9 January 1905 - Bloody Sunday - in the early afternoon, a large crowd of about 200,000, led by the priest father Gapon, marched to the Winter Palace to petition the Tsar. The square was soon packed with workers, students, women, children and old people, many wearing their Sunday best. Some carried icons and church banners. There were no speeches. Everything was peaceful. However, troops were everywhere. The soldiers began firing. The dead were counted by the hundreds, the wounded by the thousands[6].

The January massacre had a most profound effect upon the Russian proletariat; a tremendous wave of strikes swept the country, spreading to hundreds of towns and localities, factories, mines and railways. The strike involved something like a million men and women. "For almost two months, the strike ruled the land"[7].

The movement swept through Poland, and from 14-20 January the Polish capital, Warsaw, was in the grip of a revolutionary general strike. The Baltic area was also caught up in the revolutionary current and, in Riga on 13 January, 15,000 workers marched in protest and 60,000 workers staged a political general strike. The movement cut across national lines: Armenian, Georgian, Jewish, Lithuanian and Polish workers expressed their solidarity with their Russian brothers and sisters, and fought against the hated Russian autocracy. A railway strike began in Saratov on 12 January, which quickly spread to the other railway lines, spreading the news of the revolutionary wave outwards to even the most backward provinces[8].

From exile in Switzerland, Lenin immediately (18 January) greeted the January events as the beginning of the revolution in Russia: "The working class has received a momentous lesson in civil war: the revolutionary education of the proletariat made more progress in one day than it could have made in months and years of drab, humdrum, wretched existence"[9]. Lenin was also to argue that "January 9, 1905, fully revealed the vast reserves of revolutionary energy possessed by the proletariat, as well as the utter inadequacy of the Social Democratic organisation"[10]. For example, the St Petersburg Committee of the *RSDLP*, which was Bolshevik dominated, had only reluctantly agreed to participate in the 9 January demonstration, and then only a small group of about fifteen from a membership of almost 1,000 turned up[11].

The impact of 9 January pushed the whole of the workers to the left, with the mood flowing strongly in favour of militant action and support for the *RSDLP*. Bolshevik and Menshevik workers now commanded attention at factory gate meetings, Lenin was desperate to take advantage of the opportunities but believed all his efforts were floundering because of the amateurism, and disunity of the organisation largely resulting from the effects of the split[12]. Under the pressure of the mass movement, the Mensheviks in Russia moved rapidly to the left, creating unforeseen problems for the Bolsheviks. Dissatisfaction in the ranks of the St Petersburg *RSDLP*, and its supporters, with the bureaucratic methods of the local Bolshevik leadership, and its attitude to the developing mass movement, led to four of the six district organisations breaking away to join the Mensheviks[13].

In February 1905, Trotsky, aged only 25, was the first of the *RSDLP* leaders to return to Russia, reaching St Petersburg by the spring[14]. During the first months of his return, hiding from the secret police, Trotsky could do little more than write. He had a clear field, as none of the main leaders of either the Bolsheviks or Mensheviks returned to Russia until much later. Both Lenin and Martov returned after the October amnesty, Martov on 17 October and Lenin on 4 November[15]. By the summer, Trotsky was the best known name of the *RSDLP* due to a stream of articles, leaflets, letters, and (particularly) an appeal to the peasants. These included a series of newspaper articles against the notion that the liberals were the natural leaders of the revolution, and developed his idea that the working class were the decisive force in the revolution:

"Other groups in the urban population will play their part in the revolution only in so far as they follow the proletariat ... Neither the peasantry, nor the middle class, nor the intelligentsia can play an independent revolutionary role in any way equivalent to the role of the proletariat ... Consequently, the composition of the Provisional Government will in the main depend on the proletariat. If the insurrection ends in victory, those who have led the working class in the rising will gain power"[16].

Lenin was concerned with the less glamorous, but essential, problems facing the Bolsheviks: how to overcome their routine ways of working and how to establish links between their relatively small forces and the masses of workers who were moving into struggle. A key part of Lenin's plan to re-vitalise and re-organise the majority members of the *RSDLP* was the convening of the Third Congress of the *RSDLP* in the name of the (Bolshevik) Central Committee[17]. The Mensheviks were invited to attend but stayed away and organised their own conference in Geneva. Lenin remained outside Russia devoting considerable time to the preparation and convocation of the Third Congress, and on 12 April 1905, the first Bolshevik-only Party Congress met in London. Lenin drew up nearly all the main resolutions and delivered a number of reports and speeches to the Congress. Considerable attention was given to the technical and organisational preparation for the overthrow of Tsarism, and there was to be a stepping up of the political, agitational and propaganda work, including paying special attention to work in the army, e.g. troops were to be contacted using leaflets, and a commission was established, under the control of the Central Committee, to formulate a programme of transitional demands specifically for soldiers. Nevertheless, it was agreed that especially at a time when events had raised the question of armed insurrection, the fundamental task facing the party was winning over the masses[18].

Lenin was determined to open up the party to young workers "boldly and widely, and again more widely and again more boldly without fearing them"[19], and he put considerable effort into confronting the dogmatism of the committee-men (who formed the majority of delegates to the Congress), whose natural reaction was against any demands for the workers to have a greater say in the running of inner-party affairs. These attitudes, which led to Lenin losing the vote on the resolution (actually moved by Bogdanov) *'On the Relations Between Workers and Intellectuals Within the Social Democratic Organisation'*, represented a strong conservative current within Bolshevism that Trotsky would have to face in the St Petersburg Soviet some seven months later[20].

Lenin appreciated the need for such people in building the party. The Bolshevik committee-men devoted their lives to the party, and had remained loyal to the revolutionary movement despite repeated arrests, imprisonment and exile. They provided the continuity of the movement, but their clandestine life style meant they had to be conservative in their behaviour to preserve their existence[21]. "The committee-man," wrote Krupskaya:

"was usually a rather self-assured person. He saw what a tremendous influence the work of the committee had on the masses, and as a rule he recognised no inner-party democracy. 'Inner-Party democracy only leads to trouble with the police. We are connected with the movement as it is', the committee-men would say. Inwardly they rather despised the Party workers abroad who, in their opinion, had nothing better to do than squabble among themselves -'they ought to be made to work under Russian conditions'. The committee-men objected to the overruling influence of the Centre abroad. At the same time they did not want innovations. They were neither desirous nor capable of adjusting themselves to the quickly changing conditions"[22].

The events in St Petersburg stirred the provinces into action. On 1 May, workers struck in nearly 200 towns throughout Russia. The major strike, of some 70,000 workers, lasting over two months from 12 May, was in the Bolshevik stronghold of Ivanovo-Voznesensk, a textile town known as the Russian Manchester. The strike committee leading this 'first Soviet' (which pre-dated that in St Petersburg), made many important political demands such as the 8-hour day and freedom of assembly, but did not attempt to pose the question of power. The relative roles of the two Soviets was discussed later by the Commission on the History of the October Revolution of the State Publishing House, which decided that the St Petersburg Soviet under Trotsky's leadership not only exercised power but posed the question of transferring state power into the hands of the proletariat[23]. This difference in approach between the largely Bolshevik-controlled strike committee at Ivanovo-Voznesensk and the St Petersburg Soviet was confirmed by Zinoviev in his *History of the Bolshevik Party*[24] which, while omitting any mention of Trotsky's role as leader of the St Petersburg Soviet, said "The Petersburg Soviet became an embryonic government. This was the reality of the matter: either this Soviet took power in its hands and dissolved the Tsarist government or the latter would dissolve the Soviet ... ".

The increasing strength of the protests forced the Tsar to make a series of concessions; on 18 February, the Tsar issued his first Manifesto in which he hinted at a constitution and popular representation, and set in motion a separate manoeuvre intended to divide and disorient the working class. To defuse the growing militancy in the factories the government set up a commission headed by Senator Shidlovsky to investigate and identify the causes of the discontent among the workers. In an unprecedented move, it was announced that workers would be represented on the commission by means of elected delegates. The proletariat agreed overwhelmingly to participate, and this gave them the experience of electing plant representatives, experience they would use nine months later in elections to the Soviets.

On 6 August the Tsar issued a second Manifesto promising a parliament or Duma, and finally, following nation-wide political strikes, he issued his third Manifesto on 17 October promising a constitution, an amnesty for political prisoners and exiles, civil liberties and universal suffrage[25]. This October Manifesto by the Tsar, gained primarily through the actions of the workers, solved nothing fundamental, but it gave the liberals (increasingly worried by the rising militancy of the workers), a reason to unhook themselves from the revolution. As Lenin and Trotsky had foreseen, the bourgeoisie, which had all along been striving to strike a deal with Tsarism, now deserted the revolutionary camp. The big capitalists and landowners united in a reactionary bloc - the so-called "Octobrists" - which threw its weight behind the Tsar. At the same time, the "liberal" section of the bourgeoisie supporting the Constitutional Democrat Party, the "Cadets", came out in favour of a so-called constitutional monarchy, providing a pseudo-democratic, constitutional, smokescreen for the bloody reality of Tsarist rule[26].

2.3 The October Strike and Formation of the St Petersburg Soviet

The strike wave which gripped nearly all industrial areas throughout the spring and summer, took on an increasingly political character, but the end of July saw a sudden drop in the urban strike wave. During the summer there was a sharp decline in strikes in big factories, but a gradual increase in strikes amongst the most downtrodden and oppressed layers; workers in the smaller factories such as bakeries, brickyards, domestic servants, sawmills and slaughterhouses. A new impulse came from Moscow with a dispute at one print-works over whether the type-setters should be paid for setting punctuation marks. "The Bolshevik Moscow Committee immediately strained every nerve to turn the print strike into a general strike"[27].

The Committee was successful, the strike rapidly spread to other print-shops and factories and, within a few days, had become general throughout the city, spreading to the railways in and around Moscow, which started to grind to a halt on 6 October. The railways were the arteries of Russian industry and with their stoppage all major industrial activity, through necessity or sympathy, ceased. On 9 October a national conference of striking railway workers was held in St Petersburg where demands were made for an 8-hour day, civil liberties, amnesty for political prisoners and a Constituent Assembly. The strike movement was beginning to transform itself into a struggle to deprive the state of some of its power and give it to the people.

By 10 October, the entire Moscow region was in the grip of the strike which spread inexorably outwards along the railway lines in all directions, reaching the capital on the 13th. On that day the Mensheviks in Petersburg called for the creation of a revolutionary workers' council. Delegates were elected on the basis of one delegate for every 500 industrial workers[28]. Small workshops were meant to combine, but numerical norms were not observed too strictly; in some cases delegates represented only a hundred or two hundred workers, sometimes even fewer:

"The Soviet ... an organisation which ... could immediately involve a scattered mass of hundreds of thousands of people while having virtually no organisational machinery; which united the revolutionary currents within the proletariat; which was capable of initiative and spontaneous self control - and most important of all, which could be brought out from underground within twenty-four hours. ... In order to have authority in the eyes of the masses on the very day it came into being, such an organisation had to be based on the broadest representation. ... Since the production process was the sole link between the proletarian masses who, in the organisational sense, were still quite inexperienced, representation had to be adapted to the factories and plants"[29].

By mid-October, three quarters of a million railwaymen were on strike. On 16 October Finland joined in. The movement then spread swiftly to the post offices, telephones, telegrams, and professional workers. This compelled the Tsar, after consulting with his ministers, to issue the October 17 Manifesto. It was a successful ploy and on 21 October the general strike came to an end[30,31]. Not only had the strike wave spread to include ever larger numbers of urban workers, the peasantry was slowly being drawn into such revolutionary activity as burning the landlord's house, sharing out his grain stocks, etc. As would be expected, the peasant movement was both uneven geographically and lagged behind the town in revolutionary consciousness so their actions tended to be confined to their locality. Dimitrii Sverchkov has described how, for example, during the railway strike, white-collar staff often left their station by the last train owing to the danger of reprisals from the local peasants who saw the strike as an obstacle to their products reaching the towns[32].

At its peak, the St Petersburg Soviet gathered together 562 deputies from a total of 147 factories (the majority were metal workers, and these played the decisive role), 34 from workshops, 32 from the printing and paper industries, 16 from trade unions and 12 from the shop workers. The Executive Committee was formed on 17 October and consisted of 31 persons - 22 deputies and nine representatives of parties (three each from the two *SD* factions, and three from the Socialist Revolutionaries (*SR*s)). Sverchkov (a Bolshevik) reported that Trotsky, Sverchkov himself, Bogdan Mirzodzhanovich Knuniyants (member of the St Petersburg Bolshevik Committee and a former technological student) and Pyotr Aleksandrovich Zlydniev (left Menshevik, a worker in a large factory), formed the core leadership of the St Petersburg Soviet with Trotsky the undisputed ideological leader[33]. The Soviet chairman was a lawyer with links to the Mensheviks, Khrustalev-Nosar, an indecisive man who kept his position by balancing on top of the momentous forces that the Soviet represented. Trotsky, Sverchkov and Zlydniev were later chosen as a trio to replace Khrustalev-Nosar after his arrest, but the leading political figure in the Soviet was undoubtedly Leon Trotsky[34].

Here was an extremely broad, democratic and flexible organ of struggle which gradually increased its representation and authority. Through the Soviet, the workers took over the printing presses to make use of the newly-gained freedom of expression, enabling the Soviet to publish its own newspaper, *Izvestiya Sovieta Rabochikh Deputatov* (*Soviet of Workers' Deputies' News*). It also formed an armed workers' militia, initially for protection against pogroms, and even arrested (and in some cases executed) unpopular police officers. The Soviet represented practically the whole of the Petersburg proletariat but it was not all-inclusive. It did not, for example, allow representation to bourgeois-liberal or non-proletarian unions such as the 'Union of Unions', a federation of organisations and associations representing architects, doctors, economists, journalists, lawyers, professors, teachers and the intelligentsia generally[35,36].

St Petersburg, was both the Russian capital and industrial centre, and as such was the national focus of the events of the last three months of 1905. In St Petersburg itself the Soviet was the lynchpin for these events. It was the greatest workers' organisation ever seen in Russia - unique even by Western standards - and served as the model for Moscow, Odessa, and more than 50 other towns and cities[37]. This purely urban, proletarian organisation was the natural organisational focus and form of the revolution, as would be confirmed in 1917:

"The Soviet of Workers' Deputies ... represented approximately 200,000 persons, principally factory and plant workers, and although its political influence, both direct and indirect, extended to a wider circle, very important strata of the proletariat (building workers, domestic servants, unskilled labourers, cab drivers) were scarcely or not at all represented. It cannot be doubted, however, that the Soviet represented the interests of the whole proletarian mass. ... Among the proletarian masses, the political dominance of the Soviet in Petersburg found no opponents but only supporters"[38].

The name "workers' government", which both the workers and the bourgeois press gave to the Soviet, expressed the fact that the Soviet was, in essence, a workers' government in embryo, and this idea was developed by Trotsky in his *ToPR*. The Soviet represented the nascent power and revolutionary strength of the working class districts, counter posing the power still retained by the military-political monarchy. It developed a programme of political democracy (universal suffrage, republic, workers' militia, etc.) in opposition to Tsarist autocracy, and was a vital phase in the political development of the Russian proletariat[39].

Trotsky wrote most of the proclamations and manifestos of the Soviet and gained enormous popularity with the workers. Lunacharsky, who was one of Lenin's close collaborators at the time, recalled that Trotsky "held himself apart not only from us but from the Mensheviks too. His work was largely carried out in the Soviet of Workers' Deputies and together with Parvus he organised some sort of separate group which published a very militant and very well-edited small and cheap newspaper, *The Beginning*". And, he added: "I remember someone saying in Lenin's presence: 'Khrustalev's star is waning and now the strong man in the Soviet is Trotsky'. Lenin's face darkened for a moment, then he said: 'Well, Trotsky has earned it by his brilliant and unflagging work'"[40]. Trotsky was just 26 on 7 November, and became president of the St Petersburg Soviet on the 23rd.

Of all the *RSDLP* leaders, it was Trotsky who was most prominent in 1905:

"... Trotsky undoubtedly showed himself, despite his youth, to be the best prepared. Less than any of them did he bear the stamp of ... émigré narrowness of outlook which, as I have said, even affected Lenin at that time. Trotsky understood better than all the others what it means to conduct the political struggle on a broad, national scale. He emerged from the revolution having acquired an enormous degree of popularity, whereas neither Lenin nor Martov had effectively gained any at all"[41].

The advent of legal conditions created huge opportunities for the party press. Ten days after the Tsar's October Manifesto, the Bolsheviks published the first issue of the paper *Novaya Zhizn* (*New Life*), their public face until its closure in early December. Its circulation rose to 80,000, a significant achievement for a party which only a few months earlier had been underground.

Trotsky had even greater success. On 13 November, in alliance with the St Petersburg Mensheviks, he took over the liberal paper *Ruskaya Gazeta (Russian Gazette)*, changed the name to *Nachalo* (*The Beginning*) and turned it into a mass revolutionary daily paper. Its circulation reached a staggering half million by December! Whilst, theoretically, the organ of the Mensheviks, replacing the now defunct *Iskra*, the *Beginning* was, in practice, controlled by Trotsky; and the paper's political line had nothing in common with that of the Menshevik leadership, being in *de facto* agreement with Lenin and *New Life* on all important questions relating to the activities of the

Soviet. Trotsky in St Petersburg, and Lenin from Switzerland, constantly warned that the liberals would inevitably sell out.

Trotsky's literary successes would continue after 1905. Funded by A. A. Joffe and M. I. Skobolev (the son of a wealthy oil magnate) Trotsky, in exile in Vienna, would produce his own newspaper, *Pravda,* from October 1908 until 1912. At its peak this had a circulation of over 30,000, of which anything from 500 to 1,000 copies of each number reached St Petersburg. The 1910 conference of the *RSDLP*, dominated by the Mensheviks and those Bolsheviks who believed in party unity, had made it the organ of the party so even local Bolsheviks sold it, much to Lenin's annoyance, as the circulation of his own paper, *Proletarii*, in Petersburg was numbered in the few dozen[42]. In April 1912 Lenin appropriated the name and published his own *Pravda*, effectively killing Trotsky's paper[43].

Lenin, returned to Russia on 4 November, convinced of the need for the immediate re-unification of the two wings of the *RSDLP*. The rank and file members demanded it, knowing from their own experiences that continuing the split would severely damage the party's standing with the factory workers and retard the party's growth. Lenin wrote: "... it is now possible not only to *urge* unity, not only to obtain *promises* to unite, but actually *to unite* - by a simple decision of the majority of organised workers in both factions"[44].

Under the impact of the revolution, the St Petersburg Mensheviks were far to the left of the Menshevik leadership in exile, and had moved even further to the left under the influence of Trotsky. By the autumn, the members of the two factions in Russia had had established a joint committee despite the initial differences concerning attitudes to the Soviet. Both *The Beginning* and *New Life* defended the restoration of unity. The Bolshevik Central Committee (CC), with Lenin present, passed a unanimous resolution to the effect that the development of the revolution had removed the basis for the split in the *RSDLP*. The Bolshevik CC and the Menshevik Organisational Committee had also established a federative structure and were negotiating unification. Both fractions were to call their own conference preparing the way for a unity Congress as soon as possible[45].

Later, after his arrest, Trotsky questioned whether accepting representatives of bourgeois liberalism and bourgeois democracy would have added to the Soviet's strength. His reply was unequivocal, the role played by the bourgeoisie showed that the Tsar had only to promise a parliament (Duma) (with what Lenin described as the "most reactionary constitution in Europe"), to placate their opposition. The Soviet was duty-bound to remain a class organisation, an organ of struggle. Bourgeois liberal deputies would be absolutely incapable of strengthening the Soviet:

"The liberal petty-bourgeoisie and capitalists tolerated the first phase of the revolution. They saw that the revolutionary movement shook the foundations of absolutism and forced it towards a constitutional agreement. They put up with strikes and demonstrations, adopted a cautiously friendly attitude towards revolutionaries. However, after the October 17 Manifesto, which offered a deal between the liberals and the authorities, it seemed to them that all that was left to do was to put it into effect. A continuing revolution threatened to undermine that possibility. From then on the proletarian masses, united by the October strike and organised in the soviet, put the liberals against the revolution by the very fact of their existence. The soviet, on the contrary, believed that the main struggle lay ahead. Under such circumstances any revolutionary co-operation between the capitalists and the proletariat was out of the question"[46].

It was this last point that separated the *RDDPP* from the *ToPR*. For all its revolutionary ardour, Lenin's perspective was the establishment of a bourgeois-democratic state. Trotsky saw that the vanguard of the revolution was the urban proletariat, the natural organisational form of the revolution was the Soviet, and the proletariat once having seized power, would not restrict its demands to those of the bourgeois-democratic revolution.

2.4 The Bolsheviks and the Soviet

By the autumn, mass meetings were occurring almost daily in all the industrial towns and cities throughout Russia. Huge opportunities opened up as the *RSDLP* rapidly gained ground among advanced workers. Absolutely key for the successful linking of the small number of organised Marxists to the broad mass of workers in struggle, was their attitude towards the St Petersburg Soviet. Lenin immediately grasped the significance of this new phenomenon, writing from exile:

"I may be wrong, but I believe ... that politically the Soviet of Workers' Deputies should be regarded as the embryo of a provisional revolutionary government. I think the Soviet should proclaim itself the provisional revolutionary government of the whole of Russia as early as possible, or should set up a provisional revolutionary government ..."[47].

On the key issue of what attitude to take towards the Soviet and in opposition to the Bolshevik committee-men, Trotsky and Lenin were in full *de-facto* agreement:

"In Petersburg, I continued working together with comrade Krasin [one of only two the members of the Bolshevik CC not arrested in February 1905] and at the same time kept in touch with the Menshevik group. At the centre of all our discussions in that period were the question of the armed uprising, the workers' government, the democratic dictatorship of workers and peasants. In the spring the Menshevik groups supported my theses on the necessity of preparing for an armed uprising and for the seizure of power by a provisional revolutionary government."[48].

Trotsky also described the initial attitude of the leading local Bolshevik committee-men:

"The section of the Bolshevik Central Committee led by Bogdanov which was in Petersburg was flatly against the creation of a non-party organisation. ... I was present at the meeting of the Bolshevik Central Committee ... where tactics in relation to the soviet were worked out. Bogdanov put forward the following plan: to propose to the soviet in the name of the Bolshevik faction that it immediately accept the Social Democrat programme and overall leadership by the party .... the meeting adopted Bogdanov's plan. ... Some days later, after comrade Lenin's arrival, the Bolsheviks' view of the soviet changed in principle ...."[49].

Sverchkov confirmed Trotsky's description of events: "The Petersburg Bolsheviks decided that the Soviet had officially to adopt the programme of the Social Democrat Party. They put this before the Soviet with the threat that if it was rejected, they would immediately leave the Soviet. ... the vast majority of the Soviet consisted of Social Democrats ... (and) we ourselves categorically rose up in arms against this proposal"[50]. Zinoviev confirmed: "A section of the Bolsheviks had made the mistake of demanding that the Soviet officially adopt the Social Democrat Party programme. But Lenin ... soon corrected this major mistake"[51]. It was an indication of future events (in 1917) that when Lenin intervened to pull the Bolsheviks away from their sectarian attitude, his letter *Our Tasks and the Soviet of Workers' Deputies* to the Bolshevik journal *New Life* was rejected![52]. Gorev, a Bolshevik present at the time later wrote:

"Lenin put an end to this negative approach to the soviet of deputies. .... His impression of the Petersburg soviet, to which he was taken clandestinely, is particularly interesting. ... There were about 500 people there in all. It made a tremendous impression. Lenin sat silent and listened. After the session, a small group of us took him to the Vienna restaurant to celebrate his return, and we stayed there until morning.

Lenin began to chastise the members of the (Bolshevik) committee for being completely incapable of appreciating the enormous force represented by the soviet and putting forward ridiculous proposals that the soviet should subordinate itself to them. He then said that the soviet was also the embryo of the dictatorship of the proletariat and peasantry which he had been propagandising since the summer ... 'Let the peasants join it as well' he said 'and it will be a soviet of workers' and peasants' deputies, an organ of the dictatorship of the proletariat and peasantry'"[53].

In *Our Tasks and the Soviets of Workers' Deputies*, and *Socialism and Anarchism*, both written in November 1905, Lenin spelled out how he saw the development of the Soviet of Workers' Deputies into a provisional revolutionary government. Essentially the Soviet was "not a labour parliament and **not an organ of proletarian self-government**, nor an organ of self-government at all, but a fighting organisation for the achievement of definite aims"[54]. The Soviet should proclaim itself the provisional revolutionary government with a programme that included: the complete and immediate realisation of political freedom, the repeal of all legislation restricting freedom of speech, conscience, assembly, the press, association and strikes. The membership of the Soviet should be broad and mixed, and Lenin specifically called for the inclusion of the Union of Unions - rejected by the Soviet - because the goals of that organisation included the convocation of a National Assembly which fitted well with Lenin's aim of an Assembly "that would enjoy the support of a free and armed **people** and have full authority and strength to establish a new order in Russia"[55].

It has been hypothesised by, for example, Woods[56] that what prevented Trotsky from joining the Bolsheviks in late 1905 was the conduct of the Bolshevik committee-men in St Petersburg. Woods is undoubtedly correct in his appreciation of Trotsky's attitude to the formalism of the committee-men, but Trotsky, despite his outstanding and heroic role as leader of the St Petersburg Soviet, had not overcome his conciliationism, his focus on the reunification of Bolsheviks and Mensheviks, and would certainly not have made a move to join either faction prior to the Unity Conference. Additionally, Trotsky and Lenin were beginning to develop differences on the class nature of the unfolding Russian Revolution. The concept of the Permanent Revolution was stirring in Trotsky's mind, while Lenin, at the Third (Bolshevik-only) Congress, had already begun to introduce the concept of a revolutionary democratic dictatorship which he would subsequently codify and elaborate as the *RDDPP* in numerous articles and pamphlets, beginning in June-July 1905 with the publication of *Two Tactics*.

2.5 The Struggle for the 8-Hour Day

The October general strike in St Petersburg had been a major factor in forcing the Tsar to issue his Manifesto. During this great strike delegates had proclaimed that when work was resumed they, and their fellow workers, would never agree to return under the old conditions[57]. On 26 October, delegates from one of the St Petersburg districts, without the knowledge of the Soviet, decided to introduce the 8-hour working day at their factories by direct action. The following day the delegates' proposal was adopted by overwhelming majorities at several workers' meetings. At the Alexandrovsky engineering works the question was decided by secret ballot to avoid pressure; the results were 1,668 for, 14 against[58]. From 28 October, several major metalworking plants began to work the 8-hour day. On 29 October, it was reported to the Soviet, amid thunderous applause, that the 8-hour day had been introduced, "by take-over" means, at three large plants. The workers now used the same direct action methods in support of their own, specific demands, that they had previously adopted in support of the more general demands for freedom of assembly and of the press. Trotsky now asked the decisive question, "Were the rights of the factory owners, the capitalists, to be more protected than the privileges of the monarchy?"[59]. The answer was given by the thousands of workers who downed tools and left the plants and factories at the end of their 8-hours shift. These actions were an inspiration for the *ToPR*.

St Petersburg was probably the most militant city in the Russian empire throughout 1905. But the St Petersburg workers were trying to do too much, too soon. The revolutionary movement was strung out like a horse race with the St Petersburg proletariat way ahead of the proletariat in other towns and cities, and the proletariat as a whole, way ahead of the peasantry. The Soviet Executive Committee repeatedly tried to rein in the enthusiasm of the St Petersburg proletariat and, for example, argued against the immediate struggle for the introduction of the 8-hour day. But as Sverchkov said "... the demand for the 8-hour day was so precious to the workers that they did not listen to these arguments, did not think over the approaching consequences or the calamities of unemployment, and they could not give up the idea of the shortening of the working day to the desired length by direct action". In individual plants where the employers offered to reduce the working day to ten or even nine hours "the workers' response was a few dozen votes for the owners' offer and a thousand votes for the 8-hour working day"[60].

However, the situation was becoming more and more confused and difficult. Towards the end of October the government proclaimed a state of siege in Poland, and almost immediately thereafter announced that those sailors in the important naval base of Kronstadt who had supported the October general strike, would be court-martialled. In response, the Soviet called a political strike demanding the end of courts martial and the death penalty, but the balance of forces meant it was compelled to accept a compromise, that the sailors would be tried by an ordinary military court and not a court-martial, and the strike was called off on 5 November. Trotsky was aware not only of the growing weariness of the strikers, but also of the difference in level of revolutionary spirit in St Petersburg and the provinces; "We must drag out the preparation for decisive action as much as we can, perhaps for a month or two, until we can come out as an army as cohesive and organised as possible"[61]. This would be a lesson well learned and would stand Trotsky in good stead to plan and lead the October 1917 Revolution.

To the employers, each in their own factory, it appeared that the Manifesto gained by the October strike went hand-in-hand with a strengthening of the workers' stand against capital and, of course, the unilateral introduction of the 8-hour day by direct action was bound to provoke a strong reaction on their part. Now the government, the largest single employer in St Petersburg, took the lead, making an issue of the 8-hour working day, and began to close state plants while simultaneously clamping down on workers' meetings, breaking them up by force, in order to demoralise the workers. Until November, the capitalists had tended to respond individually, but with the government taking the lead, collectively declared war on the revolutionary proletariat, beginning a lock-out by which to starve the workers into submission. The fact that they had not waited and linked up with other workers nation-wide, now left the St Petersburg proletariat exposed and isolated.

A number of private factories were closed down and tens of thousands of workers were thrown onto the streets. The factory owners were recovering their confidence and now adopted a hard-line. For the workers of St Petersburg retreat was unavoidable. On 6 November the Soviet adopted a compromise resolution declaring that the 8-hour demand was no longer universal, and calling for the continuation of the struggle only in those enterprises where there was some hope of success. Such a solution was clearly unsatisfactory because it failed to provide a co-ordinating slogan and meant the movement would fragment into a series of separate struggles - each of which would be much weaker for being isolated. Workers in a small number of factories did gain a reduction in the working day of a half or even one hour, but most had to accept their former conditions or even worse. At the giant Nevsky plant, for example, not only was there no reduction in the working day, but the workers had to agree to no wildcat strikes or meetings on factory premises[62].

Trotsky pointed out that the coalition between private capital in St Petersburg and the government, had transformed the question of an 8-hour working day into a question of the authority of the state, and that the workers of St Petersburg could not, therefore, achieve victory in isolation from those of the country at large:

"Of course the eight-hour working day can only be introduced with the co-operation of state power. But state power is precisely what the proletariat was fighting for at that moment. Had it won a political victory, the introduction of the eight-hour day would have been no more than a natural consequence of the 'fantastic experiment'. But it failed to win; and therein, of course, lay its gravest 'fault'"[63].

To carry out a retreat in an organised fashion was well-nigh impossible. On 12 November, the Soviet of Workers' Deputies passed a resolution on the temporary suspension of the struggle for the introduction of the 8-hour working day. The state-operated plants re-opened for work, but under the old conditions. The gates of thirteen more private factories and plants closed and the number of workers locked-out had risen to about 100,000. On 12 November, the Soviet decided to retreat in the most dramatic of all the meetings of the workers' parliament. The vote was divided. Representatives of several textile, glassmaking, and tobacco factories wanted to continue the struggle, but Trotsky, supported by the metalworkers, won the vote[64].

Nevertheless, many workers chose to fight on. "Comrade workers from other factories and plants", the workers of a large factory who had decided to continue the struggle wrote to the Soviet, "forgive us for doing this, but we have no strength left to suffer this gradual exhaustion of ourselves both physical and moral. We shall fight to the last drop of our blood ..."[65]. These reactions of the workers were a direct source of the ideas that would, in the following year, be published as the *ToPR*.

On 14 November, Bolshevik delegates successfully proposed to the Soviet, a resolution drafted by Lenin on factory closure and unemployment, calling for all factories which had been closed to be re-opened, and all those dismissed to be re-instated. In the resolution Lenin called for the Soviet to appeal for a general strike if its demands were rejected. Whilst endorsing the sentiment, one can only wonder at the lack of appreciation of how the workers would respond to such a resolution, given that only one week before, the Soviet had to call off a political strike in support of the Kronstadt sailors, and only two days before had admitted defeat for the co-ordinated struggle for the 8-hour day[66]. Deutscher points out that during the existence of the Soviet, no alternative tactical or strategic line was ever proposed by the Bolshevik delegates (after their initial hiccup), and goes so far as to describe

Trotsky's leadership of the St Petersburg Soviet as "faultless"[67]. Any criticism of Trotsky's role is noticeable by its absence from Lenin's writings.

The defection of the bourgeois liberals had tipped the balance in favour of reaction. By 22 November, the regime felt strong enough to arrest Khrustalyov-Nosar on the premises of the Soviet Executive. Trotsky had been *de-facto* leader of the Soviet from the start and after the arrest of Khrustalev-Nosar, when he was elected temporary chairman, he was both *de facto* and *de jure* leader. However, the "heavy battalions" of labour were exhausted. The defeat of the attempt to introduce the 8-hour day by direct action, and the factory and plant closures that followed, weakened the St Petersburg proletariat and lowered its combativity, so that when, on 3 December (the day after the mutiny by the Rostov regiment in Moscow), the St Petersburg Soviet was closed down by government troops and the police, and the delegates present were arrested, there was no reaction. Now leaderless, and worn out, it was in no state to react to the December Moscow uprising.

It was the specific demand of the 8-hour day that led to the final split in the opposition to the Tsar, and turned capital into an openly counter-revolutionary force. From this, the Mensheviks drew the conclusion that in the struggle against Tsarism, the working class would have to rein in its demands to within limits acceptable to the bourgeoisie. For Trotsky, it would lead to his argument that the proletariat, as an independent revolutionary force at the head of the popular masses, could not restrict itself to limits set by the bourgeoisie.

2.6 The Moscow Uprising

The Moscow Soviet was formed on 21 November and at its first meeting there were 180 delegates representing about 80,000 workers. By the beginning of December the revolution had begun to penetrate the minds of the peasants in the army. Under the hammer blows of decisive military defeats - the battles of Yalu, Shalo and Mukden, and the fall of Port Arthur - in the war against Japan, and the influence of the general revolutionary movement, sections of the armed forces and the villages were now entering a state of ferment. Huge areas of European Russia were affected, especially the central "Black Earth" zone stretching from the Ukraine to the southern Ural mountains. However, the consciousness of the rural masses lagged substantially behind that of the towns and this proved a fatal weakness undermining the St Petersburg Soviet and the December, Moscow uprising. Although a wave of peasant discontent spread through the armed forces, the government was able to contain the mutinies that did occur. This confirmed that a major weakness of the 1905 Revolution was the lack of a firm base amongst the peasants; that the peasant-soldier revolts were not on a sufficient scale to make a fundamental difference to the outcome.

With the mutiny of the Rostov regiment in Moscow on 2 December, and the arrest of the St Petersburg Soviet on 3 December, the initiative passed to the workers of Moscow. However, the local Bolsheviks hesitated, and when the news that the soldiers of the regiment had seized weapons and thrown their officers out of the barracks, reached the Moscow Committee, it decided not to change its meeting agenda, and continued with the scheduled discussion on the agrarian question! This inaction was particularly reprehensible as the Rostov regiment, which held over half the machine guns then available in Moscow, was welcoming agitators, and representatives of the sapper regiment which guarded one of the Moscow arsenals, had approached the Soviet. The faint-heartedness of the Moscow Committee in not contacting the Rostov regiment, failing to attempt to bring it out of its barracks and link it with the Moscow Soviet, meant that in a couple of days the mutineers were demoralised, disarmed and confined to their barracks. This defeat effectively eliminated the prospect of organised units going over to the side of the workers. On 4 December, the Moscow Soviet passed a motion congratulating the soldiers on their uprising and expressing the hope that they would come over to the side of the people. But by that time the soldiers' revolt had been crushed[68].

On the other hand, the workers in the factories of Moscow were impatient for action, and on 7 December, the Soviet voted unanimously for a general political strike. Under the circumstances, no matter what the subjective intentions, this was a vote for an uprising. The general strike began the same day as the decision was taken, involving more than 100,000 workers, increasing to 150,000 on the following day. On 7 and 8 December mass meetings and street demonstrations occurred in Moscow with isolated clashes with the police. The Moscow Soviet published six issues of a daily paper from 7 to 12 of December, the Moscow *Izvestia Sovetov Robochikh Deputatov (Bulletin of the Soviet of Workers' Deputies)* which attempted to draw wider layers of the population into struggle, but made no direct mention of an armed uprising[69]. Only after the fighting had actually begun did *Izvestia* begin to give instructions to the fighting squads.

The Governor of Moscow - General Dubasov - with only 1,500 soldiers on whose loyalty he could count was, initially, confined to the centre of Moscow. Outside of this area the city was, *de facto*, in the hands of the Soviet. But Dubasov had been able to disarm and confine to barracks, those elements of the army on whose loyalty he could not rely. He also had a great stroke of luck. On the night of 7 December, the committee that linked the revolutionary parties, including the two foremost Bolshevik leaders, was arrested, leaving the movement overwhelmed by events. Dubasov was also lucky that the only railway line in and out of Moscow not brought to a halt by the strike, was the Nikolai line leading to St Petersburg, and which would bring the Semyovovsky regiment to his assistance. Revolutionaries in St Petersburg, lacked the arms, explosives, and expertise to break the Petersburg-Moscow rail link, and reinforcements loyal to the Tsar were successfully transferred to Moscow[70].

On 8 December, a mass meeting was broken up by the police and arrests made. The Soviet did not react because the Bolsheviks continued to wait for the troops to come over, but it was already too late for that. At this point, taking advantage of the hesitation, the counter-revolution struck back, On 9 December, a crowd was attacked by dragoons, and the building used for *RSDLP* meetings was surrounded by troops and machine-gunned. In the course of these clashes there were many injured, killed and arrested. On that evening, unorganised street crowds spontaneously set up the first barricades, and hostilities began in earnest. But by December 15 did the superiority of the government forces was complete, and on December 17 the Semyovovsky regiment crushed the Presnya District, the last stronghold of the uprising.[71].

Armed uprisings were not confined to Moscow[72]. There were, in fact, a whole series of armed uprisings - in Kharkov, Donbas, Yekaterinoslav, Rostov-on-Don, the Northern Caucasus, Nizhni-Novgorod and other centres. The national question also caused uprisings in Georgia and the Baltic states in particular. There were uprisings too along the railway lines in the Donetsk region and Siberia where battles occurred at several stations, attracting the support of peasants in the surrounding districts. But the Moscow uprising did not succeed in re-arousing the proletariat of St Petersburg, which meant that the government could concentrate its forces on crushing the workers of Moscow, and then put down the local movements one by one. Despite being the starting point of the October strike, Moscow had been overshadowed by St Petersburg during October and November. The Moscow uprising in December 1905 was largely a matter of a few, small, lightly-armed guerrilla groups. The Moscow Bolsheviks were too late when it came to taking advantage of the mutinous movement in the garrison. In the course of the summer of 1906 the peasant outbreaks did, again, assume mass proportions but by that time the backbone of the working class movement had been broken so the peasant revolts could be put down one by one accompanied by mass hangings, the flogging of all the males in the village, rape, and police instigated pogroms of the Jews.

2.7 Lessons Learned

For Lenin, the lessons learned confirmed the need for a party to co-ordinate and lead the uprising across all of Russia, the necessity of an alliance of the proletariat with the peasantry, and of winning over at least a section of the armed forces[73]. Trotsky did not draw up a similar detailed list. His major analysis, *Results and Prospects,* deals with the general perspective for revolution in Russia, and although it states that a class alliance between the proletariat and peasantry was essential for victory, precise details are lacking. However, in his review of the activities of the Petersburg Soviet[74], Trotsky foresaw that any new revolutionary upsurge would lead to the creation of Soviets all over the country, led and co-ordinated by an All-Russian Soviet whose programme would be based on the lessons learned in the 'Fifty Days'. In particular Trotsky proposed the same solution as Lenin for overcoming the core weakness of a purely urban revolution - to establish revolutionary co-operation with the army and the peasantry, and to create Councils of Peasants' Delegates (Peasants' Committees) as local organs of the agrarian revolution. Interestingly, also as Lenin, he also called for the Soviet to organise elections to a Constituent Assembly!

In 1905 the proletariat emerged as the key driving force of the revolution against the autocracy. However, 1905 also confirmed that no revolution could succeed in Russia without the support of the peasantry. Indeed, the Achilles' heel of the 1905 Revolution consisted of the fact that the proletarian advanced guard was exhausted before the bulk of the working people, the peasants, moved into action (for an analysis of strike statistics for 1905-06, see Lenin[75]).

The undoubted winner in 1905, in electoral terms, was the populist Socialist Revolutionary (*SR*) Party which gained the votes of the overwhelming majority of the peasantry. While mouthing Marxist and socialist phrases about land to the peasant, the *SRs* were generally reformists with a sprinkling of terrorist activists. This party would continue to receive the votes of the bulk of the peasants until at least the elections to the Constituent Assembly at the end of 1917.

To Trotsky, the general strike and creation of the Soviets proved once and for all, the superiority of town over countryside, and the proletariat as the only force capable of leading the revolution to overthrow the autocracy. Unfortunately, while he recognised the key role of the Social Democratic Party in the revolution, there was no clear recognition of the necessity of a disciplined, Leninist party; rather, Trotsky appeared more concerned with demonstrating the need for the party to work within and through the mass organisations thrown up by the class in the process of the struggle.

Nevertheless, 1905 did confirm to him the necessity of gaining the support of the peasantry, since without that support the struggle for the army could not be won. The key to winning this support was for the *RSDLP* to revolutionise feudal ownership[76].

In 1905, for the first time, revolutionary *SD* became a key force within the working class across the whole of Russia, and the decisive role of the party for any successful overthrow of the autocracy was confirmed to Lenin. Within a space of nine months, the consciousness of the workers advanced by leaps and bounds on the basis of their own experiences: from priest and petition in January, through economic strikes for better wages and conditions, to the highest expressions of the class struggle - the political general strike, workers' self-defence squads, and armed insurrection in December. Under Lenin's leadership the Bolshevik faction overcame its mistakes and advanced to the head of the revolutionary proletariat. Qualitatively, the need for an organisational weapon - the Bolshevik Party - to lead the workers to victory was proved, and its leadership was tempered in the heat of the 1905 Revolution.

2.8 References

1. Trotsky, L.D., *1905* Vintage Books, New York, 1972, pvi
2. Knei-Paz, B., *The Social and Political Thought of Leon Trotsky*, Clarendon Press Oxford, 1978, p207
3. Woods, A., *Bolshevism the Road to Revolution*, Wellred Publications, London, 1999, p173
4. Woods, A., *ibid* p160
5. Lenin, V.I., *The Two Tactics of Social Democracy in the Democratic Revolution*, June-July 1905, CW 9:15 - 140
6. Cliff, T.C., Lenin, *Building the Party, Pluto Press,* 1975, p149 - 153
7. Trotsky, L.D., *1905* Vintage Books, New York, 1972, p81
8. Woods, A., *Bolshevism the Road to Revolution*, Wellred Publications, London, 1999, p182 - 184
9. Lenin, V.I., *The Beginning of the Revolution in Russia*, Jan 1905 CW 8:97 - 100
10. Lenin, V.I., *Should We Organise the Revolution?* Feb 1905, CW 8:167 - 176
11. Cliff, T.C., Lenin, *Building the Party, Pluto Press,* 1975, p155 - 156
12. Lenin, V.I., *A Letter to A. A. Bogdanov and S. I. Gusev*, Feb 1905, CW 8:143-7
13. Somov, *From the History of the SD Movement in Petersburg in 1905 - Personal Reminiscences,* quoted in *Revolutionary History* Vol 9 No 1 p58 - 60
14. Deutscher, I., *The Prophet Armed*, Oxford Paperbacks, 1954, p110-116
15. Woods, A., *Bolshevism the Road to Revolution*, Wellred Publications, London, 1999, p237
16. Trotsky, L.D., *Iskra* No 93, 17 March 1905, quoted in Deutscher *The Prophet Armed*, Oxford Paperbacks, 1954, p118-9
17. Lenin, V.I., *A Letter to A. A. Bogdanov and S. I. Gusev*, Feb 1905 CW 8:143-7
18. Lenin, V.I., *The Third Congress of the RSDLP, April 12 April 27*, April 1905, CW 8:359 - 449
19. Lenin, V.I., *A Letter to A. A. Bogdanov and S. I. Gusev*, Feb 1905 CW 8:143-7
20. Woods, A., *Op. Cit.*, p199
21. Woods, A., *Op. Cit.*, p199 - 200
22. Krupskaya, N., *Memories of Lenin*, Panther History, 1970, p125 and p124-5

23. Sverchkov, D., *At the Dawn of the Revolution* 1925, quoted in Pete Glatter, *A Revolution Takes Shape*, Revolutionary History, Vol 9, No 1 p11-118

24. Zinoviev, G., *History of the Bolshevik Party*, New Park Publications, London, 1973, p128

25. Deutscher, I., *The Prophet Armed*, Oxford Paperbacks, 1954, p126-127

26. Trotsky, L.D., *1905* Vintage Books, New York, 1972, p157-161

27. Vasil'ev, M., *Proletarian Revolution*, Moscow 1919, quoted in *Revolutionary History* Vol 9 No 1 p169 - 170

28. Sverchkov, D., *At the Dawn of the Revolution* 1925, quoted in Pete Glatter, *A Revolution Takes Shape*, Revolutionary History, Vol 9, No 1 p112

29. Trotsky, L.D., *1905* Vintage Books, New York, 1972, p104

30. Woods, A., *Op. Cit.*, p210 - 216;

31. Glatter, P. and Ruff, P., *The Decisive Days*, in *Revolutionary History*, Vol 9 No 1 p107-111

32. Sverchkov, D., *At the Dawn of the Revolution* 1925, quoted in Pete Glatter, *A Revolution Takes Shape*, Revolutionary History, Vol 9, No 1 p114

33. Sverchkov, D., *At the Dawn of the Revolution* 1925, quoted in Pete Glatter, *A Revolution Takes Shape*, Revolutionary History, Vol 9, No 1 p117 - 118

34. Deutscher, I., *The Prophet Armed*, Oxford Paperbacks, 1954, p140

35. Sverchkov, D., *At the Dawn of the Revolution* 1925, quoted in Pete Glatter, *A Revolution Takes Shape*, Revolutionary History, Vol 9, No 1 p112

36. Wolfe, B.D., Three Who Made a Revolution, Pelican, London, 1984, p318

37. Trotsky, L.D., *1905* Vintage Books, New York, 1972, p104

38. Trotsky, L.D., *1905* Vintage Books, New York, 1972, p254

39. Trotsky, L.D., *1905* Vintage Books, New York, 1972, pix

40. Lunacharsky, A., *Revolutionary Silhouettes*, London, 1967, p60-1

41. Lunacharsky, A., *Revolutionary Silhouettes*, London, 1967, p60

42. McKean, R.B. *St Petersburg Between the Revolutions*, Yale University Press, 1990, p54 and 59

43. Trotsky, L.D., *1905* Vintage Books, New York, 1972, p49

44. Lenin, V.I., *The Reorganisation of the Party*, Nov 1905, CW 10:37-8

45. Woods, A., *Op. Cit.*, p236 - 237

46. Trotsky, L.D., *1905* Vintage Books, New York, 1972, p254

47. Lenin, V.I., *Our Tasks and the Soviet of Workers' Deputies*, Nov 1905, CW 10:21

48. Trotsky's letter to the Commission on the History of the October Revolution and the RCP(B) of the State Publishing House saying he did not have time to write an introduction to Sverchov's book, quoted in *Revolutionary History*, Vol 9 No 1 p117

49. Trotsky's letter *ibid* p117 - 119

50. Sverchkov, D., *At the Dawn of the Revolution* 1925, quoted in Pete Glatter, *A Revolution Takes Shape*, Revolutionary History, Vol 9, No 1 p120

51. Zinoviev, G., *History of the Bolshevik Party*, New Park Publications, London, 1973, p128

52. Cliff, T.C., Lenin, *Building the Party, Pluto Press,* 1975, p161

53. B Gorev *The Bulletin of Revolutionary History* No 1 January 1922, quoted in *Revolutionary History* Vol 9 No 1 p123

54. Lenin, V.I., *Socialism and Anarchism,* 24 Nov 1905, CW 10:71

55. Lenin, V.I. *Our Tasks and the Soviet of Workers' Deputies,* 4 Nov 1905, CW 10:24-25

56. Woods, A., *Op. Cit.*, p236

57. Trotsky, L.D., *1905* Vintage Books, New York, 1972, p179-186

58. Trotsky, L.D., *1905* Vintage Books, New York, 1972, p180

59. Trotsky, L.D., *1905* Vintage Books, New York, 1972, p181

60. Sverchkov, D., *At the Dawn of the Revolution* 1925, quoted in Pete Glatter, *A Revolution Takes Shape*, Revolutionary History, Vol 9, No 1 p159

61. Trotsky, L.D., *Investia* No 7, 7 Nov 1905, quoted in Deutscher, I., *The Prophet Armed*, Oxford Paperbacks, 1954, p132 - 134

62. Glatter, P. and Ruff, P., *The Decisive Days*, in *Revolutionary History*, Vol 9 No1 p161

63. Trotsky, L.D., *1905* Vintage Books, New York, 1972, p185

64. Deutscher, I., *The Prophet Armed*, Oxford Paperbacks, 1954, p135

65. Quoted in Trotsky, L.D., *1905* Vintage Books, New York, 1972, p184

66. Lenin, V.I., *Resolution of the Executive Committee of the St Petersburg Soviet of Workers' Deputies on Measures for Counter-Acting the Lock-Out.* Nov 1905, CW 10:50-51

67. Deutscher, I., *The Prophet Armed*, Oxford Paperbacks, 1954, p135

68. Vasil'ev, M., *Proletarian Revolution*, Moscow 1919, quoted in *Revolutionary History* Vol 9 No 1 p169 - 170

69. Pokrovsky, M.N., *The Year 1905 - A History of the Revolutionary Movement*, State Publishing House, Moscow, 1925, quoted in

Revolutionary History Vol 9 No 1 p172. [Pokrovsky was a Party historian loyal to the Stalinist faction. It is now recognised that his history of 1905 was the commencement of the re-writing of events to play down the role of Trotsky - Deutscher, footnote, p135 *The Prophet Armed*]

70. Vasil'ev, M., *Proletarian Revolution*, Moscow 1919, quoted in *Revolutionary History* Vol 9 No 1 p169 - 170

71. Lenin, V.I., *Lessons of the Moscow Uprising*, Aug 1906, CW 11:171-178

72. Glatter, P. and Ruff, P., *The Decisive Days*, in *Revolutionary History*, Vol 9 No1 p166-167

73. Lenin, V.I., *Lessons of the Moscow Uprising*, Aug 1906, CW 11:171-178

74. Trotsky, L.D., *The Soviet and Our Revolution*, 1907, see www. marxists.org/archive/trotsky/1918/ourrevo/ch05.htm

75. Lenin, V.I., *Strike Statistics in Russia*, Jan 1911, CW 16:393-421

76. Trotsky, L.D., *1905,* Vintage Books, New York, 1972, p49

Chapter 3
LENIN AND THE REVOLUTIONARY-DEMOCRATIC DICTATORSHIP OF THE PROLETARIAT AND PEASANTRY

3.1   Introduction
3.2   The Peasants Replace the Liberal Bourgeoisie as a Major Driving Force in the Russian Democratic Revolution.
3.3   Social-Democrats in a Revolutionary Government?
3.4   Prospects for a Socialist Revolution
3.5   What Form for the Revolutionary-Democratic Dictatorship of the Proletariat and Peasantry?
3.6   Inner Tensions in the Revolutionary-Democratic Dictatorship of the Proletariat and Peasantry
3.7   Lenin and the Peasantry
3.8   References

3.1 Introduction

To demonstrate that Lenin did, indeed, fundamentally change his revolutionary perspective during 1917, it is necessary to understand what he had previously proposed and what Lenin's pre-1917 demand for a democratic dictatorship actually entailed. Thus, this chapter explores the origins, content and predicted likely outcomes of the slogan of the *RDDPP*, which encapsulated the Bolshevik strategy for the seizure of power in the forthcoming Russian Revolution. It discusses the slogan itself, identifies what was new in it and what elements Lenin retained in common with his Menshevik opponents, and argues that Lenin placed clear limits on the nature of the changes that a revolutionary-democratic dictatorship would introduce to Russian society and its economy. It describes how Lenin, himself, indicated such a dictatorship would function, the form it might take, and the key measures it would need to take to successfully carry through the bourgeois-democratic revolution. This is important for any analysis of the limitations of the *RDDPP*, and for understanding how, pre-1917, Lenin's concept of the Russian Revolution differed from Trotsky's.

The chapter also discusses inherent tensions and contradictions in the perspective of a *RDDPP*, and ends with a review of how Lenin believed, until 1917, that the *RDDPP* would solve the agrarian question in Russia in a way that would strengthen capitalism and that this would be achieved before the Russian socialist revolution. The latter would occur after, and as a consequence of, the socialist revolution in Western Europe. Additionally, the chapter introduces the idea that the political education that Bolshevik leaders, such as Zinoviev, Kamenev and others, received in the period 1905-1917 (the time span over which the *RDDPP* was an essential part of the Bolshevik programme), contributed to their actions over the February-October period prior to the October 1917 Revolution, which were so heavily criticised by Lenin.

Between 1903 - when he presented the agrarian programme of the *RSDLP* to the Second Congress in London - and 1905, Lenin completed an important leap in viewing the petty bourgeois peasantry rather than the urban petty bourgeois, as the major ally of the working class in the bourgeois-democratic revolution. At that time all currents within the *RSDLP* agreed that the Russian Revolution towards which they were working, was a bourgeois-democratic revolution, the outcome of which would be a capitalist state with a capitalist government. It was generally accepted by Marxists, even before the experiences of the first Russian Revolution, that the Russian big bourgeoisie would play no independent progressive role in the actual revolution:

"We told you already in 1848, brothers, that the German liberal bourgeoisie would soon come to power and would immediately turn its newly won power against the workers. You have seen how this forecast came true. It was indeed the bourgeoisie which took possession of the state authority in the wake of the March movement of 1848 and used this power to drive the workers, its allies in the struggle, back into their former oppressed position. Although the bourgeoisie could accomplish this only by entering into an alliance with the feudal party, which had been defeated in March, and eventually even had to surrender power once more to this feudal absolutist party, it has nevertheless secured favourable conditions for itself"[1].

Bolshevism, specifically emphasised the view that the Russian bourgeoisie, liberal or otherwise, was incapable of leading its own revolution to the end.

Prior to the experiences of 1905, international *SD* marched in step because it saw the major ally of the proletariat in the bourgeois-democratic revolution as the urban petty bourgeois not the peasantry, and certainly not the peasantry as a whole. Lenin was at one with the leading theoreticians of the Second International on his attitude to agrarian questions. So wedded was Lenin to the views of Plekhanov and Kautsky, that in an 1899 review he wrote that Kautsky's book (*Die Agrarfarge (The Agrarian Question)*) was the most important event in economic literature since the third volume of *Capital*[2].

It was expected that during the bourgeois-democratic revolution the working-class would lead the fight supported by revolutionary elements of the urban and rural petty-bourgeoisie, liberal bourgeoisie and intelligentsia; would defend its specific interests (8-hour day, existence of trade unions, right to strike, minimum wage, freedom to form its own political parties and struggle for socialism, etc.), but would not attempt to replace the bourgeoisie as the ideological leaders of the revolution. Plekhanov's Marxism, while leading him to the conclusion that "the revolutionary movement in Russia will triumph only as a working class movement or else it will never triumph"[3] also led him to ignore key specificities of Russia's social structure and of her revolutionary development, and to see that development as a shadow following Marx's theory of Western historical development[4,5].

The revolution of 1905 produced three key tendencies within Russian Marxism, which would separate into the Bolsheviks, Mensheviks and a small group around Trotsky. Naturally, their differences centred on the historical character of the Russian Revolution, how it would be realised and the path of its development - because the answers to these questions defined the strategy, tactics and practical day-to-day activities to be undertaken.

3.2 The Peasants Replace the Liberal Bourgeoisie as a Major Driving Force in the Russian Democratic Revolution

By 1905, the leaders of the *RSDLP* were well aware that the masses rise to revolution only in their own interests; the workers against the factory owner, and the great peasant mass of the Russian people against the landlords. The differences between *SDs* lay in the answers to the questions: What would be the character of the revolutionary government? What tasks would confront it, and in what order? How far would the revolution go?

For *SDs*, the answers to these important questions would determine which bourgeois and petty bourgeois block(s) the proletariat allied with in the coming bourgeois revolution - the liberal bourgeoisie, the urban petty bourgeois and intellectuals, or the peasantry. The Menshevik leadership retained the view that the bourgeoisie would remain the hegemonic class and so chose to attempt an alliance with the former groups. While critically supporting the bourgeoisie during the 1905 Revolution, they argued against Social-Democratic participation in the transitional revolutionary government, and by 1917 had become apologists for the bourgeoisie and their policies. In this, they constituted a block to the revolutionary progress of both the proletariat and peasantry, and it was against this that Lenin concentrated most of his fire during and after 1905, beginning with, for example, *Should We Organise the Revolution*[6] and *Two Tactics*[7].

Lenin had viewed the peasantry - over 80% of the Russian population - as potential allies of the proletariat in the democratic revolution since 1894, but it was re-assessing them as the major allies that became the basis of the historic disagreement between the two factions. The 'land programme' or 'agrarian question' or 'land question' were names for the process that would release the land to the peasant, and - and this was the more important issue for many peasants - end the feudal duties owed by peasants to their landlord. Lenin saw this programme of bourgeois progress as the key question of the bourgeois-democratic revolution because it affected the lives of so many.

Nevertheless, for the next twelve years, in common with the Mensheviks, Lenin continued to support the classical Marxist analysis, that a bourgeois-democratic revolution, particularly the agrarian revolution, was necessary **before** the question of the socialist revolution could be posed in Russia. In none of his writings before 1917-18 did Lenin ever, for a moment, pose the question of the peasantry becoming an ally of the proletariat in the socialist revolution. On the contrary, at that time he considered the socialist revolution in Russia impossible before the solution of the agrarian question, precisely because of the overwhelming preponderance of the peasantry in Russian society[8]. This idea underpins all his articles which touch directly or indirectly upon the agrarian question. However, whether the allies of the proletariat were the urban petty-bourgeoisie or the peasantry, both Bolsheviks and Mensheviks agreed that the autocratic rule of the Romanovs could be broken only if a majority of the population supported the revolution and the resulting regime rested on majority rule, as expressed in a Constituent Assembly[9].

However, Lenin, in contrast to Plekhanov, insisted that the destruction of Tsarist feudalism was not possible under the political leadership of the Russian bourgeoisie. The triumph of the bourgeois-democratic revolution in Russia was possible only if the working class waged the struggle for democracy independently of and, in fact, in opposition to, the bourgeoisie. The necessary mass base of the democratic revolution could not be provided by the working class alone, but the Russian proletariat, would be able to mobilise and lead the Russian peasantry if it consistently advanced an uncompromisingly radical resolution of the agrarian issues[10].

Lenin was not the only leading *SD* to revise his views on the role of the peasantry in the Russian Revolution. Kautsky, the Second International's leading Marxist theoretician, in his article *The Driving Forces and Prospects of the Russian Revolution*[11], was strongly in support of the new Leninist position and was quoted with enthusiasm by Lenin:

"Kautsky ... points out that in Russia .... the urban petty bourgeoisie 'will never be a reliable support of the revolutionary parties' ... Kautsky determines that peculiar relation between Russian liberalism and the revolutionary character of the peasants, ... 'The more the peasants become revolutionary, the more do the big landowners become reactionary, ... *the more unstable become the liberal parties*, and the more the *liberal professors and lawyers* in the towns shift to *the right*, so as not to lose all connection with their previous mainstay'"[12].

The Russian urban bourgeoisie would not be one of the driving forces in the Russian Revolution. Their function would be performed by the peasantry and the central problem for the democratic revolution in Russia would be the 'land question'. Only the proletariat and peasantry were authentic revolutionary forces and their alliance would be a *RDDPP*. Lenin was firmly of the opinion that the peasantry could only carry out an agrarian revolution if they abolished the old regime, the standing army and the bureaucracy, because all these were supports of landlordism, bound to it by ties of family, friendship, and financial interest[13]. The Russian bourgeois revolution would be a bourgeois revolution made largely without and, most likely, against the urban bourgeoisie.

At the Third (Bolshevik) Congress of the *RSDLP* in 1905, Lenin formalised significant changes to his 1903 strategy, and proposed a new scenario for the Russian Revolution that differed substantially from that of Plekhanov and the Mensheviks. The Congress agreed that, notwithstanding the bourgeois character of the coming revolution, the Russian liberal bourgeoisie was hostile to the expropriation of landlords' estates; instead they wanted a compromise with the monarchy on the basis of a constitutional regime. Lenin now argued that an alliance of workers and the entire peasantry would play the leading role in carrying out the tasks of the bourgeois revolution. Not that Lenin had any illusions about the extent to which the peasantry as an estate would support the working class struggle, nor the limits on the reciprocal support the proletariat would show for the peasants' struggle to obtain possession of the land and abolish serfdom. In September 1905, Lenin might have seen the semi-proletarian, landless elements in the Russian village as allies in the struggle for socialism, but never the peasantry as a whole:

"We support the peasant movement to the extent that it is revolutionary democratic. We are making ready (doing so now, at once) to fight it when, and to the extent that, it becomes reactionary and anti-proletarian. The essence of Marxism lies in that double task, which only those who do not understand Marxism can vulgarise or compress into a single and simple task"[14].

Lenin over the period 1905-1909, charted the two possible and alternative capitalist developments for Russian agriculture which he called the Prussian path and the American path[15]. In the former, the semi-feudal system slowly evolved into a bourgeois landed gentry style economy under a constitutional monarchy, this was the favoured option of the liberal bourgeoisie. Here, the process was evolutionary, from feudal bondage to capitalist exploitation on the land of the descendants of the feudal landlords, which condemned the peasants to decades of deprivation and subjugation. In the second case, revolutionary bourgeois democracy eliminated feudal relations on the land by confiscation without compensation, the feudal estates to be seized and divided between the peasants by the peasants themselves. Initially small-holdings would predominate, but eventually the peasant would evolve into a bourgeois farmer. Lenin believed that the seizure of the land, and its distribution to the peasants by the peasants, would turn the peasantry into a conservative force protecting its new interests. For Lenin's most complete description of the processes involved see *The Agrarian Programme of Social Democracy in the First Russian Revolution* in particular in Section 5, *Two Types of Bourgeois Agrarian Evolution*[16]. Of course, there is no suggestion in Lenin's works that by the use of the term 'American path' he was implying that Russia could become a capitalist world power, as had the USA. He was making the point that for the peasants and workers of Russia, the most beneficial development of capitalism would be a revolutionary resolution of the land question.

In the postscript to the 1917 edition of *The Agrarian Programme of Social Democracy in the First Russian Revolution*, Lenin would say something very different, in clear confirmation that in 1907 the demand for nationalisation of the land was **not** seen as a step towards socialism:

"At the present time [September 1917] the revolution poses the agrarian question in Russia in an immeasurably broader, deeper, and sharper form than it did in 1905-07. ... *neither* the proletariat *nor* the revolutionary petty-bourgeois democrats *can* keep within the limits of capitalism.

Life has already overstepped those limits and ... the question of the nationalisation of the land must inevitably be presented **in a new way** in the agrarian programme, **namely: nationalisation of the land is not only 'the last word' of the bourgeois revolution, but also a step towards socialism.**"[17]

If Lenin had expected the Russian Revolution to proceed from its bourgeois phase to its proletarian phase with no significant period of time between, he would have been unlikely to have spent so much time discussing and describing which was the most beneficial form of capitalist agricultural property relations for the struggle for the socialist revolution[18]. Also, it should be obvious that Lenin's preferred option, the transition of peasant farmers into capitalist farmers is hardly the task of a few months or years, but of decades. Indeed, Lenin, in describing the development of these capitalist farmers, compared them to the growth of capitalist farms after the fall of serfdom in 1861 (a period of over forty years) and predicted the process might take "several revolutionary decades"[19]. The crucial issue is that Lenin considered the expropriation of the land necessary for the American path, could be carried through by an alliance of the proletariat and the peasantry, with the support of the revolutionary democratic petty bourgeoisie, later to be legitimised by the bourgeois Constituent Assembly. During the period, 1905-1915, there was never any suggestion in his writings that it would be necessary for the proletariat to hold state power, for a proletarian, socialist revolution to take place before the land question could be resolved.

Lenin was quite clear, the peasants wanted the land for themselves: small-scale capitalist cultivation was fighting large-scale feudal land-owners. He stressed that the **proletarian** leadership of the bourgeois liberation movement, had to rally the **peasantry as a whole** behind it and lead a **bourgeois** revolution in its most consistent and decisive form. "In the Russian revolution the struggle for the land is nothing else than a struggle for the renovated path of capitalist development"[20].

If there was to be a significant period of time between the bourgeois-democratic and socialist revolutions then, in the sense that the bourgeois-democratic revolution had at its core the solution of the 'agrarian problem', and could only succeed to the extent it solved that problem, it could be said that Lenin was proposing a dominance of peasant interests. Indeed, on certain occasions, Lenin appeared to say just that. For example, at the Stockholm Unity Congress[21] Lenin, in refuting Plekhanov who came out against the 'utopia' of seizing power, said that to be victorious, the 'peasant agrarian revolution' must become the central authority throughout the state[22].

This point was not, of course, in contradiction to his more common and frequent declarations that "Our party holds firmly to the view that the role of the proletariat is the role of leader in the bourgeois-democratic revolution ...", rather it was confirmation that the proletarian party would not be making demands of the democratic dictatorship which were against or went beyond the interests of the peasantry. That is, the demands of the *RSDLP* within the revolutionary dictatorship would be limited, essentially, to the *SD* minimum programme[23]. Implicit in Lenin's strategy was that the workers and peasants could successfully make a revolution in favour of a third class, the bourgeoisie, which did not want such a revolution!

3.3 Social Democrats in a Revolutionary Government?

In the early part of 1905, prior to the Third Congress in London, Lenin published a series of articles in *Vyperod* proposing that the *RSDLP* participate in any revolutionary government that came into being in the struggle against the autocracy. Articles such as *The Revolutionary Democratic Dictatorship of the Proletariat and the Peasantry*[24] argued for two new concepts, both in opposition to the Mensheviks. Firstly, Lenin proposed (see previous section) that the main petty bourgeois allies of the proletariat would be the peasantry. Lenin's thinking had developed under the direct impact of the peasant uprisings beginning in 1902, followed by the rural explosion(s) of 1903-05. These led to *To the Village Poor* which introduced the concept of a reciprocal alliance of the poor peasant and the industrial worker[25]. This proposal was agreed and adopted as the policy and programme of the Bolsheviks at the Third Congress. (See Lenin's *Report on the Question of the Participation of the Social Democrats in the Provisional Revolutionary Government* [26].)

Secondly, he proposed that, in addition to participating in the armed uprising in fighting unity with the revolutionary democrats, the *RSDLP* should not shrink from taking part in any provisional revolutionary government to secure the best conditions for the workers from the Russian bourgeois-democratic revolution. Of course, the *RSDLP* representatives in any provisional revolutionary government would be subject to strict control by the party. At that time, in *Social-Democracy and the Provisional Revolutionary Government*[27], Lenin had cause to criticise Parvus' call for a Social-Democratic government on the grounds that such a perspective had the insurmountable failing in the Russian context of effectively excluding the peasants. Parvus' statement appeared in his introduction to Trotsky's pamphlet *Before the Ninth of January,* where he had proposed the possibility of a *Social Democratic* government arising from the Russian bourgeois-democratic revolution. This was the first time such an idea had been mooted and, for many (including Lenin), Parvus' introduction overshadowed the pamphlet it introduced. Indeed, there is evidence that Lenin believed that the body of the pamphlet carried the same message as the introduction. In his response to Parvus, Lenin gave an insight into his own understanding of the likely composition of the *RDDPP* when he absolutely ruled out any possibility that the provisional revolutionary dictatorship could be exclusively *SD*, and went so far as to say that even a *SD* majority was:

"*impossible*, unless we speak of fortuitous, transient episodes, and not of a revolutionary dictatorship that will be at all durable and capable of leaving its mark in history. This is *impossible*, because only a revolutionary dictatorship supported by the vast majority of the people can be at all durable ... The Russian proletariat, however, is at present a minority of the population in Russia. It can become the great, overwhelming majority only if it combines with the mass of semi-proletarians, semi-proprietors, i.e., with the mass of the petty-bourgeois urban and rural poor"[28].

The irony here is that the debate in 1905 *et seq* was about whether or not the *RSDLP* should **participate** in a revolutionary government. Lenin considered a Social Democratic majority in the *RDDPP* as "*impossible*", but in 1917 he would defend a revolutionary government initially composed entirely of Bolsheviks! Lenin's insistence on majority support should also be noted. If land distribution ended the peasants' revolutionary fervour, then the requirement for majority support (i.e. peasant support) placed a severe constraint on the revolutionary dictatorship. However, in 1917, Lenin would recognise that the party that enabled land distribution would gain the support of the peasantry as a whole, so that a revolutionary proletarian regime could - at least in its initial stages - gain the support of the overwhelming majority of the Russian population.

In June 1905, Lenin wrote the pamphlet *Two Tactics of Social Democracy in the Democratic Revolution*[29]. The title of the pamphlet is interesting because it made clear that Lenin was addressing differences in tactics; the aim of the revolution remained that of a (bourgeois) democratic state and this was not, apparently, in dispute. One of the main themes of the pamphlet was a sharp rebuttal of the Menshevik arguments that the *RSDLP* should not play a leading role in any provisional revolutionary government since such a presence would inevitably mean attempting to put into effect the entire Social-Democratic programme - including its maximum, socialist programme. The theoretical basis of the Menshevik argument was an extract from Engels' *The Peasant War in Germany*[30] to the effect that the leadership of an "extreme party" should avoid taking over as a government when the historic conditions were not ripe for the domination of the class which it represented, nor for the implementation of those measures which that domination required.

Lenin, in a series of pamphlets and articles, roundly attacked the argument that the *RSDLP* in taking the leading part in the struggle to establish the *RDDPP*, and then playing a major role in any subsequent government, would necessarily have to lead an attempt at a socialist revolution. He gave two separate answers to the criticisms made by Martynov, the delegate from - and former editor of - *Workers' Cause* who did not quit the Second Congress, and who symbolised the transition of the Mensheviks to reformism.

The first part of his answer is particularly interesting because it concerned the subjective factor, the role of the party leaders and their aims and objectives in participating in the provisional revolutionary government. Lenin argued it was acceptable for the *RSDLP* to participate in the transitional revolutionary government precisely because it would **not** attempt to introduce socialist measures! Because the *RDDPP* was not the period of the overthrow of the bourgeoisie, the *RSDLP* leadership would voluntarily restrict its demands to the minimum programme. The *RSDLP* itself would eliminate the subjective factor of leadership of the socialist revolution.

This argument gave rise to criticisms from rank and file members of the *RSDLP*, which Lenin had to answer. His proposal that the party participate in the revolutionary democratic government and limit its demands to the minimum programme was interpreted by some as meaning the *RSDLP* would be endorsing and continuing the repressive measures of a bourgeois state! This was an ideal opportunity for Lenin to correct any misapprehensions Bolsheviks might have had on the speed of the transition from bourgeois to socialist revolution and, if it was the case, to correct the misinterpretation that there would be at least several decades of bourgeois rule before the socialist revolution. In *The Revolutionary Dictatorship of the Proletariat and Peasantry* he replied:

> " ... Participation in the provisional government with the bourgeois revolutionary democrats, they [Lenin's critics] weep, means sanctioning the bourgeois order; it means sanctioning the perpetuation of prisons and the police, of unemployment and poverty, of private property and prostitution. ... Social-Democrats do not hold back from struggle for political freedom on the grounds that it is bourgeois political freedom. Social-Democrats regard this "sanctioning" of the bourgeois order from the historical point of view. ... they sanction it, not for its prisons and police, its private property and prostitution, but for the scope and freedom it allows to combat these charming institutions"[31].

Here, Lenin clearly accepted that *RSDLP* representatives in the provisional dictatorship would, indeed, be operating within a 'republican-democratic bourgeois order'. The class rule of the bourgeois would be 'sanctioned', there is no suggestion that essential elements of the bourgeois state, e.g. prisons and police, were to be abolished during the period when the *RDDPP* held power. There can be little doubt that, in the given context, Lenin was envisaging a revolutionary dictatorship initiating, and resting on, bourgeois state norms. It will be shown later that such a state was expected to be ratified and exist for a significant period of time under the governance of a Constituent Assembly.

The second part of his answer was the huge numbers of peasants who were capable of supporting the democratic revolution but were not interested in supporting the socialist revolution[32], that is the forces necessary for carrying out the socialist revolution would be missing. Having the peasantry as the major ally imposed severe limits on the aims of the revolution. In *The Peasant, or "Trudovik", Group and the RSDLP,* written in May 1906, Lenin's perspective was that the bourgeois-democratic revolution came to an end when the peasants solved the land problem, because they had achieved their objective of taking ownership of the land for themselves. He explained that a period of time ('decades') would be required during which class differentiation would occur in the countryside, before the victory of the struggle against capitalist society as a whole.

The peasant movement was not proletarian, it was a struggle waged by small proprietors to cleanse Russia of serfdom. It was not a struggle against the foundations of capitalism. The proletariat would lead the successful bourgeois-democratic revolution as a necessary step on its way to a genuine socialist revolution, but the masses of the peasantry were not interested in any immediate struggle against capitalist society. When the peasantry won the bourgeois-democratic revolution, the peasantry as a whole would have exhausted its revolutionary energy[33]. In *Social-Democracy's Attitude Towards the Peasant Movement,* 1 Sept 1905, Lenin argued:

"At first we support the peasantry *en masse* against the landlords, support it to the hilt and with all means, ... we shall bend every effort to help the entire peasantry achieve the democratic revolution, *in order thereby to make it easier* for us, the party of the proletariat, to pass on as quickly as possible to the new and higher task - the socialist revolution. We promise no harmony, no egalitarianism or 'socialisation' following the victory of the *present* peasant uprising, on the contrary, we 'promise' a new struggle, new inequality, the new revolution we are striving for"[34].

Lenin never saw the peasantry as an ally in the fight for the socialist revolution. If he had, he would not have had the slightest grounds for insisting upon the *bourgeois* character of the revolution and for limiting the *RDDPP* to purely democratic tasks. Lenin correctly foresaw that land distribution would transform the poor peasants into middle peasants, ending their revolutionary dynamic. Their concern would then be to protect their newly-gained ownership of the land, not risk it by launching a struggle for a socialist revolution[35]. All Lenin promised was that after the victory of the struggle against the landlords for the democratic revolution, when no-one could know the balance of class forces, there would begin a new struggle for the socialist revolution, the victory of which would first require class differentiation within the peasantry.

3.4 Prospects for a Socialist Revolution

Despite their differences and the heat of the discussion, Plekhanov and Lenin still shared elements of their previous, common, approach. Both separated the bourgeois revolution from the socialist revolution, on the grounds that each revolution required an entirely different combination of social forces to carry it through to success. Plekhanov postponed the socialist revolution to some indefinite future. Political freedom was to be achieved by the proletariat in alliance with the liberal bourgeoisie; after many decades and on a higher level of capitalist development, the proletariat would then carry out the socialist revolution in direct struggle against the bourgeoisie.

The constraints Lenin imposed on the democratic revolution flowed directly from the economic analysis, spelled out in great detail in *The Development of Capitalism in Russia*[36]. The destruction of the feudal system by the democratic revolution was the key that would open the development of capitalism in Russia, so Lenin placed at the heart of Bolshevik strategy, a revolutionary alliance that had as its essential task, the abolition of feudal relations in agriculture. The main forces in the alliance would be the proletariat and the peasantry, and the alliance would have the governmental form of the *RDDPP*. The democratic dictatorship as he envisaged at that time had a certain structural fluidity, being defined more as the mechanisms required to enforce and defend the sum-total of changes proposed in the *RSDLP* minimum programme, than a given form of government[37].

Lenin's response to the Mensheviks' concern over a too-rapid transition to a socialist revolution also included pointing out that the concrete circumstances in which the bourgeois-democratic revolution would occur eliminated any such possibility. It is important for any proposed comparison of the *RDDPP* with Trotsky's *ToPR* to be unambiguous on this point. Lenin's stated position in his pamphlet *The Revolutionary Dictatorship of the Proletariat and Peasantry* (March 30th, 1905), was:

"... Social-Democracy has constantly stressed the bourgeois nature of the impending revolution in Russia and insisted on a clear line of demarcation between the democratic minimum programme and the socialist maximum programme. ... [The] march of events will assuredly confirm this more and more fully as time goes on. It is the march of events that will 'impose' upon us the imperative necessity of waging a furious struggle for the republic and, in practice, guide our forces, the forces of the politically active proletariat, in this direction. It is the march of events that will, in the democratic revolution, inevitably impose upon us such a host of allies from among the petty bourgeoisie and the peasantry, whose real needs will demand the implementation of our minimum programme, that any concern over too rapid a transition to the maximum programme is simply absurd."[38]

That the working class was in a small numerical minority was given prominence, the numerically superior "host of allies" would act as a block on any attempts at a "too rapid transition" to a socialist revolution. That is: to preserve its allies in the *RDDPP,* it would be 'absurd' for the *RSDLP* to do anything more than enact its minimum programme. In 1905, Lenin was proposing that the actual events of the bourgeois-democratic revolution would, themselves, eliminate the possibility of its growing over into a socialist revolution.

The primacy of actual events in determining the pace and extent of the bourgeois-democratic revolution (and the likelihood of a subsequent socialist revolution) is methodologically important, since the emphasis on reality as the determining factor gives Lenin's analysis a certain algebraic character. A different quantification of the objective factors allowed for a different qualitative outcome from the same methodology, which is as it should be. In 1918 Lenin would use exactly the same method to justify the socialist nature of the 1917 October Revolution.

In 1905, Lenin believed that both the objective conditions (the degree of economic development and alliance with the peasantry) and subjective conditions (degree of class consciousness) in which the working class found itself, made the too rapid transition to a socialist revolution impossible[39]. In 1917, the impossible would be accomplished within a year.

In *Two Tactics* Lenin clearly explained that between the democratic and socialist dictatorships there would be a series of intermediary stages of revolutionary development, at the start of which, capitalism would receive an impetus, and during which, the bourgeoisie would rule as a class:

"Marxists are absolutely convinced of the bourgeois character of the Russian revolution. ... the democratic reforms in the political system and the social and economic reforms, which have become a necessity for Russia .. will, for the first time, really clear the ground for a wide and rapid, European, and not Asiatic, development of capitalism; they will, for the first time, make it possible for the bourgeoisie to rule as a class. ... even the complete success of a peasant insurrection, even the redistribution of the whole of the land for the benefit of the peasants and in accordance with their desires ... will not destroy capitalism at all, but will, on the contrary, give an impetus to its development and hasten the class disintegration of the peasantry itself.

... the only force capable of gaining 'a decisive victory over Tsarism,' is the people, i.e., the proletariat and the peasantry, ... the revolutionary-democratic dictatorship of the proletariat and the peasantry. ... But of course it will be a democratic, not a socialist dictatorship. It will not be able (without a series of intermediary stages of revolutionary development) to affect the foundations of capitalism. At best it may bring about a radical redistribution of landed property in favour of the peasantry..."[40].

There is no suggestion here of an uninterrupted transition to a socialist revolution, rather several revolutionary decades of capitalist rule would be required for the class disintegration of the peasantry[41]. This viewpoint can be followed in Lenin's writings from one article to the next, year by year, volume by volume. The language and examples vary, but the basic thought remains the same, the aim of the struggle was to overthrow Tsarism and bring about the conquest of governmental power by the proletariat relying on the support of the revolutionary peasantry. In 1911 in *"The Peasant Reform" and the Proletarian-Peasant Revolution*, Lenin showed that he remained convinced that the tasks of the bourgeois-democratic revolution would be finally accomplished by the convocation of a popular Constituent Assembly and the establishment of a democratic republic[42]. To this end, he proposed at the *1913 Joint Conference of the Central Committee of the RSDLP and Party Officials* that the task of the *SDs* was to conduct widespread revolutionary agitation among the masses for the overthrow of the monarchy and the establishment of a democratic republic, which would legitimise the confiscation of the landed estates, an 8-hour day and freedom of association[43].

In 1914 in *Left-Wing Narodism and Marxism*, Lenin remained insistent that the economic development of Russia would proceed from feudalism to capitalism, and through large-scale, machine-based, capitalist production to socialism. He was clear that he considered the only route to socialism was through the further development of capitalism. Suggestions for any other route he considered pipe-dreams, and characteristic of the liberals or of "petty proprietors"[44].

In November 1915 in *On the Two Lines in the Revolution*, he called for the proletariat to wage a courageous revolutionary struggle against the monarchy based on the 'three pillars' of Bolshevism: a democratic republic; confiscation of the landed estates; an 8-hour day. He remained convinced that such a struggle would gather in its wake the democratic masses, i.e., the bulk of the peasantry. At the same time the proletariat would wage a ruthless struggle in alliance with the European proletariat for the socialist revolution in Europe[45].

Lenin saw the *RDDPP* establishing the democratic republic, in parallel with which, the proletarians would struggle to gain as much as they could and lay the most advantageous basis for the struggle for socialism. It will be shown later that Lenin retained this approach until at least the early spring of 1917 and it was still, at least partially, present in his *Letters from Afar*[46].

So where was the socialist revolution? For Lenin in 1905 the **complete victory** of the democratic revolution marked the **beginning of the struggle** for the socialist revolution:

"... The complete victory of the present revolution will mark the end of the democratic revolution and the beginning of a determined struggle for a socialist revolution. The satisfaction of the demands of the present-day peasantry, the utter rout of reaction, and the winning of a democratic republic will mark the complete end of the revolutionism of the bourgeoisie and even of the petty bourgeoisie - will mark the beginning of the real struggle of the proletariat for Socialism. The more complete the democratic revolution, the sooner, the more widespread, the purer and the more determined will be the development of this new struggle. ... when not only the revolution but the complete victory of the [bourgeois] revolution becomes an accomplished fact, we shall 'substitute' (perhaps amid the horrified cries of new, future, Martynovs) for the slogan of the democratic dictatorship, the slogan of a socialist dictatorship of the proletariat, i.e., of a complete socialist revolution"[47].

On a number of occasions Lenin was disarmingly frank about his assessment of the likelihood for a Russian socialist revolution growing directly out of the bourgeois-democratic. For example, at the Unity Congress in 1906, Lenin went so far as to argue that instead of progressing towards a socialist revolution, the Russian working class could hope to retain the democratic gains of the bourgeois-democratic revolution only if the workers in Western Europe came to their aid. He believed then, and for the rest of his life, that the only guarantee against restoration was a socialist revolution in the West. Indeed without such help, restoration would be positively inevitable. He formulated his proposition as:

"the Russian [bourgeois-democratic] revolution can achieve victory by its own efforts, but it cannot possibly hold and consolidate its gains by its own strength. It cannot do this unless there is a socialist revolution in the West. .... After the complete victory of the democratic revolution the small proprietor will inevitably turn against the proletariat; and the sooner the common enemies of the proletariat and of the small proprietors, such as the capitalists, the landlords, the financial bourgeoisie, and so forth are overthrown, the sooner will this happen. Our democratic republic has no other reserve than the socialist proletariat in the West"[48].

The theme of the better-off peasants becoming positively anti-working class after the revolution is also present in the *ToPR*, as will be shown in the next chapter. But the comments above were not unique. In May 1905 Lenin gave the warning:

"Our victory in the coming democratic revolution will be a giant stride forward towards our socialist goal; we shall deliver all Europe from the oppressive yoke of a reactionary military power and help our brothers, the class-conscious workers of the whole world who have suffered so much under the bourgeois reaction and who are taking heart now at the sight of the successes of the revolution in Russia, to advance to socialism more quickly, boldly, and decisively. With the help of the **socialist** proletariat of Europe, we shall be able, not only to defend the **democratic republic**, but to advance with giant strides towards socialism."[49].

In *The Stages, the Trend and the Prospects of the Revolution* (written late 1905 or early 1906), Lenin further elaborated his idea of the socialist revolution in Western Europe being the safe-guard of the gains of the Russian bourgeois-democratic revolution. His more detailed scenario was: in the bourgeois-democratic revolution, the Russian workers and peasants break the power of the landlords but face a counter-revolutionary upsurge by the liberal bourgeoisie (which includes the well-to-do peasants and a section of the middle peasants) to take away from the proletariat the gains of the revolution. The proletariat fights to retain its democratic gains including the 8-hour day and the right to free trade unions. The Russian workers' if left to fight alone, face inevitable defeat, but the socialist revolution in Europe comes to their aid, and the European and Russian workers together bring about the socialist revolution in Russia:

"... 4. The working-class movement achieves victory in the *democratic* revolution, the liberals passively waiting to see how things go and the *peasants* actively assisting. ... The rising of the peasants is victorious, the power of the landlords is broken. ('The revolutionary-democratic dictatorship of the proletariat and the peasantry.')

5. The liberal bourgeoisie ... becomes downright counter-revolutionary, and organises itself in order to take away from the proletariat the gains of the revolution. Among the peasantry, the whole of the well-to-do section, and a fairly large part of the middle peasantry ... turn to the side of the counter-revolution in order to wrest power from the proletariat and the rural poor, who sympathise with the proletariat.

6. ... a new crisis and a new struggle develop and blaze forth, **with the proletariat now fighting to preserve its democratic gains** for the sake of a socialist revolution. ... at this stage, the liberal bourgeoisie and the well-to-do peasantry (plus partly the middle peasantry) organise counter-revolution. The Russian proletariat *plus* the European proletariat organise revolution. In such conditions the Russian proletariat can win a second victory. The cause is no longer hopeless. The second victory will be the *socialist revolution in Europe*. The European workers will show us 'how to do it', and then together with them we shall bring about the socialist revolution"[50].

This argument can be followed until at least November 1915 when Lenin again re-iterated that the *RDDPP* would rid bourgeois Russia of Tsarism the better to bring about a socialist revolution in alliance with the proletarians of Europe[51]. To paraphrase; in 1905-06 Lenin's predicted scenario for the Russian Revolution was a victorious uprising leading to the *RDDPP*. This would face a determined counter-attack by the forces of reaction but the Russian Revolution would generate a socialist revolution in the West which would "save the day". The direct translation of the *RDDPP* into a socialist revolution in Russia alone was excluded. We can say, with certainty, that in Lenin's writings during the period when the slogan of the provisional *RDDPP* was a key programmatic demand of the Bolsheviks, there was no suggestion of either:

- The socialist revolution occurring in Russia before the socialist revolution in Western Europe, or
- The land question in Russia being solved by a socialist rather than a bourgeois-democratic revolution; by the dictatorship of the proletariat rather than the provisional *RDDPP*.

To end this section it is appropriate to consider the public face of the Bolsheviks. Here is the relevant section of a leaflet distributed prior to 1 May 1905:

"Down with the tsarist government! We will overthrow it and set up a provisional revolutionary government to convene a Constituent Assembly of the people. Let people's deputies be elected by universal, direct, and equal vote, through secret ballot. ...

This is what the Social-Democrats ... call upon you to fight for, arms in hand: for complete freedom, for the democratic republic, for the eight-hour day, for peasants' committees. ... Freedom or death! Workers of all Russia, we will repeat that great battle-cry, we will not shrink from any sacrifices: through the uprising we will win freedom; through freedom, socialism! ...

Bureau of Committees of the Majority Editorial Board of Vperyod[52].

3.5 What Form for the *RDDPP*?

The victory of the bourgeois-democratic revolution, Lenin wrote in *Two Tactics,* would require a dictatorship because without a dictatorship, it would be impossible to break the desperate resistance of the landlords, big business and Tsarism, and repel their counter-revolutionary attempts[53]. By its origin and fundamental nature, such a democratic dictatorship must be the organ of popular insurrection. But what would be its form? Investigating this question shows that Lenin intended the democratic dictatorship to be a stage on the path to a bourgeois-democratic Constituent Assembly.

Lenin argued that the Russian Revolution was of a bourgeois-democratic character, but recognised that such a description did not define the balance of class forces and the governmental power in the revolution. For Lenin, always sensitive to the needs of the peasants, the heart of this democratic revolution was the resolution of the agrarian question - the destruction of all remnants of feudalism. Lenin insisted that the task of the working class was to strive, through its independent organisations and efforts, for the widest and most radical development of the bourgeois-democratic revolution. He was for an utterly uncompromising struggle to demolish all economic, political and social vestiges of feudalism. The struggle against Tsarism was to be used to create the most favourable conditions for the establishment of a genuinely progressive constitutional democratic framework for the benefit of the Russian workers' movement.

Initially, Lenin was more concerned with defining the tasks the democratic dictatorship would have to carry out, and at this stage was severely critical of those who, in his opinion, showed 'lifeless scholasticism' in attempting to define too closely the form. For him the *RDDPP* was the movement, the alliance of workers and peasants that overthrew Tsarism, after which it was any form of revolutionary government required to repulse all attempts at restoration[54] [occasionally he added the condition that the participation of the proletariat in the government was necessary].

The formation of the St Petersburg Soviet suggested to Lenin that the Soviet of Workers' Deputies should be regarded as the embryo of the *RDDPP*[55]. However, the formal purpose of the *RDDPP* was to convene a popular Constituent Assembly; to put into effect the minimum programme of proletarian democracy which was the only programme capable of safeguarding the interests of the people which had risen against the autocracy. Somebody had to convene the Constituent Assembly, somebody had to guarantee the freedom and fairness of the elections, somebody had to invest the Assembly with power and authority. Obviously only a revolutionary government, the organ of the insurrection, could genuinely desire this and be capable of doing what was necessary to achieve it[56]. The Soviet perfectly fitted that specification.

Lenin made it clear: the major political task of the provisional revolutionary government, the government of the victorious popular insurrection, would be to secure and convene a Constituent Assembly that would express the will of all the people with full power and authority. This Constituent Assembly was, of course, a democratic institution elected by universal suffrage - that is, a bourgeois institution. The Constituent Assembly would be the Russian governmental form that rested on the bourgeois state relations resulting from the seizure of power by the proletariat and peasantry. This sets a clear limit on the tasks and duration of the *RDDPP*.

Nevertheless, Lenin felt it necessary to explain in some detail its practical tasks and political programme. In 1905, in *The Revolutionary Army and the Revolutionary Government*[57], Lenin listed six fundamental points that he considered had to become the political banner and the immediate programme of any provisional revolutionary government. These were designed to enlist the sympathy of the people for that government and were to be regarded as the most urgent tasks, on which the entire revolutionary energy of the people would be concentrated. There was, of course, as was usual with Lenin, considerable overlap with what he wrote elsewhere. (See, for example, *The Democratic Tasks of the Revolutionary Proletariat*[58] and *Victorious Revolution*[59].)

The six points were:

(1) Convening a Constituent Assembly of all the people, elected by secret ballot in universal, direct, and equal elections (one person one vote, etc.). However, this slogan did not stand in isolation, but in conjunction with the following Bolshevik slogans:

- the revolutionary overthrow of the Tsarist autocracy, and its replacement by the democratic republic, and

- the sovereignty of the people, safeguarded by a democratic constitution, i.e., the concentration of supreme governmental authority entirely in the hands of a legislative assembly composed of representatives of the people and forming a single chamber.

(2) Creation of a democratic political system. Political freedom was economically equivalent to:

- free development of capitalism, but no privileges for either the capitalists or the landlords,
- abolition of all survivals of serfdom, and
- the raising of the living and cultural standards of the masses, especially of the lower strata.

(3) Arming the people, no independent power for either the police or the officials; their complete subordination to the people. All power - wholly, completely and indivisibly - in the hands of the whole people.

(4) Complete freedom for the oppressed and disfranchised nationalities.

(5) Introduction of the Bolshevik minimum programme: 8-hour day, free trade unions, the working class be free to struggle for socialism, etc.

(6) Formation of peasant revolutionary committees with responsibility for distributing the land seized without compensation by the revolutionary activities of the peasants during the democratic revolution. The provisional revolutionary government resting on the *RDDPP* would enact land to the peasant, and this would be formally approved by the subsequent bourgeois-democratic Constituent Assembly.

Of course, Lenin could give only a list of the most important factors required for winning the democratic republic. He did not claim his list was complete. Rather, his emphasis was on the revolutionary government striving to secure the support of the masses, as without the active revolutionary support of the people it would be a mere nothing.

The lynch-pin of the class alliance that would form the basis of the provisional *RDDPP* was item 6 on the list, proletarian support for the bourgeois measure of an end to serfdom: seizure of the land without compensation, and its distribution amongst the peasants by the peasants themselves. Here, the task is to be performed as an integral and essential part of the bourgeois-democratic revolution by a provisional revolutionary democratic dictatorship consciously restricting itself to bourgeois measures and resting on bourgeois property relations.

To sum up:

1. The *RDDPP* was, in practice, whatever governmental structure was required to implement the sum-total of bourgeois-democratic changes envisaged in the Bolshevik **minimum** programme, and for the defence of the

gains of the bourgeois-democratic revolution, until reaction had been defeated.

2. The form of the government was not essential: the Soviets appeared suitable as did revolutionary peasant committees.

3. A key and essential purpose of the provisional *RDDPP* was to ensure that a Constituent Assembly would be freely and fairly elected to be the government of a bourgeois Russian state.

4. To preserve its alliances in the *RDDPP* the Bolshevik Party would limit its demands to its minimum programme.

It is quite clear that in 1905-06, Lenin's schema for the Russian Revolution was a victorious uprising of the democratic forces, overthrowing the Tsarist autocracy, solving the land problem and leading to the provisional *RDDPP*. This would be followed by an elected bourgeois-democratic government (Constituent Assembly) resting on a capitalist state. During this last period there would be a determined counter-attack by the forces of reaction to take back some or all of the gains made, but the day would be saved by a socialist revolution in the West. **The direct translation of the RDDPP into a socialist revolution in Russia alone was excluded.** This was a scenario that ran through Lenin's works up to, and including, early 1917. For example, in September 1914, he again drew attention to the link he placed between the socialist revolution in Europe and bourgeois-democratic revolution in Russia. He explained that while in all the advanced countries the war had placed socialist revolution on the order of the day, in Russia it still remained the task of Russian *SDs* to achieve the three fundamental conditions for consistent democratic reform [a democratic republic with complete equality and self-determination for all nations, confiscation of the landed estates, and an eight-hour working day][60].

Lenin's perspective may be briefly expressed as follows: The belated Russian bourgeoisie was incapable of leading its own revolution to the end. The complete victory of the revolution through the medium of the provisional *RDDPP* would purge the country of serfdom, invest the development of Russian capitalism with an "American" dynamic, strengthen the proletariat in the city, its allies in the country, and would open up broad possibilities within a democratic Russia for the struggle for socialism. Simultaneously, the victory of the Russian Revolution would provide a mighty impulse for the socialist revolution in Western Europe, and this latter would not only shield Russia from the dangers of restoration but also permit the Russian proletariat to achieve the conquest of power in a comparatively short historical interval.

3.6 Inner Tensions in the *RDDPP*

In 1905, Lenin's conception of the bourgeois-democratic transition in Russia represented an enormous step forward as it proceeded not from the constitutional reform of Tsarism as demanded by the liberal bourgeoisie, but from the revolutionary overthrow of agricultural relations, and it also proposed a workable combination of real social forces for the accomplishment of this task.

The weak point in Lenin's conception was a major internal contradiction within the *RDDPP*. A fundamental limitation of this dictatorship was that it was defined as revolutionary democratic, and therefore, while it was revolutionary in origin and actions, its class content was pre-determined as bourgeois. By this, as has been shown above, for the sake of preserving its alliance with the peasantry, the proletariat would restrict itself to the *RSDLP* minimum programme and forego directly posing socialist tasks. That is, the proletariat would renounce any possibility of moving directly to its own dictatorship and the socialist revolution. Today, it is hard to credit Lenin with believing the armed workers would not use their power to protect and extend their own, specific, interests in the factories, the government and the state. But Lenin was writing in 1905, before the St Petersburg Soviet and twelve years before the activities of the Red Guards in 1917-1918.

Lenin's perspective was not tested in 1905 because the revolution was defeated before that could happen. His formula attempted to avoid the problem of the probable conflict between a bourgeois state power and a revolutionary government based, at least to a significant extent, on proletarian Soviets, by simply stating that the democratic Constituent Assembly would be their mutual goal. In 1917 the reality had to be faced and, it will be argued later that, from April 1917, Lenin was compelled, in a direct struggle against the most experienced cadres of the party, to drop his 1905 perspective and adopt a radically new stance.

The pamphlet *Two Tactics*[61] provided the governmental slogan of the *RDDPP* and also delineated Bolshevik tactics and strategy for the unfolding Russian Revolution. It contained and developed a number of very important ideas and strategies that were crucial for success in the October Revolution. These were summed up in the resolution passed at the Third Congress, the text in full is printed in *Two Tactics,* and the elements of the resolution occur as themes in *Two Tactics.* In later years Lenin would frequently refer back to these points as demonstrating the continuity of Bolshevik ideas, in direct line from Marx and Engels, in particular:

(1) Lenin re-emphasised and reaffirmed Engel's and Marx's position on the necessity for the destruction of the (autocratic) state.

(2) Lenin made clear the necessity for a separate, strictly class party of *SD* which must maintain its complete organisational and political independence.

(3) Lenin insisted that, for the success of the revolution, the proletariat must ally with the peasantry.

(4) Lenin insisted that the working class would lead the struggle against the autocracy.

(5) Lenin argued that, in its struggles the proletariat should be armed and the revolution would be an armed uprising.

(6) Lenin predicted that the outcome of the armed uprising would be a dictatorship since without a dictatorship it would be impossible to break down resistance and to repel counter-revolutionary attempts.

(7) Lenin argued that the *RSDLP* should be prepared to participate in a provisional revolutionary government (subject to strict control by the party over its representatives).

There are a wealth of quotations in *Two Tactics* and other works from about that time that show that Lenin was determined to push the bourgeois-democratic revolution as far as possible and this shows an inner tension, or possibly even a degree of contradiction, in Lenin's writings. The dilemma is the antagonism between bourgeois factory owner and proletarian. For the bourgeois revolution to have been successful, the workers - guns in hand - would have already taken the lead. To suppose that the proletariat participates in the democratic revolution independently of the bourgeoisie, and as the leader of the revolution, is to invite the proletariat to overstep bourgeois-democratic limitations. In such circumstances, the proletarian would not accept control by the provisional *RDDPP*. For example, in the struggle for the bourgeois-democratic republic, revolutionary workers would push for demands outside the Bolshevik minimum programme; nationalisation of their industry under workers' control, say. In 1905 Lenin removed this potential contradiction from his schema by stressing the overwhelming proportion of peasants in the population and the lack of political and social development of the working class. As a minority within the *RDDPP*, the Bolshevik Party recognised the:

"incontestably bourgeois nature of the revolution, which is incapable of *directly* overstepping the bounds of a mere democratic revolution, our slogan *pushes forward* this particular revolution and strives to mould it into forms most advantageous to the proletariat; consequently, it strives to make the very most of the democratic revolution in order to attain the greatest success in the further struggle of the proletariat for Socialism"[62].

The contradictions between the consistent revolutionary core of Lenin's policies, in 1905 and afterwards, and its bourgeois-democratic shell, would be a factor in the party crisis - the paralysis of the Bolshevik leadership for days and weeks - during and after the February 1917 Revolution. Lenin's combativity and determination, expressed in 1905 by wanting to take the struggle against the regime as far as possible, would be crucial in resolving the 1917 crisis in the Bolshevik Party and the success of the October Revolution.

Lenin insisted that the Bolsheviks would participate in the revolutionary-democratic government, and the leadership of the Bolshevik Party was educated in, and Bolshevik culture was imbued with, the idea of participating as leading figures in the democratic dictatorship. For over a decade, the Bolshevik cadres were educated in the notion that the coming revolution was bourgeois because of its governmental form, its immediate programme and its socio-economic content (free capitalist farmers leading to the unfettered development of capitalism). An essential part of this strategy was that the proletarian party would limit its demands to the *RSDLP* minimum programme.

In 1917 did the Old Bolsheviks see the existing Soviets as the revolutionary government? Did the Old Bolsheviks believe that the line the party had pushed since 1905 was coming to fruition, that everything they had worked and called for was actually beginning to happen? Part of the answer is given by Zinoviev, one of Lenin's closest comrades for many years and one of the Bolshevik Party's leaders from 1907. In his book, *History of the Bolshevik Party,* published in 1923, he stated:

"Beginning with 1905 we considered that Russia was moving towards a dictatorship of the proletariat and peasantry ... when a wave of revolution was already forming [1916], we were still, however, talking about a democratic revolution ... Some of us (including myself) for too long upheld the idea that in our peasant country we could not pass straight onto the socialist revolution, but merely hope that if our revolution coincided with the start of the international proletarian one it could become its overture."[63].

3.7 Lenin and the Peasantry

Lenin had researched the agrarian development of Russia thoroughly, and was the leader of the *RSDLP* most concerned with the so-called peasant question. As we have seen, from at least 1905 Lenin was convinced that the abolition of feudal relations in agriculture would strengthen the development of capitalism in Russia. Before 1917 there is no suggestion that the solution of the agricultural question would require a workers' socialist revolution.

Three points need to be made here about the 1905 theories developed by Lenin concerning the peasantry. For many years Lenin was iconised in public by the Soviet bureaucracy and its supporters, who presented him as a man who never made a political mistake, nor had to change his policies. See, for example, Sorin[64] and Hill[65]. The reality is different. In response to the peasant upsurge of 1903-1905, Lenin recognised that the then existing party programme, regarding the agrarian question, was inadequate. Lenin's consistent use of the Marxist method, which required analysis of the actual, concrete circumstances of the given stage of the 1905 Revolution, caused him to make a significant change to this element of the party programme during the revolution itself.

The second point to appreciate is the manner in which Lenin presented the changes in policy and programme to the party. Until the Third (Bolshevik) Congress, the party's agrarian programme consisted of little more than the return to the peasants of the so-called "cut-off lands", the land which had been withheld from the peasants when the serfs were emancipated in the Peasant Reform of 1861. By 1905 the general sentiment among the peasants, clearly expressed in their spontaneous uprisings across most of Russia, was unquestionably in favour of seizing all the landlords' lands and estates. In this respect the old party programme was well out of date.

Lenin re-drafted the agrarian programme to include the confiscation of all landowners', government, church, monastic, and crown lands. In his address to the Congress on the Peasant Movement. Lenin was at pains to stress the continuity of his position:

"The Resolution speaks of measures that will not halt at the expropriation of the landed estates. It has been said that this formulation modifies our agrarian programme. I consider this opinion wrong. ... we see nothing in our Resolution that modifies our agrarian programme. ... Both Plekhanov and I have stated in the press that the Social-Democratic Party will never hold the peasantry back from revolutionary measures of agrarian reform, including the 'general redistribution' of the land. Thus, we are not modifying our agrarian programme"[66].

Lenin was quite correct to point out that both he and Plekhanov had never sought to impose limits on the revolutionary activities of the peasants, and to draw attention to the continuity of the Marxist method that led to the proposed change in the party programme, but he is stretching things a bit too far to say there was no modification of the party programme.

Indeed, Krupskaya in her *Memories of Lenin* tells just how Lenin was finally convinced that a change in programme was necessary. Lenin met Father Gapon in Geneva early in 1905. Independently present was a sailor from the Potemkin, Matinshenko, later to be a leading participant in the mutiny. Together they convinced Lenin that the 'pieces of land' slogan was inadequate and that a much broader slogan must be launched - one of confiscation of landowners' estates, crown and church lands. The result was that at the December Conference in Tammerfors, Finland, Lenin tabled a motion to drop this point on the peasants' land from the programme. In its place a paragraph was inserted on support for the revolutionary measures of the peasantry, including confiscation of landowners' estates, crown and church lands[67].

As if to confirm that significant changes had, indeed, been made to the party programme, Krupskaya describes how Lenin addressed a fringe meeting, organised by the Bolsheviks, at a Teachers' Congress. The meeting was attended by 'a few score' teachers. Lenin spoke on the agrarian question (which may be an indication of how important he felt this to be). The *SRs* present challenged Lenin on the changes in the *RSDLP* agrarian programme, quoting his previous writings against his new position and claiming that the Bolsheviks had adopted the *SR* land programme. Krupskaya says that Lenin made a "rather angry reply"[68].

It might be argued that Lenin was faced with a Congress dominated by committee-men and he had enough on his hands in persuading them to open the party to new members. Was stressing the elements of continuity, and downplaying differences, the best way to get the committee-men to vote to agree a new policy towards the peasants? As we shall see later, Lenin adopted a similar approach after 1917, when many times, he stressed the continuity of such key strategies as the revolutionary alliance between the workers and the peasantry as a pre-requisite for solving the agrarian problem, strategies which were integral to Bolshevik success in the 1917 October Revolution. Unfortunately, the stress placed on 'continuity' appears to have blinded some authors to the qualitative change in Bolshevik policy between the first (1905) and second (1917) Russian Revolutions.

The third point is to understand the development of Lenin's ideas and just what he proposed as the policy of the *RSDLP* in 1905, and for twelve years subsequently. From very early in his political life Lenin studied the agrarian question; in 1899 he proposed some minor changes to the *RSDLP* agrarian programme[69], in 1901 he made his first serious attempt to elaborate his own agrarian programme in *The Workers' Party and the Peasantry*[70], he developed these ideas in *The Agrarian Programme of Russian Social-Democracy*[71], and persuaded the *RSDLP* to adopt them as its agrarian programme at the Second Congress, in 1903. The central demands of this programme were, as we already noted, for the return of the 'cut-off' lands [which in some areas amounted to nearly 40% of the peasants' land], and the abolition of feudal relations in the countryside.

Lenin always wanted any demands to be concrete and correspond as closely as possible to the actual needs and consciousness of the peasants. He had to defend himself against those who (correctly) objected that limiting the *RSDLP* demand to the restitution of the cut-off lands was far too meek an approach. He replied: "We maintain, and shall endeavour to prove, that the demand for the 'restitution of the cut-off lands' is the maximum that we can at present advance in our agrarian programme."[72]. But the breadth and depth of the 1903-1906 peasant uprising made it clear that Lenin's 1903 programme was far too conservative. Later (1907), Lenin was to admit that the fundamental mistake in the agrarian programme of 1903 was that the Bolsheviks had failed to appreciate that the political awareness of the peasant masses had risen to a level such that they could be directed against landlordism in general[73].

As Lenin became increasingly convinced that the only meaningful ally for the workers in their struggle to overthrow the autocracy consisted in the peasantry, his vision of the revolution became one of the broadest possible movements to overthrow Tsarism and establish a provisional revolutionary government which, without going beyond the limits of capitalism, would carry through the most radical and far-reaching democratic programme, first and foremost the confiscation of the big estates and "land to the peasants". It is quite correct for Barnes, for example, to draw attention to Lenin's emphasis on the alliance between the proletariat and the peasants as a whole, to carry through the bourgeois-democratic revolution[74]. Indeed it was a significant progression in Lenin's thinking that, during and after 1905, he proposed an alliance not with the liberal bourgeoisie but with the "entire peasantry against the landlords"[75], and that the revolutionary peasant committees to be set up would be committees representing the peasants as an estate[76]. But Barnes and other writers are quite wrong to refrain from mentioning that in 1917, from the *April Theses* onwards, Lenin was at pains to emphasise the divisions between the wealthy and middle peasants (capitalists and petty capitalists) on the one hand, and agricultural labourers, wage-workers and poor peasants (the semi-proletarians), on the other, and that the aim of the Bolsheviks for the October Revolution was for the dictatorship of the **proletariat and poor peasantry**[77] to hold state power.

In 1905 Lenin was clearly arguing that the solution of the agrarian problem was achievable within capitalism and would strengthen capitalist development:

"A bourgeois revolution is a revolution which does not go beyond the limits of the bourgeois, i.e., capitalist, social and economic system. A bourgeois revolution expresses the need for the development of capitalism, and far from destroying the foundations of capitalism, it does the opposite, it broadens and deepens them. This revolution therefore expresses the interests not only of the working class, but of the entire bourgeoisie as well. ... Marxism has irrevocably broken with the ravings of the Narodniks and the anarchists to the effect that Russia, for instance, can avoid capitalist development, jump out of capitalism, or skip over it and proceed along some path other than the path of the class struggle on the basis and within the framework of this same capitalism"[78].

He continued this theme until at least 1915, stating clearly that the outcome of the democratic revolution (land reform) would be a bourgeois state. In chronological order, there follow are a number of passages to show that Lenin had a consistent overall appreciation of what the bourgeois-democratic revolution meant for Russia. In March 1906 he wrote "... In its social and economic aspect, the impending agrarian revolution will be a bourgeois-democratic revolution; it will not weaken but stimulate the development of capitalism and capitalist class contradictions"[79]. In 1907 he wrote:

"... the aims of the revolution that is now taking place in Russia do not exceed the bounds of bourgeois society. Even the fullest possible victory of the present revolution - in other words, the achievement of the most democratic republic possible, and the confiscation of all landed estates by the peasantry - would not in any way affect the foundations of the bourgeois social system. ...

... This struggle for the land inevitably forces enormous masses of the peasantry into the democratic revolution, for only democracy can give them land by giving them supremacy in the state ... the complete victory of the peasant uprising, the confiscation of all landed estates and their equal division will signify the most rapid development of capitalism, the form of bourgeois-democratic revolution most advantageous to the peasants. ... It is just as advantageous to the proletariat. The class conscious proletariat knows that there is, and there can be, no path leading to socialism otherwise than through a bourgeois-democratic revolution. ... The more complete the victory of the peasantry, the sooner will the proletariat stand out as a distinct class, and the more clearly will it put forward its purely socialist tasks and aims"[80].

Lenin continued this theme and in May 1914 re-affirmed that anyone acquainted with even the ABC of political economy must have known that Russia was undergoing a change-over from the system of serf-ownership to capitalism, that there was no third economic system for Russia, and that there was no way of achieving the ideals of labour democracy other than by ensuring the most rapid elimination of serfdom and the rapid development of capitalism[81]. In June of the same year he wrote:

"What is the economic essence of the agrarian question in Russia? It is the reorganisation of Russia on bourgeois-democratic lines. ... Capitalism will develop more widely, more freely and more quickly from such a measure. This measure is very progressive and very democratic. ... But, we repeat, this is a bourgeois-democratic measure. ... Marx advised class-conscious workers, while forming a clear idea of the bourgeois character of all agrarian reforms under capitalism (including the nationalisation of the land), to support bourgeois-democratic reforms as against the feudalists and serfdom. But Marxists cannot confuse bourgeois measures with socialism."[82]

Before 1917 Lenin considered that the effective solution of the land question would strengthen the growth of capitalism in Russia. The *RDDPP* would gain most for the working class by ensuring land distribution was achieved by the revolutionary seizure and distribution of the land by the peasantry - to whom, and in what proportions, was left undecided until 1917[83,84]. The organisational form of the revolution could well be Soviets supported by peasant committees but these would be temporary institutions which yielded power to a bourgeois-democratic Constituent Assembly.

3.8 References

1. Marx, K. and Engels, F., *Address of the Central Committee to the Communist League,* March 1850, Marx-Engels Selected Works, FLPH Moscow 1962, Vol 1, p106 - 117
2. Lenin, V.I., *Review of Karl Kautsky's The Agrarian Question,* 1899, CW 4:94
3. Quoted in Harding, N., *Lenin's Political Thought, Vol 1 Theory and Practice of the Democratic Revolution,* Macmillan Press, London 1977, p46. See also Wolfe, B.D., *Three who made a Revolution,* Penguin, London, p112
4. Trotsky, L.D., *Stalin,* Hollis and Carter, London, 1947, p426
5. Knei-Paz, B., *The Social and Political Thought of Leon Trotsky,* Clarendon Press, London, 1978, p4
6. Lenin, V.I., *Should We Organise the Revolution,* Feb 1905, CW 8:167-176
7. Lenin, V.I., *The Two Tactics of Social Democracy in the Democratic Revolution,* June-July 1905, CW 9:13-140
8. Lenin, V.I., *The Revolutionary Democratic Dictatorship of the Proletariat and the Peasantry,* March 1905, CW 8:295
9. Shanin, T., *Russia, 1905-07, Revolution as a Moment of Truth,* Macmillan, London, 1986, p296
10. Lenin, V.I., *Report on the Resolution on the Support of the Peasant Movement,* April 1905, CW 8:400-404
11. Kautsky, K. *The Driving Forces and Prospects of the Russian Revolution (abridged translation),* Journal of Trotsky Studies No 2 1994, p200-223
12. Lenin, V.I., *The Proletariat and its Ally in the Russian Revolution,* Dec 1906, CW 11:363-375
13. Lenin, V.I., *The Agrarian programme of Russian Social-Democracy,* March 1902, CW:13 349
14. Lenin, V.I., *Social-Democracy's Attitude Towards the Peasant Movement,* Sept 1 1905, CW 9:230-239
15. Lenin, V.I., *The Agrarian Programme of Social-Democracy in the First Russian Revolution 1905 - 1907,* Nov-Dec 1907, CW 13:239
16. Lenin, V.I., *The Agrarian Programme of Social Democracy in the First Russian Revolution,* Nov-Dec 1907, CW 13:238-242
17. Lenin, V.I., *The Agrarian Programme of Social-Democracy in the First Russian Revolution 1905 - 1907,* Nov-Dec 1907, CW 13:430
18. Cliff, T.C., *Lenin: Building the Party, Pluto Press,* 1975, p200
19. Lenin, V.I. *Social-Democracy and the Provisional Revolutionary Government,* March 1905, CW 8:288

20. Lenin, V.I., *The Agrarian Programme of Social-Democracy in the First Russian Revolution 1905 - 1907*, Nov-Dec 1907, CW 13:229 and 292-3

21. Lenin, V.I., *Report on the Unity Congress of the RSDLP*, May 1906 CW 10:342

22. Lenin, V.I., *The Agrarian Programme of Social-Democracy in the First Russian Revolution 1905 - 1907,* Nov-Dec 1907, CW 13:333

23. Lenin, V.I., *The Aim of the Proletariat in Our Revolution*, March 1909, CW 15:379

24. Lenin, V.I., *The Revolutionary Democratic Dictatorship of the Proletariat and the Peasantry,* March 1905, CW 8:293-303

25. Krupskaya, N., *Memories of Lenin*, Panther History, 1970, p79 and 108 - 111

26. Lenin, V.I., *Report on the Question of the Participation of the Social Democrats in the Provisional Revolutionary Government,* April 1905, CW 8:382-395

27. Lenin, V.I., *Social-Democracy and the Provisional Revolutionary Government,* March 1905, CW, 8:277-292

28. Lenin, V.I., *The Revolutionary Democratic Dictatorship of the Proletariat and the Peasantry,* March 1905, CW 8:291

29. Lenin, V.I., *The Two Tactics of Social Democracy in the Democratic Revolution,* June-July 1905, CW 9:15-140

30. Engels, F., *The Peasant War in Germany*, International Publishers, New York, 2000, p70

31. Lenin, V.I., *The Revolutionary Democratic Dictatorship of the Proletariat and the Peasantry,* March 1905, CW 8:300

32. Lenin, V.I., *The Rev```olutionary Democratic Dictatorship of the Proletariat and the Peasantry,* March 1905, CW 8:298

33. Lenin, V.I., *The Peasant, or "Trudovik", Group and the R.S.D.L.P.* May 1906, CW 10:411

34. Lenin, V.I., *Social-Democracy's Attitude Towards the Peasant Movement,* Sept 1905, CW 9:237

35. Lenin, V.I. *Agrarian Programme of Social Democracy in the First Russian Revolution 1905-1907*, Nov-Dec 1907, CW 13:230

36. Lenin, V.I., *The Development of Capitalism in Russia*, 1899, CW 3:21-607

37. Lenin, V.I., *The Democratic Tasks of the Revolutionary Proletariat,* June 1905, CW 8:511-518

38. Lenin, V.I., *The Revolutionary Dictatorship of the Proletariat and Peasantry*, March 1905, CW 8:297

39. Lenin, V.I., *Two Tactics of Social Democracy in the Democratic Revolution*, June-July 1905, CW 9:29

40. Lenin, V.I., *The Two Tactics of Social Democracy in the Democratic Revolution,* June-July 1905, CW 9:48 and 52

41. Lenin, V.I. *Social-Democracy and the Provisional Revolutionary Government*, March 1905, CW 8:288

42. Lenin, V.I., *"The Peasant Reform" and the Proletarian-Peasant Revolution,* March 1911, CW 17:128

43. Lenin, V.I., *Resolutions of the Summer, 1913, Joint Conference of the Central Committee of the R.S.D.L.P. and Party Officials,* September 1913, CW19:420

44. Lenin, V.I., *Left-Wing Narodism and Marxism,* June 1914, CW 20:372

45. Lenin, V.I., *On the Two Lines in the Revolution,* November 1915, CW 21:418

46. Lenin, V.I., *Letters from Afar,* 1917, CW 23:295-342

47. Lenin, V.I., *Two Tactics of Social Democracy in the Democratic Revolution,* July 1905, CW 9:130

48. Lenin, V.I., *Speech in Reply to the Debate on the Agrarian Question,* 1906, CW 10:280

49. Lenin, V.I., *Report on the Third Congress of the RSDLP,* May 1905, CW 8:438-439

50. Lenin, V.I., *The Stages, the Trend and the Prospects of the Revolution,* late 1905 or early 1906, CW 10:91-92

51. Lenin, V.I., *On the Two Lines in the Revolution,* November 1915 CW 21:420

52. Lenin, V.I., *Bureau of Committees of the Majority Editorial Board of Vperyod,* May 1905, CW 8:350-351

53. Lenin, V.I., *Two Tactics of Social Democracy in the Democratic Revolution,* July 1905, CW 9:56

54. Lenin, V.I., *On the Provisional Revolutionary Government,* May 1905, CW 8:464-465

55. Lenin, V.I., *Our Tasks and the Soviet of Workers' Deputies*, 1905, CW 10:21

56. Lenin, V.I., *Two Tactics of Social Democracy in the Democratic Revolution,* July 1905, CW 9:21

57. Lenin, V.I., *The Revolutionary Army and the Revolutionary Government, 1905,* CW 8:566-567

58. Lenin, V.I., *The Democratic Tasks of the Revolutionary Proletariat,* June 1905, CW, 8:511-518

59. Lenin, V.I., *Victorious Revolution,* May-June 1905, CW8:450-451

60. Lenin, V.I., *War and Russian Social Democracy*, Sept 1914, CW 21:33

61. Lenin, V.I., *Two Tactics of Social Democracy in the Democratic Revolution,* July 1905, CW 9:15-140

62. Lenin, V.I., *Two Tactics of Social Democracy in the Democratic Revolution,* July 1905, CW 9:87

63. Zinoviev, G., *History of the Bolshevik Party,* New Park Publications, London, 1973 p177-178

64. Sorin, V., *Vladimir Ilyich Lenin (1870-1924)* Marx Engels Institute, Moscow, USSR, 1936

65. Hill, C., *Lenin and the Russian Revolution,* Pelican Books, London, 1971

66. Lenin, V.I., *Report on the Resolution on the Support of the Peasant Movement* CW 8:400-404

67. Krupskaya, N., *op cit,* p108 - 110

68. Krupskaya, N., *op cit,* p137

69. Lenin, V.I., *A Draft Programme of our Party,* 1899, CW 1:227-254

70. Lenin, V.I., *The Workers' Party and the Peasantry,* 1901, CW 4:420-428

71. Lenin, V.I., *The Agrarian programme of Russian Social-Democracy,* March 1902, CW 6:107-150

72. Lenin, V.I., *Ibid,* March 1902, CW 6:116

73. Lenin, V.I., *The Agrarian Programme of Social Democracy in the First Russian Revolution 1905 - 1907,* November-December 1907, CW 13:257-258

74. Barnes, J., *Their Trotsky and Ours: Communist Continuity Today,* Fall 1983, New International, Vol. 1 No 1 pp9-89.

75. Lenin, V.I., *The Proletariat and the Peasantry,* Nov 12, 1905, CW 10:43

76. Lenin, V.I. *On Our Agrarian Programme,* March 16, 1905, CW 8:250

77. Lenin, V.I., *Can the Bolsheviks Retain State Power,* Oct 1, 1917, CW 26:87-136

78. Lenin, V.I., *Two Tactics of Social Democracy in the Democratic Revolution,* July 1905, CW 9:48-49

79. Lenin, V.I., *Revision of the Agrarian Programme of the Workers' Party,* March 1906, CW 10:193

80. Lenin, V.I., *Fifth Congress of the RSDLP.* May 1907, CW 12:466

81. Lenin, V.I., *Left-Wing Narodism and Marxism,* June 1914, CW 20:299

82. Lenin, V.I., *The Agrarian Question in Russia,* June 1914 CW 20:376

83. Lenin, V.I., *Social-Democracy's Attitude Towards the Peasant Movement,* Sept 1905, CW 9:236-237

84. Lenin, V.I., *The Proletarian Revolution and the Renegade Kautsky,* 1918, CW 28: 313

Chapter 4
TROTSKY AND THE THEORY OF PERMANENT REVOLUTION

4.1   **Introduction**
4.2   **What is the Theory of Permanent Revolution?**
4.3   **Who Would Make the Revolution?**
4.4   **What Kind of Revolution?**
4.5   **The Proletariat and the Revolution**
4.6   **The Proletariat in Power and the Peasantry**
4.7   **The Proletarian Regime**
4.8   **A Workers' Government in Russia, and Socialism**
4.9   **What was Innovative in the Theory of Permanent Revolution?**
4.10   **Which Class Would Lead the Revolution?**
4.11   **Comparison with Revolutionary Democratic Dictatorship**
4.12   **References**

4.1 Introduction

Trotsky's ideas formed the third, relatively tiny current, that developed within the *RSDLP* after 1905, being differentiated by his daring conclusion that the Russian proletariat, having taken power, would not limit itself to the *RSDLP* minimum programme (see for example *Our Differences*[1]). Based on his experience of the struggle for the 8-hour day in St Petersburg, and a perspective which placed the Russian Revolution in both an international and historic context, Trotsky concluded that the reality of class relations would compel the working class, as the leading force in the revolution, to exercise its political domination in its own economic interests, and against those of the bourgeoisie. It would be in this way, he predicted in the *ToPR,* that the struggle of the working class for an end to feudalism would, necessarily, carry over into a struggle for state power, that is, it would take on a socialist character. Trotsky was alone, until 1917, in proposing an explanation for how and why a socialist revolution could be on the immediate agenda in semi-feudal Russia, before it occurred in Western Europe[2].

It must be realised that whilst Lenin was alive, no leader of the *RSDLP*, from any faction or grouping, declared that Russia was ready for socialism. Tsarist Russia's industrialisation was primarily for military, not social, purposes. Indeed, the industrialisation of Russia was largely state directed, and accompanied by mechanisms of mass repression precisely to minimise any consequent social changes that might occur and threaten the privileges of the aristocracy. Russia lagged too far behind the West educationally, culturally, economically and industrially for any socialist to believe that socialism could be reached by her own efforts. All Russian socialists agreed that the immediate tasks facing Russia were bourgeois-democratic. The differences were in how these would be achieved.

Despite his behaviour during and after the 1903 Congress of the *RSDLP*, Trotsky was, in fact, in fundamental political disagreement with the core Menshevik strategy of a revolutionary alliance with the liberal bourgeoisie. Woods describes how, in an article in the (new) *Iskra* on 15 March 1904, he severely criticised the liberals as indecisive and treacherous[3]. Later, he would suggest that *RSDLP* support for the liberals should be a noose around their neck dragging them forward until liberalism was left a corpse on the path of history[4]. Incensed, Plekhanov demanded his removal from the editorial board. Whatever his intentions, Trotsky was outside the two major groupings within the *RSDLP* and was more or less politically isolated by the end of 1904[5].

Trotsky's campaign against the Menshevik policy of gaining the support of the liberal bourgeoisie culminated in a pamphlet, *Before the Ninth January*, that would appear early in 1905, after Bloody Sunday. The pamphlet was a sweeping and devastating indictment of the Mensheviks, arguing - in agreement with Kautsky and Lenin - that the liberal bourgeoisie was more afraid of revolution than of the Tsar, and incapable of revolutionary activities[6]. This pamphlet predicted that the town would be the main area of revolutionary events - the armed uprising of the proletariat - but that the urban proletariat was not strong enough on its own to determine the outcome of the revolution. The peasantry represented the necessary reservoir of energy and support, and the pamphlet strongly underlined the dangers of the urban proletariat becoming isolated from the peasantry in a situation where the vast majority of soldiers were peasants in uniform. Trotsky considered that Bloody Sunday, the subsequent strike wave, and the initial armed clashes which supplemented the strike wave, were a "vivid confirmation of the prognosis" contained in his pamphlet[7].

It was in the period between Bloody Sunday and the October strike, in the heat of the strike wave spreading across Russia, that the *ToPR* took shape in Trotsky's mind, to be systematised and articulated after his experience of the St Petersburg Soviet. Essentially, he proposed that the urban proletariat, the necessary leader of the revolution would seize power in the urban centres, and once having power in its hands, would not remain within the bourgeois limits of universal suffrage, a republic, etc. On the contrary, precisely in order to protect the gains it had made, the proletarian vanguard would, from the very first stages of its rule, have to make deep inroads not only into feudal but also into bourgeois property relations. The attempts by the proletariat to implement its own, specific, measures - both democratic and transitional (e.g. 8-hour day, end to unemployment) would bring it into hostile conflict, not only with those bourgeois groups which had supported it during the initial stages of the revolutionary struggle, but also with the broad masses of the peasantry, with whose collaboration it - the proletariat - had come to power[8].

As a matter of record, in his *Results and Prospects*[9], Trotsky does not use the phrase 'Permanent Revolution'. This title appears to have been given to Trotsky's theory by Martynov[10], and has little to do with what Trotsky actually wrote at that time. It is unfortunate that Trotsky accepted this designation, but he did, and that is the name by which his theory is now known. In fact, Trotsky used the description "uninterrupted revolution"[11], and referred to a process which combined the bourgeois with the proletarian revolution, moving without interruption from one historical stage (the bourgeois) to another (the socialist). The revolution would begin as bourgeois-democratic but its internal dynamic, largely determined by the leading role of the urban proletariat, flows through in an uninterrupted process to the dictatorship of the proletariat and the first steps towards socialism.

Results and Prospects, written while Trotsky was in prison for his leading role in the Soviet, and which succinctly described the *ToPR*, was originally published as an 80-page final chapter in the book *Our Revolution*. The immediate influence of the theory that would come to define 'Trotskyism' was negligible:

- An important factor in the lack of impact of the new theory was that Trotsky had antagonised all the leading Russian Marxists and had become a political lone wolf, outside of both major factions whose leaders had no interest in any theory that Trotsky might develop, nor in popularising him or his ideas.
- Despite Trotsky's undoubted popularity as head of the St Petersburg Soviet, the revolution was on the downturn and the idea of "uninterrupted" or Permanent Revolution was out of synchronisation with the pessimistic mood of the time.
- Most copies of the book were seized by police and only a few copies were actually circulated.
- By publishing his new theory as the last chapter in a book mainly composed of old essays, Trotsky could hardly have found a better way to hide it.
- Trotsky was only 26 years old and in a society which, at that time, gave weight to age. His relative youth - he was some 20 years younger than Plekhanov - meant he was considered too young for his novel ideas to be

taken as a serious threat to the ideological hegemony of the older generation.

It is likely that far more *SDs* met Trotsky's ideas on Permanent Revolution in his short polemical article *Our Differences*[12] and the first four chapters of *1905*[12], than read the original Russian text[13]. The article was published in 1908, in a Polish journal edited by Rosa Luxembourg, and the book, *1905*, was published in 1910, in German, under the title *Russland in der Revolution*. The significance of the title of the article was not lost on its readers - it was the same as that used by Plekhanov in 1885 for his major work against the non-Marxist, People's Will group.

To critically review the development of Lenin's theory of the provisional *RDDPP* a large number of texts and references must be read, studied and compared. This is not the situation with Trotsky's *ToPR*. Before 1917 there is really only one major text - *Results and Prospects*. In the time between the first Russian Revolution and the second, it is noticeable that there was no work that significantly extended or deepened his initial writing. Thus, the *ToPR* as described below, deliberately relies on *Results and Prospects* since this was the definitive text describing the theory which was contemporaneous with Lenin's writings on the revolutionary democratic dictatorship and the most finished form of the theory existing before the 1917 October Revolution. Of course, later Trotsky would be forced, by the faction fights in the *CPSU* after Lenin's death, to revisit and generalise his arguments[14] .

4.2 What is the Theory of Permanent Revolution?

It is always tempting to look for the roots of new ideas in the writings of the past, and it is incontestable that an important historic trend had already been noted by Marx and Engels, that the big bourgeoisie were ever more reluctant to take a revolutionary path to complete even the bourgeois revolution. Instead, their political perspective was to seek a compromise with the monarchy and aristocracy. Marx and Engels praised the revolutionary power of the bourgeois in the Great French Revolution in 1789, but after the revolution of 1848 were forced to recognise that the German bourgeoisie was prepared, even eager, to compromise with the aristocracy[15]. In their *Address to the Central Committee Communist League*, Marx and Engels presented their most developed permanentist position:

"while the democratic petty-bourgeoisie wants to bring the revolution to an end as quickly as possible ... it is in our interest and our task to make the revolution permanent until all the more or less propertied classes have been driven from their ruling positions, until the proletariat has conquered state power and ... at least the decisive forces of production are concentrated in the hands of the workers"[16].

One month later Engels published his analysis of the constitutional campaign in Germany and concluded that since June 1848 the question had stood as either the rule of the revolutionary proletariat or the rule of the landed aristocracy:

"A middle road is no longer possible. In Germany, in particular, the bourgeois has shown itself incapable of ruling; it could only maintain its rule over the people only by surrendering it once more to the aristocracy and bureaucracy. ... the revolution can no longer be brought to a conclusion in Germany except with the complete rule of the proletariat"[17].

Three years later Engels was to further refine his attitude to the workers' party taking power in the bourgeois revolution:

"In a backward country such as Germany which possesses an advanced party ... at the first serious conflict, and as soon as there is *real danger*, the turn of the advanced party will inevitably come, and this in any case will be *before* its normal time. ... we shall start off straight away with the *Manifesto*... "[18].

The bourgeoisie is neither willing nor able to carry through the bourgeois-democratic revolution, the "advanced party" will be forced by events to take the power and once in power has no choice but to start with the *Communist Manifesto* and make "communist experiments". It could, then, be sensibly argued that the seeds of the *ToPR* may be found in the writings of Marx and Engels[19].

4.3 Who Would Make the Revolution?

Trotsky's own analysis began with a description and review of the peculiarities of Russian historical development: the nature and growth of the highly centralised and conservative Russian state, its uniquely low population density and enormous size, the brief Russian summers, and long, bitter Russian winters. By the end of the nineteenth century the autocracy rested upon a highly centralised bureaucratic machine which was quite useless for taking economic, social or political initiatives, but very experienced and effective at carrying out systematic repression. Relative uniformity of action by the administration and secret police could be achieved across the country, despite the enormous distances involved, due to the introduction of the telegraph. The railways, limited though they were, made it possible to transfer military forces relatively rapidly from one end of the country to the other. The army may have proved useless in the Japanese War, but it was sufficient for internal domination.

The Russian government appeared to the world as a colossal military-bureaucratic power, even if it depended to a high degree upon loans from the British Stock Exchange and, even more so, the French Bourse[20]. In *1905* Trotsky gives some figures to show the degree of dependence. In 1908, after the ending of the Russo-Japanese war, interest payments to the "Rothschilds and the Mendelssohns" amounted to some 40% of the entire state budget[21]. Nearly a decade later Lenin would include much the same information in *Imperialism*, but would draw more general conclusions on how the economic domination of the banks had developed a commonality of interests of the nobility, landowners and capitalists.

The autocracy appeared so strong militarily and financially that it seemed to exclude any chance whatsoever for a successful Russian Revolution. The greater the military strength of the Russian autocracy, the longer it could hold state power after it had ceased to satisfy even the most elementary needs of social development. The longer such a state of affairs dragged on, the less likely - even impossible - it became psychologically for Tsarism to voluntarily take the parliamentary path. Thus, a democratic solution to the agrarian problem, the essence of the Russian democratic revolution, was blocked by the autocracy, leaving a revolution by the masses as the only possible means forward[22]. The entire preceding social development of the country made revolution inevitable, and what was more, argued Trotsky, the revolution would be all the more radical because of the delay imposed by the autocracy.

What social forces would make this revolution? Trotsky noted that Russia's low economic level together with the disproportionate amount of national wealth taken by the state for military purposes and debt repayment, resulted in an indigenous manufacturing industry that had remained small scale, and an adjunct to agriculture. From the second half of the nineteenth century, when large-scale capitalist industry began to develop widely in Russia it was largely a foreign import. Foreign and national capitalists and industrialists received substantial support from the autocracy and met few obstacles in their path to **economic** domination - however, the more support they received from the autocracy, the less significant was the role they needed to play politically. Trotsky concluded there would be no serious challenge to the Tsar from this quarter[23].

Trotsky's scenario was that in an economically-enslaved and backward country such as Russia, European capital had introduced the most advanced methods of production and in doing so had short-circuited a whole series of intermediate technical and economic stages through which it, itself, had had to pass in its own countries. For example, factories had arrived in Russia before the widespread development of town handicrafts, short-circuiting the creation of the craftsman class which provided the bulk of the revolutionaries of Paris during the Great Revolution[24]. The consequence was that the nucleus of the population of a Russian town at the turn of the last century, at least of those towns possessing sufficient industry to be of some economic and political significance, was not self-employed artisans but wage-workers. This fact was destined to play a decisive role in the Russian Revolution[25]:

> "The factory industrial system not only brings the proletariat to the forefront but also cuts the ground from under the feet of bourgeois democracy. In previous revolutions the latter found its support in the urban petty-bourgeoisie: craftsmen, small shop-keepers, etc"[26].

Foreign capital had set up enormous factories, employing tens of thousands of workers, making the political weight of the working class employed in those factories, their number, strength and influence, out of all proportion to that of the national bourgeoisie.

Trotsky had begun his political activity by taking part in a small group of mainly student activists - the Southern Russian Workers' Union - where he gained first hand experience of the rapid industrialisation that could occur due to foreign investment. He saw the number of factory workers increase more than fivefold in just a few years. But, and just as important, he saw that the workforce was predominantly young with a higher than average level of literacy[27]. This was valuable practical experience in determining the likely motor forces of the Russian Revolution.

The late development of Russia created a new situation not previously met by Marxists, an entirely new combination of social and economic forces was created by the introduction of the latest capitalist techniques into a society where the vast majority lived in near feudal conditions. Trotsky argued that one consequence of this unevenness in the economic and social development of Russia was the rapid and extensive growth of Marxism and the *RSDLP* before the bourgeois revolution.

Trotsky had to answer the question of why the majority of the oppressed people of Russia, the peasants, would not be the leaders of the revolution. His argument was that there was no tradition in Russia of victorious, concerted political struggle by the peasantry; the peasants were scattered in small communities separated by enormous distances and, even in 1905-1906, had significantly failed to overcome this geographical separation. Trotsky summed up this aspect with his much quoted line "Local cretinism is history's curse on all peasant riots"[28]. He pointed out that the main aim of the peasants during the agrarian riots of 1905 and 1906, appeared to be restricted to driving out their own landowners from their own localities. However, against the peasant revolts the land-owners had the centralised resources of the state:

"The peasantry could have overcome this obstacle only by means of a resolute uprising unified both in time and in effort. But, owing to all the conditions of their existence, the peasants proved quite incapable of such an uprising. They liberate themselves from this curse only to the extent that they cease to be purely peasant movements and merge with the revolutionary movements of new social classes"[29].

Lenin had also addressed this question in, for example *What the Friends of the People Are*, where he said of agricultural workers: "Scattered, individual, petty exploitation ties the working people to one locality, divides them, prevents them from becoming conscious of class solidarity, prevents them from uniting ..."[30].

4.4 What Kind of Revolution?

Trotsky accepted that as far as its first, most direct tasks were concerned, the Russian Revolution was a "bourgeois" revolution because it set out to free the country from the restrictions of semi-feudalism, particularly in land ownership. But would a revolution against the autocracy be carried through to a satisfactory conclusion if led by the bourgeoisie?

Trotsky sketched the development of the bourgeois-democratic revolution by briefly considering the revolutions of 1789, 1848 and 1905, and followed the analysis made by Engels in *Revolution and Counter Revolution in Germany*[31], who had argued that in 1848, the bourgeois revolution would have had to be carried out not by the German bourgeoisie, but against it, since to the German bourgeois, democratic institutions represented not an aim to fight for but a menace to its interests. For the revolution against the monarchy to have succeeded, a class was needed that could have taken charge without, and in spite of, the bourgeoisie. Neither the urban petty-bourgeoisie nor the peasants were able to do that. Only the workers were brave enough to face and fight the reaction, but were neither sufficiently organised nor sufficiently conscious in 1848, to take the lead and carry the revolution through[32].

Having introduced the idea of the proletariat as the key fighting force in any future revolution to overthrow the autocracy, Trotsky emphasised that things had come a long way in nearly sixty years, and that the consciousness of the Russian working class of 1906 was way ahead of, say, that of the workers of Vienna of 1848. In Russia, the principal driving force of the

Revolution would be the armed proletariat, this would mean that proletarian methods and organisational forms would, by-and-large, be adopted in the struggle - in particular the political general strike and Soviets. His decisive evidence was the springing up all over Russia, of Soviets of Workers' Deputies, potential organs of government created by the masses themselves for the purpose of co-ordinating their revolutionary struggle and organising the political strikes. "And these Soviets, elected by the masses and responsible to the masses, were unquestionably democratic institutions, conducting a most determined class policy in the spirit of revolutionary socialism"[33].

In support of his thesis Trotsky pointed out that in the revolutions of 1789 and 1848 (whether in Berlin, Paris, Vienna or Italy), the first demand was for a militia, a National Guard - the arming of the propertied and the 'educated' classes to protect the liberties won from the monarchy and to make the further existence of despotism impossible, but also to protect bourgeois private property from attacks by the proletariat, a guarantee for the propertied classes against possible disorder from below. The militia had been a clear class demand of the bourgeoisie[34]. However, in Russia the liberal bourgeois had not formed its own militia and was most definitely hostile to a **proletarian** militia. This, Trotsky argued, showed that the liberal democrats feared arming the proletariat more than they feared the soldiers of the autocracy[35].

4.5 The Proletariat and the Revolution

It was in considering the role of the proletariat in the bourgeois revolution that Trotsky introduced the concept that most startled his readers. He began by reminding them of the most basic of Marxist views on the state and revolution. The state is only a machine in the hands of the dominating social force, driven by the class interests of that social force; its "motor and transmitting mechanisms" such as the church, courts, press and schools rest on its police, its prisons and its armed forces. Revolution is an open struggle for state power between social forces and "Every political party worthy of the name strives to capture political power and thus place the State at the service of the class whose interests it expresses"[36]. Trotsky drew the obvious conclusion that the *RSDLP*, being the party of the proletariat, should naturally strive for political domination by the working class.

Trotsky then develops the core of the *ToPR*, and the lessons of the St Petersburg Soviet resonate through:

"The proletariat grows and becomes stronger with the growth of capitalism. In this sense the development of capitalism is also the development of the proletariat towards dictatorship. But the day and the hour when power will pass into the hands of the working class depends directly not upon the level attained by the productive forces but upon relations in the class struggle, upon the international situation, and, finally, upon a number of subjective factors: the traditions, the initiative and the readiness to fight of the workers. ...

It is possible for the workers to come to power in an economically backward country sooner than in an advanced country. ... To imagine that the dictatorship of the proletariat is in some way automatically dependent on the technical development and resources of a country is a prejudice of 'economic' materialism simplified to absurdity. This point of view has nothing in common with Marxism"[37].

Trotsky argued that the political importance and strength of the industrial proletariat was not linearly related to a country's industrial development, that numerous social and political factors of a national and international character had to be considered, and these could sometimes completely alter the normal political expression of economic relations[38]. In Trotsky's view, the Russian Revolution would create conditions in which power could pass into the hands of the workers. Given that the workers would provide the core of the revolutionary fighters, the major force in the armed insurrection, it would not be possible for the revolution against the Tsar to be victorious without actual power - power on the ground - passing into the hands of the armed workers. But, if this happened, real power would be in the hands of the proletariat before the bourgeois liberal politicians could assume the government - whether or not in the form of a Constituent Assembly - and begin to govern the country.

As support for his views, Trotsky drew on Kautsky's authority quoting from his book, *American and Russian Workers*, in which Kautsky pointed out that there was no direct relation between the political power of the proletariat relative to the bourgeoisie and the level of capitalist development. Kautsky compared the specific social weights of the Russian and American working classes, concluding that the militant proletariat had nowhere acquired such importance as in Russia, and that this importance would undoubtedly increase, because Russian workers had only just begun to take part in the modern class struggle[39].

Seeking to answer in advance some of the expected criticisms from those Russian Marxists such as Plekhanov, Trotsky particularly recommended the following extract from Kautsky:

"It is indeed most extraordinary that the Russian proletariat should be showing us our future, in so far as this is expressed not in the extent of the development of capital, but in the protest of the working class. The fact that this Russia is the most backward of the large states of the capitalist world would appear to contradict the materialist conception of history, according to which economic development is the basis of political development; but really this only contradicts the materialist conception of history as it is depicted by our opponents and critics, who regard it not as a *method of investigation* but merely as a ready-made *stereotype*'"[40].

Trotsky then gave a final quotation from Kautsky in support of his argument;
"'struggle for the interests of *all* Russia has fallen to the lot of the *only now-existing strong class in the country* - the industrial proletariat. For this reason the industrial proletariat has tremendous political importance, and for this reason the struggle for the emancipation of Russia from the incubus of absolutism which is stifling it has become converted into a *single combat between absolutism and the industrial proletariat,* a single combat in which the peasants may render considerable support but cannot play a leading role'"[41].

Later, Trotsky published his own annotated translation of Kautsky's *The Driving Forces of the Russian Revolution* as support for the *ToPR*, claiming that the line of thinking of the two articles was "precisely the same"[42]. It is here that Trotsky asserted, with Kautsky's apparent support, that the political domination of the proletariat would inevitably lead to civil war and the ultimate defeat of the proletariat, if the revolution remained within a national framework. Trotsky's conclusion was the proletariat in power should use all the resources at its disposal to turn a Russian revolution into the first episode of the European revolution. Trotsky gave a somewhat novel twist to what Kautsky had written. It would be more exact to say that Kautsky, as Lenin, believed that the Social Democrats, as the victorious party of the revolution, could go no further in the implementation of their programme than the interests of the peasantry permitted. The peasants could not be expected to become socialists, so to introduce socialist measures in the economy would conflict with interests of the majority of the population, a conflict that could be resolved successfully only with the assistance of the European working class[43].

Whether or not the revolution was bourgeois-democratic, the experience of the St Petersburg Soviet showed that expecting the political domination of the proletariat to be only a passing episode ignored the reality that once the proletariat had taken power, it would not give it up unless it was torn from its hands by armed force. On taking power, the proletariat would, by the very logic of its position, move towards the introduction of state intervention into industry, would itself take the first steps towards collectivisation and the socialist transformation of society. Defining the Russian Revolution, generally, as a bourgeois revolution, neither defined nor answered the specific political and strategic problems which the actual revolution would throw up.

Trotsky asked the rhetorical question as to whether revolutionary *SDs* should consciously work towards a proletarian government or regard it as an event to avoid[44]. He answered: "In the revolution whose beginning history will identify with the year 1905, the proletariat stepped forward for the first time under its own banner in the name of its own objectives"[45].

4.6 The Proletariat in Power and the Peasantry

In a country in which the overwhelming majority of the population was peasants, the obvious question was what would be the relationship between the urban proletariat and the rural petty bourgeois, i.e. in the event of a victory of the revolution.

Obviously, with a decisive victory of the revolution, the class that played the leading role would take power (especially if that class dominated in the capital, towns and industrial centres and controlled the only national transportation network) - in other words, power would pass into the hands of the proletariat. To Trotsky, as Lenin, it was axiomatic that *SDs* would participate in such a revolutionary democratic government, any other perspective would have been senseless. To retain power for any significant period of time the proletarian government would have to contain influential representatives of revolutionary non-proletarian social groups - especially the peasantry. Trotsky was open to suggestion on how such a government might be described; as the dictatorship of the proletariat and peasantry, as a dictatorship of the proletariat, peasantry and intelligentsia, or even as a coalition government of the working class and the petty bourgeoisie. However, whatever the name of the government, the real issue would be: who determined the content of the government's policy, who wielded hegemony in the government and through it, in the country at large?[46].

In later years Trotsky would come under fire from the bureaucratic wing of the Bolshevik Party for proposing, in 1906 and after, a "Workers Government", in the sense of a government composed of workers' parties only. However, in *Results and Prospects* there is clearly no intention to exclude the participation of representatives of the peasantry from government, rather the success of the revolution is predicated on peasant participation. Trotsky never doubted that in order for the proletariat to stay in power, it had to widen the base of the revolution. Drawing on the events of 1905, he proposed that there would be an inevitable delay before many sections of the working masses, particularly those in the countryside, would be drawn into the revolution and become politically organised, primarily thorough Soviets. In many cases it would be after the advance-guard of the revolution, the urban proletariat, had taken state power into its hands. Indeed, having governmental power, the proletariat would be expected to use that power to enact legislation that would revolutionise the rural masses in support of its government, and so give the proletariat an invaluable advantage. (We shall see later, that Lenin, having gone through the experience of the October 1917 Revolution, would propose precisely the same concept.) Governmental recognition of all revolutionary expropriations of land carried out by the peasants would mean *"The proletariat in power will stand before the peasants as the class which has emancipated it"*[47].

Thus, the fundamental interests of Russia's peasants (even including the kulaks) were bound up with the outcome of the revolution, and the fate of the proletariat. The *ToPR* predicted that in Russia the fundamental problems of democracy, and for the peasants this meant the end of feudal relations on the land, would be solved by a workers' revolution. The majority of the Russian peasantry would, in the first and most difficult period of the revolution, actively seek to maintain the proletarian government which guaranteed its new property holdings. In such a situation, created by the transfer of power to the proletariat, the peasantry as a whole would rally to support the workers' regime. However, Trotsky also sounded a cautious and somewhat pessimistic note, warning that in both the revolutions of 1789 and 1848, the peasantry, having achieved its aims, lost all interest in progressing the revolution, and betrayed it by placing itself as the foundation-stone of 'order'[48].

For factional reasons, Stalin, in *The October Revolution and the Tactics of the Russian Communists*[49], wrote that Trotsky, in 1905, simply forgot about the peasantry as a revolutionary force and advanced the slogan of "No tsar, but a workers' government", that is a revolutionary government without the peasantry. In the interests of the Soviet bureaucracy, the weight of the Russian state was placed behind a campaign that lasted until the collapse of the Soviet Union, to the effect that Trotsky under-estimated the peasantry:

> "Stalin quotes from a leaflet which Trotsky did not write and simply forgot about the slogan which Trotsky *actually* advanced in 1905: *Neither Tsar nor Zemtsi* (i.e. liberals), *but the People*! i.e. a slogan embracing the workers and peasants. The leaflet in which this occurs is to be found, along with numerous appeals to the very peasantry which Trotsky "forgot", in Trotsky's *Collected Works* (vol. 2, page 256) which were printed in Russia after the October Revolution"[50].

However, Trotsky's use of the phrase "a workers' government" does need clarification because of the apparent similarity between his use of the term and its use by Parvus, a co-worker and colleague, who helped Trotsky launch *Nachalo (The Beginning)* in 1905. Parvus wrote the introduction to *Before the Ninth of January*, and there stated that the revolutionary government would be a *Social Democratic* government. We have seen that Lenin criticised Parvus' call for a workers' government for excluding the peasantry. But Parvus limited the tasks of the workers' government to the **democratic** tasks, and argued that the "Workers' Government" brought to power by the revolution would be a **reformist** workers' government not a dictatorship of the proletariat, not a workers' socialist government[51]. Writing in *Our Differences,* on the differences between his ideas on "a Workers' Government" and those of Parvus, Trotsky said that at that time (1904), Parvus' views on the Russian Revolution "bordered closely on mine, without however being identical with them"[52]. Trotsky's differences with Parvus were twofold: the degree of peasant participation in the government, and whether the workers' government limited itself to the *RSDLP* minimum programme or took the first steps towards socialism[53,54].

As we know, until 1905, Lenin was of the opinion that return of the cut-off lands was all that could be realistically proposed as party policy. In 1905 Trotsky held the view: "... we cannot undertake to carry out a programme of equal distribution ... This policy, being directly wasteful from the economic standpoint, could only have a reactionary-utopian ulterior motive, above all would politically weaken the revolutionary party"[55]. These prognostications had to be tested against reality and, in 1917, recognition of the need for the support of the peasantry meant that both Trotsky and Lenin agreed to the Bolshevik Party adopting, without alteration, the agrarian programme of the *SRs*.

4.7 The Proletarian Regime

While stressing that the proletariat could achieve state power only through a nation-wide upsurge, and would enter government as the champion of the nation in the revolutionary democratic struggle against absolutism and feudalism, Trotsky pointed out that once in power, the proletariat would have to make policy. The first measures would include restructuring all social and state relations (most importantly, land to the peasant), which would have the active support of the whole nation. However, "the workers' government" would also be immediately confronted by other important issues such as the length of the working day and the problem of unemployment.

Drawing once again on his experience of leading the St Petersburg Soviet, Trotsky considered the demand for the 8-hour day, explaining that the introduction of such a measure in a time of intense class antagonisms (as in November, 1905), would almost certainly meet the organised and determined resistance of the capitalists, even to the extent of lockouts and the closing down of factories. In such a situation the workers would demand maintenance and support from the revolutionary government they had created, and a government relying upon the workers could not refuse them. (Of course, Trotsky was making a point in principle, the 8-hour day would not be such a significant issue in 1917 as it had been in 1905 due to supply shortages limiting war-time production. The issue in 1917 would be much more to do with employer sabotage of production and laying-off workers.)

In such circumstances, which would occur more or less immediately after power was transferred into the hands of a revolutionary government with a *SD* majority, the division between minimum demands (demands which are compatible with private property in the means of production), and maximum demands (demands that would form the first steps towards socialism and presupposed a proletarian dictatorship), would lose its significance, since a proletarian government would be faced with enacting policies which cannot be divided so neatly.

If the employers resorted to a lock-out as they did in 1905, and threw hundreds of thousands of workers onto the streets, what should the revolutionary government do? A bourgeois-democratic government would retreat, but a government based to a large extent on workers' Soviets would call for workers' occupation of the closed factories and the introduction, in at least the largest of them, of state supported communal production. The speed with which the proletariat would advance towards such collectivist measures would, naturally, depend upon the balance of forces. It will be shown later that in the 1917 October Revolution, the workers moved almost immediately to the demand for nationalisation. Trotsky, if anything, under-estimated the likely proletarian pressures on "a workers' government".

Trotsky, like Lenin, was hypothesising about possible activities by a future revolutionary government, and both came to similar pessimistic conclusions. Trotsky's prognosis was that as the "workers' government" took actions on behalf of the working class and its policy ceased to be general-democratic and became more a class policy, the revolutionary ties between the proletariat and the nation would be broken. Like Lenin, Trotsky saw the activities of the post-revolutionary government in carrying the class struggle into the villages, as generating the active opposition of the upper, and possibly middle sections, of the peasantry which would have an influence on a section of the intellectuals and the petty-bourgeoisie of the towns. The more definite and determined the policy of the proletariat in power became, the narrower would its base become.

Trotsky's pessimism bears a strong resemblance to that of Lenin who saw the liberal bourgeoisie becoming downright counter-revolutionary, and organising itself with the whole of the well-to-do peasants, and a fairly large part of the middle peasantry, to take away from the proletariat the gains of the revolution[56]. Both Lenin and Trotsky concluded that despite their foreboding it was the business of *SDs* to enter the revolutionary provisional government and, during the period of revolutionary-democratic reforms, lead the fight for these to have a most radical character, relying for this purpose upon the organised proletariat and, eventually, the support of the revolutionary proletariat in the West.

4.8 A Workers' Government in Russia, and Socialism

Marx had already answered, in principle, the question of whether the transfer of governmental power into the hands of the Russian proletariat would be the beginning of the transformation of the national economy into a socialist one. In May 1871 in Chapter 5 of *The Civil War in France*, entitled *The Paris Commune*, he had written: "The political rule of the producer cannot co-exist with the perpetuation of his social slavery. The Commune was therefore to serve as a lever for uprooting the economical foundation upon which rests the existence of classes, and therefore of class rule"[57].

Trotsky's principal testing ground for his innovative hypothesis was the experience of the St Petersburg Soviet. Put simply: If the workers formed the government and dominated politically, would they allow their economic enslavement to continue? If the proletariat took power through an armed uprising, and controlled the means of coercion, would they continue to tolerate the conditions of capitalist exploitation? Would such a government, even if it wished to limit itself to the *SD* minimum programme (as Lenin proposed for the provisional *RDDPP*), nevertheless, by the logic of its position, have to take collectivist measures?

The first thing the proletarian regime would have to do on coming to power would be to solve the agrarian question, more precisely it would legitimise all the revolutionary changes (expropriations) in land relationships carried out by the peasants themselves. The interests of the peasantry **as a whole**, as an **estate**, would be bound up with the fate of proletarian revolution. The way in which the agrarian policy would be carried out and the speed of its introduction, would be determined by the need to retain the peasant masses as allies and avoid pushing them into the ranks of the counter-revolution. In the first period of its existence the legislation enacted by the revolutionary government would be a powerful instrument for revolutionising the masses, and would give it invaluable advantages. Once the honeymoon was over, the rate of social change enacted by the regime would have to be a balance between the interests of the proletariat and the hostility likely to be generated amongst the petty-bourgeois masses.

Trotsky, like Lenin, was at pains to stress that it would not be the passing of this or that specific measure which would be the deciding factor; what was key was organising and mobilising the masses to carry out for themselves the necessary practical measures. Political power would not give the regime omnipotence, but the proletariat could use that political power to mobilise the maximum active support and so minimise the obstacles on the path towards collectivism[58]. Trotsky concluded:

"*Without the direct State support of the European proletariat the working class of Russia cannot remain in power and convert its temporary domination into a lasting socialistic dictatorship.* Of this there cannot for one moment be any doubt. But on the other hand there cannot be any doubt that a socialist revolution in the West will enable us directly to convert the temporary domination of the working class into a socialist dictatorship. ... The revolution in the East will infect the Western proletariat with a revolutionary idealism and rouse a desire to speak to their enemies 'in Russian'"[59].

This bears a striking resemblance to Lenin's opinions at that time:

"The Russian proletariat *plus* the European proletariat organise revolution. In such conditions the Russian proletariat can win a second victory. The cause is no longer hopeless. The second victory will be the *socialist revolution in Europe*. The European workers will show us 'how to do it', and then together with them we shall bring about the socialist revolution"[60].

Both Lenin and Trotsky were optimistic and, correctly, believed the influence of the Russian Revolution upon the European proletariat would be "tremendous", not only would the revolution destroy Russian absolutism, it would create a "revolution in the consciousness and temper of the European working class"[61].

4.9 What was Innovative in the Theory of Permanent Revolution?

The *ToPR* has undoubtedly been one of the most significant and widely discussed contributions (even if as a topic of factional dispute) made by a Marxist in the 20th century. The theory, which Trotsky initially restricted to

Russia, addressed one of the most pressing problems of the day: What would be the class character of the revolution that would overthrow autocratic rule, solve the agrarian problem and free the mass of the population (the peasants) from poverty and hunger?

Trotsky's proposals on the nature of the Russian Revolution were a radical departure from the dominant ideas and methodology of the Second International, particularly on the subject of the future of semi-feudal Russia. His analysis, and the theory developed from it, represented an astonishing theoretical breakthrough. Einstein's theory of relativity, published in 1905, fundamentally altered the conceptual framework within which man viewed the universe, so Trotsky's *ToPR* fundamentally shifted the analytical perspective from which revolutionary processes were viewed. Without wishing to develop the analogy too far, it can also be said that, initially, both revolutionary changes were largely ignored by the establishment of the day.

Prior to 1905, the development of revolutions tended to be seen as a progression of national events, each outcome determined by the logic of its own internal socio-economic relations. Trotsky proposed that in the modern era another approach was required: revolution must be viewed as a world-historic process of social transition from class society, rooted in nation-states, to a classless society based on a global economy and the international working class[62].

There were four distinct characteristics to the young Trotsky's contribution to the theory of the coming Russian Revolution, and these implicitly contained a number of fundamental criticisms of the mechanistic Marxism of the older leaders of Russian socialism.

1. First, and most importantly, Trotsky addressed the problem of the transition from the democratic revolution to the socialist and, in a truly Marxist manner, began with a study of the reality of the development of capitalism in Russia. Many senior Russian Marxists (e.g. Plekhanov) tended, probably because of their polemics with Populism, to play down any specificity of Russian social formations, and insisted on an inevitable similarity between the social and economic development of Western Europe and the future of Russia. Trotsky sited the coming Russian Revolution squarely in terms of Russian history, and observed that at a time when the development of capitalism in Russia was still in its relative infancy, the joint action of state and foreign capital had parachuted into semi-feudal Russia, a number of large-scale industries employing tens of thousands of workers in some of the largest factories in the world. This made the working-class relatively much stronger with respect to the bourgeoisie than in any previous bourgeois revolution. Trotsky also determined from his analysis that because

of the links which the Russian liberal and urban petty-bourgeoisie had with the land, they would play a counter-revolutionary role[63].

Trotsky argued that Plekhanov[64] had proposed a pattern of historical development according to which democracy and socialism for all peoples and in all countries, were two stages in the development of society which were entirely distinct and, in time, were separated by generations. Plekhanov, the father of Russian Marxism, considered the idea of the dictatorship of the proletariat in semi-feudal Russia, to be a delusion, a view that was not only that of the Mensheviks but also of the overwhelming majority of the Bolshevik 'Old Guard'[65].

Up to this point in the debate, Trotsky had much in common with Lenin and Kautsky, but the *ToPR* then proposed that, in the present epoch, the democratic tasks of the backward bourgeois nations led directly to the dictatorship of the proletariat and this put socialist tasks on the order of the day. In complete contradiction to both the vulgar Marxists and Lenin, the *ToPR* established that for semi-feudal and backward countries, the road to democracy passed through the dictatorship of the proletariat. The major tasks of the bourgeois-democratic revolution (in particular the solution of the agrarian problem), could not be carried through unless under the dictatorship of the proletariat[66].

2. Trotsky, Lenin and Kautsky observed that in the conditions of the early 20th century, industry and landlords were economically entwined with the banks through loans and credit, and socially through family links, and common education, etc. Kautsky and Lenin drew the conclusion that the urban petty bourgeois would be anti-revolutionary and that the proletariat, with the support of, and in alliance with, the peasantry, would be the armed vanguard of the bourgeois revolution. Trotsky went qualitatively further and concluded that the revolutionary agrarian reforms necessary to end feudal relations on the land, would be such a massive blow against the economic, social and political interests of the bourgeois classes, that these could be carried through only under the dictatorship of the proletariat. Lenin would come to the same conclusion some ten years later, in 1917[67], while Kautsky would join the camp of counter-revolution.

3. Trotsky explicitly rejected the economist traits of Plekhanov's Marxism. This is one of the fundamental methodological presuppositions of the *ToPR*, as shown by the well-known passage from *Results and Prospects*:

"To imagine that the dictatorship of the proletariat is in some way automatically dependent on the technical development and resources of a country is a prejudice of 'economic' materialism simplified to absurdity. This point of view has nothing in common with Marxism"[68].

Trotsky recognised that the immediate social conditions of the Russian factory workers meant their consciousness was very different from that generated by the general technical and economic level of peasant Russia. This was re-enforced by his experience as leader of the St Petersburg Soviet which convinced him that the workers, once committed to revolutionary struggle and having taken governmental power, would not voluntarily restrain themselves and allow the bourgeoisie to take control, but would rapidly progress to placing socialist demands on their government.

Of course, the urban proletariat had to win the support of the peasantry - without this it could not hold power. But the only way for it to attract the mass of small rural proprietors was (a) firstly to show the necessary vigour, strength, organisation and determination through taking power in an armed uprising, and (b) then to solve the agrarian problem by ending feudal relations on the land. We shall see that this first ... then approach, would later become an important element in Lenin's analysis and plan of action for the October Revolution. The role of the revolutionary Social Democratic Party would be crucial in such a process. By appearing before the peasants as their liberators, the revolutionary proletariat could take state power long before they became the majority in Russian society.

Trotsky, while clearly stating that the active support of the peasantry was necessary for a successful Russian Revolution, placed certain limits on its role: the peasantry would be unable to play an independent role due to its dispersion and class heterogeneity; the Russian bourgeois-democratic revolution could only triumph under proletarian, socialist leadership. He argued, that a working-class which had just achieved victory - including taking state power - against both Tsarism and all politically conservative forces (including the bourgeoisie), could not be expected, on the following day, to return to the workplace and voluntarily submit to unarmed capitalists. It would be ridiculous to expect the proletariat to agree to rule outside the factory gate but not inside.

Trotsky recognised that the working class could actually conquer power before, and instead of, the bourgeoisie in a relatively backward country. Here Trotsky's conception of the task of Marxists was as instigators, not interpreting history, but working to change it in a radically new way. This would be an argument that Trotsky would later use to justify the Bolshevik's dissolving of the Constituent Assembly in 1918, the revolution was actively creating a majority not statically reflecting the electoral balance at a given instant[69]. However, it must be recognised that Trotsky did downplay the subjective factor and, in 1906 and for many years subsequently, failed to recognise the necessity for the centralised, disciplined, revolutionary party.

4. It was one of Trotsky's great achievements that he grasped the impact of the world economy on Russia's national, social and political life and was then able to develop a consequent practical approach to Russian politics, and elaborate an effective revolutionary strategy. With Lenin, Trotsky accepted the international context of the Russian Revolution but, more than Lenin in 1905, he posed the question of the character of that revolution in terms of the world-wide capitalist system and in this way rose above national restrictions. From this he rejected Lenin's division between bourgeois and proletarian revolutions as not corresponding to Russian reality. The international situation, was an essential consideration in determining what form of state power should be the goal of the Russian revolutionary movement. Trotsky concluded that because of the weight of European capital in Russia, the huge superiority of foreign industry and its virtual domination of world markets, the lack of a radical agrarian revolution meant the Russian bourgeoisie would be unable to carry through any thorough-going industrialisation of its own.

It was the synthesis of these innovations which transformed them into something new and made *Results and Prospects* unique[70]. Starting from a weak and largely foreign bourgeoisie, and a modern and exceptionally concentrated proletariat - Trotsky came to the conclusion that only the workers' movement, supported by the peasantry, could accomplish the democratic revolution in Russia, by overthrowing the autocracy and the power of the landowners. The novelty of Permanent Revolution was not so much in its definition of the class leadership of the coming Russian Revolution (all *SDs* agreed that the proletariat would take the leading role in the armed struggle), than in its definition of the historic tasks (bourgeois-democratic or proletarian) to be undertaken. Trotsky's novel contribution was the idea that the Russian proletarian revolution would carry through the bourgeois-democratic tasks more thoroughly than the bourgeoisie itself, and then transcend those limits and begin to take anti-capitalist measures with a clearly socialist content.

However, Trotsky warned that while the Russian socialist revolution would undoubtedly begin on national foundations, the maintenance of the proletarian revolution within a national framework could only be provisional. An isolated proletarian state must finally fall to imperialism. The way out for it lay in the victory of the proletariat of the advanced countries, an opinion that Lenin agreed with both in terms of the provisional *RDDPP* in 1905, and the dictatorship of the proletariat in 1917. It was this conclusion, which has now been proved correct, that was the main butt of Stalinist venom and the source of many slanders alleging Trotsky's hostility to the Soviet Union. That it was also Lenin's opinion was always conveniently ignored.

4.10 Which Class Would Lead the Revolution?

Lenin like Trotsky agreed on the likely counter-revolutionary role of the Russian bourgeois. Both agreed that the peasantry would not play an independent leading political role. However, Trotsky, more than Lenin, emphasised the reasons why:

"because of its dispersion, political backwardness, and especially of its deep inner contradictions which cannot be resolved within the framework of a capitalist system, the peasantry can only deal the old order some powerful blows from the rear, by spontaneous risings in the countryside, on the one hand, and by creating discontent within the army on the other. ... Because the town leads in modern society, only an urban class can play a *leading* role and because the bourgeoisie is not revolutionary (and the urban petty-bourgeoisie in any case is incapable of playing the part of *sans-culottes*), the conclusion remains that only the proletariat in its class struggle, placing the peasant masses under its revolutionary leadership, can carry the revolution to the end"[71].

Lenin would reinforce this idea of the town as the leader of modern society in *The ... Renegade Kautsky*[72] but, of course, that would be written a full year after the October Revolution, while Trotsky was writing twelve years before the October Revolution.

Both Lenin and Trotsky explained that only the working class, in alliance with the peasant masses, could carry out the tasks of the bourgeois-democratic revolution, and both agreed that the proletariat must assume the leadership of the armed struggle and would, at least initially in so far as it solved the agrarian question, have the support of the vast majority of the peasantry. Both agreed that the Social Democratic Party should participate in the revolutionary dictatorship and any subsequent government. To the extent that both Lenin and Trotsky considered the support of the mass of the peasants as essential for the success of the revolution, both placed the same qualitative emphasis on the peasantry. In 1917 both Lenin and Trotsky would see the key to gaining the necessary peasant support for the proletarian, socialist revolution as legitimising the peasants' seizure of the land.

However, neither saw the worker-peasant alliance as an alliance of equals. Lenin presented the democratic dictatorship as being led by the proletariat whose actions would be constrained by the need to preserve the alliance. Trotsky presented the peasantry as being led by the proletariat which would inevitably carry out collectivist measures in its own interest[73].

In his article *The Aim of the Proletarian Struggle in Our Revolution*, Lenin reviewed the discussions in the *RSDLP* on the slogan of the provisional *RDDPP*. His debate was with Martov and other leading Mensheviks, and one issue was whether, in the alliance of workers and peasants, the joint actions were the activities of equals. Lenin was quite clear - the workers would lead the revolution assisted by the peasants. He pointed out that his unease with the phrase; the proletariat "relying on" the peasantry, as it could give the impression that the proletariat were the weaker party in the alliance, relying on a stronger peasantry. He favoured the phrase "the proletariat with the help of the peasantry"[74].

In 1906 Trotsky, while still in prison, wrote *Our Tactics* (a small pamphlet which was published by the Bolsheviks):

"The proletariat will be able to support itself upon the uprising of the village, and in the towns, the centres of political life, it will be able to carry through to a victorious conclusion the cause which it has been able to initiate. Supporting itself upon the elemental forces of the peasantry, and leading the latter, the proletariat will not only deal reaction the final triumphant blow, but it will also know how to secure the victory of the revolution"[75].

Trotsky's use of such phrases as "supported by the peasantry"[76] may be considered as not qualitatively different from those of Lenin. What separated Lenin and Trotsky was not so much the degree and kind of peasant support needed by the proletariat, but the class nature of the state that would immediately follow the revolution. With armed power in the hands of the proletariat and the Social Democratic Party participating in the revolutionary dictatorship, Lenin's and Trotsky's analyses parted company.

Lenin argued that the proletariat, arms in hand, would lead the revolution in an alliance with the revolutionary peasantry, would implement the essential bourgeois-democratic tasks of solving the agrarian problem in a revolutionary manner (the provisional *RDDPP*), establish a Constituent Assembly, and hand governmental and state power to the bourgeois and petty bourgeois parties in open, free elections.

Four months before the St Petersburg Soviet, Lenin denounced, in *Two Tactics,* the very conclusions that Trotsky would come to:

"... by making it the task of the provisional revolutionary government to put into effect the minimum programme, the resolution eliminated the absurd, semi-anarchist ideas about ... the conquest of power for a socialist revolution. The degree of economic development of Russia (an objective condition) and the degree of class consciousness and organisation of the broad masses of the proletariat (a subjective condition inseparably connected with the objective condition) make the immediate complete emancipation of the working class impossible. Only the most ignorant people can ignore the bourgeois nature of the democratic revolution which is now taking place; only the most naive optimists can forget how little as yet the masses of the workers are informed about the aims of Socialism and about the methods of achieving it. ... a socialist revolution is out of the question unless the masses become class conscious and organised, trained and educated in open class struggle against the entire bourgeoisie. In answer to the anarchist objections that we are putting off the socialist revolution, we say: we are not putting it off, but we are taking the first step towards it in the only possible way, along the only correct road, namely, the road of a democratic republic. Whoever wants to reach Socialism by a different road, other than that of political democracy, will inevitably arrive at conclusions that are absurd and reactionary both in the economic and the political sense. If any workers ask us at the given moment why we should not go ahead and carry out our maximum programme, we shall answer by pointing out how far the masses of the democratically-minded people still are from Socialism, how undeveloped class antagonisms still are, how unorganised the proletarians still are. ... in order to achieve this organisation, in order to spread this socialist enlightenment, we must achieve the fullest possible measure of democratic reforms"[77].

There is little ambiguity here: the workers' party would seek to limit the revolution to the minimum demands ('the three pillars' - a democratic republic, confiscation of the landed estates, and an 8-hour working day) and, convinced of the general unpreparedness of society for socialism, would dissuade the workers from pressing their maximum demands. The idea that the workers' party should immediately struggle for socialism, was "absurd" but in any case, it was "impossible" that the Social Democratic Party would be a majority in the revolutionary government.

The purpose of the coalition of the proletariat and the peasantry in a bourgeois revolution, was to democratise economic and political relations within the limits of private ownership of the means of production. Lenin saw the low level of productive forces objectively barring any immediate transition to the hegemony of the armed working class. His answer to why should the working class restrict its demands, was to make a distinction of principle between the socialist revolution led by the armed proletariat, and the revolutionary democratic (i.e. bourgeois) revolution led by the armed proletariat. If the attempt to achieve a socialist revolution would inevitably be defeated, it was necessary for the proletariat, having achieved power together with the peasantry, to agree that its dictatorship would be merely "democratic". The contradiction between the proletariat's self interests and the bourgeois limitations of the revolution would be solved by raising the proletariat's consciousness to such an extent that it would accept the political limitation imposed upon it by its *SD* leaders, in order to retain the mass of peasants as collaborators or co-dictators. This self-limitation would be the result of the proletariat's own party, the *SDs*, having the necessary theoretical awareness to limit its demand to those acceptable within the limits imposed by private ownership of the means of production - the minimum demands.

Trotsky's response in *Our Differences* was founded on the actuality of the St Petersburg Soviet and the lessons learned. He pointed out that the proletariat, despite the best intentions of its leaders, had ignored the formal boundary which confined it to a democratic dictatorship. Arguing by analogy, Trotsky drew upon the events at the end of 1905, and the factory owners' response to the (minimum programme) demand for the 8-hour day: the shutting down of factories and plants. He explained that with a revolutionary democratic (bourgeois) dictatorship, the factory owners would believe they were secure in their actions because the response of the proletariat would be constrained by that democratic dictatorship. Trotsky then asked the question which exposed Lenin's schema to reality: Initially the revolutionary government would be a workers' government, and what would that do when faced with factory and plant closures? and answered, "It must re-open them and resume production at the government's expense. But is that not the way to socialism? Of course it is. What other way do you suggest?"[78]. Whatever Lenin predicted, Trotsky's experience told him that a revolutionary dictatorship in Russia would be a government dominated by workers who would not restrict their actions to what was acceptable to the factory owners.

Trotsky elaborated this point by asking whether the alliance with peasant representatives or peasant parties, would refuse state support for those workers striking for the 8-hour day, or publicly-funded work for those laid off by the factory owners. Would the peasant parties oppose the government opening of factories closed down by the owners and the commencement of production under workers' control? If so, Trotsky concluded, then very early in the coalition the proletariat would enter into conflict with the revolutionary government.

There is a symmetry here in the analysis and predictions of both men - Lenin foresaw a counter-revolutionary upsurge by the liberal bourgeoisie, the well-to-do peasants and a section of the middle peasants with the proletariat fighting to retain its **democratic** gains[79]. Trotsky went further, he drew the conclusion that dictatorship by coalition would not work, and foresaw a counter-revolutionary upsurge by the liberal bourgeoisie, the well-to-do peasants and a section of the middle peasants with the proletariat fighting to retain its **socialist** gains. It occurred to neither man, in 1906, that the vast majority of the peasantry might be so grateful for the solution of the agrarian problem and so preoccupied with implementing it, that it would accede to the demands of the working class and defend a proletarian state against the restoration of the landlords.

What hope was there for the success of the Russian Revolution? The hegemonic role of the working-class meant the growing over and intermingling of the democratic revolution into the socialist revolution, but the *ToPR* never suggested that Russia could be carried straight into socialism. Trotsky was convinced that the working class would play the leading role in the Russian Revolution, and would then be confronted with the objective problem of taking the first steps towards socialism. These measures would very rapidly conflict with the country's economic backwardness. The reality of the victory of the revolution would be the transfer of power into the hands of a party that enjoyed the support of the armed urban population, but Trotsky saw socialism as unattainable in a predominantly peasant country within the framework of a national revolution. Trotsky cut the Gordian knot: the workers' government would have to unite its forces with those of the socialist proletariat of Western Europe. This was the only realistic way its temporary revolutionary hegemony could develop into a socialist dictatorship[80].

Lenin drew the conclusion that the *RSDLP* (a minority in the *RDDPP*) should limit itself to its minimum demands, and only the victory of the proletariat in the West would protect Russia from Tsarist restoration and secure the possibility of a socialist transformation: "The European workers will show us 'how to do it', and then together with them we shall bring about the socialist revolution"[81].

It can be seen that Trotsky and Lenin had crucial differences on the social character of the revolutionary dictatorship which would be brought to power in the Russian Revolution. In 1905, Lenin correctly indicated the general direction of the struggle, but failed to predict the rate with which it would progress after the overthrow of the autocracy and the taking of power by the urban proletariat, and thus failed to recognise its class nature. This inadequacy was not revealed because the 1905 revolution was defeated.

Lenin publicly attacked Trotsky's ideas on the *ToPR* some two years before the October Revolution, in *On the Two Lines in the Revolution*. Here he spends two pages of a six page article, replying to *The Struggle for Power* written by Trotsky and published in *Nashe Slovo,* 17 October 1915[82]. In his article Lenin used a description of Trotsky's *ToPR* that was to become famous:

"From the Bolsheviks Trotsky ... has borrowed their call for a decisive proletarian revolutionary struggle and for the conquest of political power by the proletariat, while from the Mensheviks [he] has borrowed "repudiation" of the peasantry's role"[83].

In fact, Trotsky had (correctly) pointed out that the capacity of the Russian peasantry for **independent** political activity as an estate had declined even further as it had become increasingly socially differentiated since 1905: the overthrow of Tsarism would not be the result of an independent revolutionary uprising of the peasantry "as a whole". Nor would Tsarism be overthrown by an alliance between labour and the bourgeoisie, it would be overthrown by a revolution led by the proletariat whose allies would (initially) be the peasantry as an estate, but in the long term would be the landless labourers and semi-proletarians in the villages[84]. Superficially, this scenario may appear to be much the same as Lenin's. The difference, however, was crucial: what would be the class nature of the state resulting from the revolution? For Trotsky the alliance with the peasantry as a whole would follow the revolutionary seizure of state power by the urban workers. We shall see later that this is just the realisation that Lenin came to in 1917, during and after the October Revolution.

In 1915, Lenin argued that **if** Trotsky believed that in the era of imperialism, a Russian "national" revolution was impossible (that is the bourgeois-democratic revolution could only succeed if the proletariat seized power), **then** Russia faced a socialist revolution and Trotsky should have been calling not for a revolutionary workers' government, but for a workers' socialist government[85]. Of course, the *ToPR* did not differentiate between the two in this way, and in that lay one of its great strengths - the former would necessarily include the first steps towards the latter.

The distinction Lenin made between a workers' revolutionary, and a workers' socialist government gives the distinct impression that he confused the positions of Trotsky and Parvus. This is confirmed because Lenin went on to say "Trotsky has not realised that if the proletariat induce the non-proletarian masses to confiscate the landed estates and overthrow the monarchy, then that will be the consummation of the 'national bourgeois revolution' in Russia; it will be a revolutionary-democratic dictatorship of the proletariat and the peasantry!"[86]. The implication was that the class nature of the regime necessary to solve the land question, was of little real consequence, confirming that Lenin was not familiar with the *ToPR*. Interestingly, within two years Lenin, himself, would be calling for the socialist October Revolution and the transfer of all state power to the proletariat.

Lenin, in the final of paragraph of his article, repeats his perspective that it would require an alliance of the Russian and Western European proletariat to bring about a Russian socialist revolution:

"The proletariat are fighting, and will fight valiantly, to win power, for a republic, for the confiscation of the land, *i.e.* to win over the peasantry, make *full* use of their revolutionary powers, and get the "*non*-proletarian masses of the people" to take part in liberating *bourgeois* Russia from *military-feudal* "imperialism" (tsarism). The proletariat will at once utilise this ridding of bourgeois Russia of tsarism and the rule of the landowners ... to bring about the socialist revolution in alliance with the proletarians of Europe"[87].

We should examine Lenin's proposition. Was he really saying the Russian workers would lead the revolution, arms in hand, would at once attempt to ally with the European proletariat to bring about the socialist revolution in Russia, **without** itself taking the first steps for this very purpose? Or was he saying the Russian proletariat would lead the revolution, arms in hand, would at once attempt to ally with the European proletariat to bring about the socialist revolution in Russia and, **simultaneously**, itself take the first steps for this very purpose? Reader make up your own mind - but the latter scenario had no principled differences with the *ToPR*.

In either case, however, the limits previously imposed on *RSDLP* participation in the *RDDPP* (specifically the impossibility of being in a majority and restricting its demands to the minimum programme), are now put in serious doubt. It could be argued that this article, while on the face of it being a criticism of Trotsky and the *ToPR,* was in fact an early indication that Lenin was prepared to reconsider the *RDDPP* and the role of *SDs* within it.

The analyses of the two men, as they stood at that time, were shown in their writings on the 1916 Easter Rebellion in Ireland. It is possible to find Trotsky's *Lessons of the Events in Dublin* juxtaposed with the section from Lenin's *The Discussion on Self-determination Summed Up*[88], as though one was a reply to the other, in an effort to imply political differences between the two men on issues current today[89]. Both Lenin and Trotsky condemned the British imperialists' execution of the heroic defenders of the Dublin barricades and demanded self-determination for Ireland.

Lenin defended the uprising as a blow delivered against the English imperialist bourgeoisie, a symptom of the general crisis of imperialism that he expected to lead to revolutions across Europe. Within the context of his support for a genuinely revolutionary nationalist movement, he simultaneously emphasised that it was a premature revolutionary outburst by a section of the urban petty bourgeoisie supported by elements of the workers movement that had yet to find its real, socialist, leaders. Lenin presented this analysis of the Easter uprising in the context of his debate with Rosa Luxemburg on the national question, and so he was concerned with emphasising its revolutionary potential, thus this "article" contained no mention of the failure of the uprising to gain the support of the Irish peasantry.

It was left to Trotsky, who had supposedly "repudiated" the necessity of an alliance with the revolutionary peasantry, to criticise the uprising, specifically, for taking place in a situation where it did not have, and was unlikely to gain, peasant support. Trotsky, just like Lenin, also criticised the uprising because it was led not by socialist, proletarian elements, but petty bourgeois. The workers had allowed the "ascendancy of the green flag over the red"[90]. Of course, for Trotsky this meant that the workers should have had a strategy for moving uninterruptedly to the dictatorship of the proletariat instead of stopping at the national, bourgeois revolution.

However, we now have some ninety years since the Easter Rebellion and can trace the historic direction taken by the forces involved. How far even the most radical current amongst the nationalists has moved towards becoming part of the governmental structure of the English imperialist state was made clear when, on 25 July 2005, the Irish Republican Army officially decommissioned its weaponry and Sinn Fein, at a national gathering on 28 January 2007, endorsed co-operation with the power of the state (the Police Service of Northern Ireland). Clearly, the analyses proposed by both men agreed on key fundamentals: without a socialist perspective and leadership, even the most radical trend amongst the rebels could become a component part of the British state structure. In 1916, of course, Lenin had not yet made his transition to a permanentist perspective, and this would be reflected in his comments on the Easter Rebellion.

4.11 Comparison with the Revolutionary Democratic Dictatorship

Until Trotsky proposed the *ToPR* in 1906, backward countries, such as Russia, which had not passed through the bourgeois-democratic revolution, were supposed to follow the path of America, England, France and Germany: the primary tasks facing Russian revolutionaries were seen as ending Tsarism, ending feudal relations on the land, and the establishment of a Constituent Assembly[91]. For example, even Lenin, in one of his major works of this period, *Development of Capitalism in Russia*[92], concentrated on what was classical in the development of capitalism in Russia.

There has been a long-standing tendency amongst the supporters of Trotsky to minimise the differences between Lenin's theory of the provisional

RDDPP and the *ToPR*. Apparently, the first to make this argument explicitly was Karl Radek who was not present in Russia for the October Revolution but who, according to Trotsky in *Permanent Revolution*, "more than once intended to write a pamphlet dedicated to proving the idea that the theory of the Permanent Revolution and Lenin's slogan of the democratic dictatorship of the proletariat and peasantry, taken on an historical scale ... were ... essentially the same"[93]. Many Trotskyists, e.g. Ted Grant, former leader of the Militant Tendency in the UK Labour Party, in reply to Stalinist attempts to magnify the differences between Lenin and Trotsky, naturally emphasised the similarities between the two theories[94].

Let us follow Grant's lead: as we have seen, both theories agreed on many of the fundamental questions of the revolution; the counter-revolutionary role of the bourgeoisie, the need for an alliance of workers and peasants to carry through the democratic revolution, the international significance of the revolution, and so on. Both Lenin and Trotsky considered it essential that the proletariat participate in, and lead, the revolution, and play a leading role in any interim provisional revolutionary dictatorship that would eradicate feudal forms. Both agreed that the revolutionary gains could be preserved only if the revolution extended to Western Europe; that socialism in Russia could occur only after the socialist revolution in Western Europe. Incidentally, we shall see later that it is precisely these similarities that form the basis of claims that the Bolshevik regime after October 1917 was the *RDDPP* and not the dictatorship of the proletariat.

Notwithstanding efforts to reconcile the two theories, it must be recognised that from 1905 until early 1917, a major difference between Trotsky and Lenin was their characterisation of the class nature of the state resulting from the coming revolution in Russia, the class nature of the revolutionary dictatorship that would carry through the bourgeois tasks of the revolution: for Lenin this would be the bourgeois-democratic *RDDPP*, while for Trotsky it would be the dictatorship of the proletariat.

Lenin was clear that the outcome of the Russian Revolution would be to introduce a bourgeois state with a bourgeois form of government. Trotsky predicted that the necessary state framework within which the alliance between proletariat and the peasants would carry through the bourgeois-democratic revolution, would be a dictatorship of the proletariat.

Trotsky criticised Lenin's formulation for its vagueness; there would be a two-class dictatorship which would be led by the proletariat, even though its party, the *RSDLP*, would be a minority in the governing body of the *RDDPP*, but it was not clear **which class** would exercise the dictatorship. The **implication** was, of course that the working class would lead, but would simultaneously limit its actions to what was acceptable to the peasantry as a whole. Lenin's vagueness may have been intentional as the formula for the democratic dictatorship of the proletariat and peasantry contained a number of variables that would have to be filled in by the revolution itself.

However, the Bolshevik idea of a proletariat in power, whether in an alliance or not, imposing bourgeois-democratic limitations on itself meant that there was a potentially anti-revolutionary aspect to Bolshevism. But unlike Menshevism, which was openly opportunistic before the revolution, Bolshevism would show its possible anti-revolutionary face only after the Tsar was overthrown and during the revolutionary dictatorship. That it was possible for the Marxist Party to perform such an anti-revolutionary role was confirmed in 1927, when the Chinese Communist Party followed the instructions of the Comintern and disarmed its militia, handing over its weapons to the Kuomintang, only to be massacred weeks later.

When one considers the profound implications of Trotsky's development of Marxist theory, one can better appreciate his attitude to both the Bolsheviks and the Mensheviks. For Trotsky, what determined his attitude to all tendencies within the *RSDLP* was their perspective, their programme. The Bolshevik leadership in Russia in 1905 had opposed participation in the Soviets, but while indicative, this was of less importance than whether or not their political programme was based on a correct assessment of the world forces that would determine the evolution and fate of the Russian Revolution. From this standpoint, Trotsky, particularly in *Our Differences,* was justifiably critical of the programme and orientation of the Bolsheviks .

Lenin's and Trotsky's views summarised

LENIN - Provisional Revolutionary Democratic Dictatorship of the Proletariat and Peasantry	TROTSKY - Theory of Permanent Revolution
1. A bourgeoisie which arrives late on the scene is fundamentally different from its predecessors. It is incapable of providing a consistent, democratic, revolutionary solution to the problems posed by feudalism and is incapable of carrying out the thoroughgoing destruction of feudalism and achieving real political democracy. It has ceased to be revolutionary and is an absolutely conservative force.	
2. The decisive revolutionary role falls to the proletariat, even though it may be very young and small in number.	
3. Incapable of independent action, the geographically dispersed and socially heterogeneous Russian peasants would follow the towns and, if won to a revolutionary perspective, will follow the leadership of the industrial proletariat.	
4. The solution to the key agrarian question (end of feudal relations on the land) will be achieved by a dictatorship, the *RDDPP*, a class alliance of proletariat and peasantry to carry through the bourgeois-democratic revolution in the most thoroughgoing manner to the advantage of the proletariat, clearing the way for the struggle for socialism. The alliance of workers and peasants will be embodied as the Soviets. *SDs* will participate in the revolutionary dictatorship but there is no question of a *SD* only dictatorship, or even of a *SD* majority in the *RDDPP*. The Soviets will ensure the fair and free election of a	4. The consistent solution to the key agrarian question (end of feudal relations on the land) will be achieved by a dictatorship, the policy and programme of which will be determined by its proletarian elements. The resulting governmental form will have representation from all the revolutionary petty bourgeois elements, especially the peasantry, but will rest on the dictatorship of the proletariat. The priority of the regime will be abolishing feudalism, but simultaneously it will take the first steps towards collectivisation, moving beyond the bounds of bourgeois private property at the same time as it carries through the remaining bourgeois-democratic tasks.

Constituent Assembly resting on a bourgeois-democratic state.	
5. Revolution in Russia would lead to convulsions in the advanced European countries. The inevitable backlash in Russia itself will be defeated, and the gains of the revolution retained and extended, only with the support and aid of the workers in Western Europe. Russian workers would use all their resources to spread the revolution to the rest of Europe as rapidly as possible.	
6. The socialist revolution in Russia takes place only with/after the socialist revolution in Europe.	**6. The socialist revolution in Russia will precede the socialist revolution in Europe, but cannot be completed until after the socialist revolution in Europe.**
7. 'The final victory of socialism in Russia is, of course, 'impossible'[95], it is 'inconceivable'[96], a reactionary, narrow dream. The socialist revolution is completed only with the victory of a new society 'in all lands' on the planet[97].	

4.12 References

1. Trotsky, L.D., *Our Differences* in *1905* Vintage Books, New York, 1972, p299-318
2. Knei-Paz, B., *The Social and Political Thought of Leon Trotsky*, Clarendon Press Oxford, 1978, p5
3. Woods, A., *Bolshevism the Road to Revolution*, Wellred Publications, London, 1999, p162
4. Trotsky, L.D., *On the Road to the Second Duma* in Journal of Trotsky Studies No 2, 1994, p62-63. - Note Lenin was to use a similar analogy in *Left-Wing Communism - an Infantile Disorder*, when he likened Communist support for the Labour leaders to a rope that supports a hanged man CW 31:88)
5. Deutscher, I., *The Prophet Armed*, Oxford Paperbacks, 1954, p88 - 97
6. Knei-Paz, B., *The Social and Political Thought of Leon Trotsky*, Clarendon Press, London, 1978, p34-38
7. Trotsky, L.D., *Our Differences* in *1905* Vintage Books, New York, 1972, vi
8. Trotsky, L.D., *My Life* Penguin Books, 1984, p171-2
9. Trotsky, L.D., *Results and Prospects,* New Park Publications, London, 1962
10. Knei-Paz, B., *ibid*, p153
11. Trotsky, L.D., *Results and Prospects,* New Park Publications, London, 1962, p212
12. Trotsky, L.D., *Our Differences* in *1905* Vintage Books, New York, 1972, p299-318
13. White, J.D. *Lenin The Practice and Theory of Revolution*, Palgrave, 2001, p10
14. See the introduction to *Permanent Revolution* written in 1928 and the introduction to the 1919 reprint of *Results and Prospects* (both in one volume, New Park Publications, 1962).
15. Marx, K. and Engels, F., *Address to the Central Committee Communist League* (March 1850) MESW, Vol 1 p107
16. Marx, K. and Engels, F., *Ibid,* p110
17. Engels, F., *The Campaign for the German Imperial Constitution*, April 1850, www.marxists.org/archive/marx/works/1850/german-imperial/ch04.htm)
18. Engels, F., Letter to Joseph Weydmeyer 12th April 1853 MECW Vol 39 p303
19. Trotsky, L.D., *My Life* Penguin Books, 1984, p194

20. Trotsky, L.D., *Results and Prospects,* New Park Publications, London, 1962, p175
21. Trotsky, L.D., *1905,* Vintage Books, New York, 1972, p6
22. Trotsky, L.D., *Results and Prospects,* New Park Publications, London, 1962, p176
23. Trotsky, L.D., *Ibid* p181 - 182
24. Trotsky, L.D., *Ibid* p180
25. Trotsky, L.D., *Ibid* p181
26. Trotsky, L.D., *Ibid* p181
27. Thatcher, I. D., *Trotsky,* Routledge, London and New York, 2003, p23-24
28. Trotsky, L.D., *1905,* Vintage Books, New York, 1972, p48
29. Trotsky, L.D., *Ibid,* p48
30. Lenin, V.I., *What the 'Friends of the People' Are,* 1894, CW 1:300
31. Engels, F., *Revolution and Counter Revolution in Germany,*
32. Trotsky, L.D., *Results and Prospects,* New Park Publications, London, 1962, p190
33. Trotsky, L.D., *Ibid,* p192
34. Trotsky, L.D., *Ibid,* p192-193
35. Trotsky, L.D., *Ibid,* p193
36. Trotsky, L.D., *Ibid,* p194
37. Trotsky, L.D., *Ibid,* p194-195
38. Trotsky, L.D., *Ibid,* p197
39. Trotsky, L.D., *Ibid,* p197
40. Trotsky, L.D., *Ibid,* p198
41. Trotsky, L.D., *Ibid,* p198
42. Trotsky, L.D., *Kautsky on the Russian Revolution,* Journal of Trotsky Studies No 2 1994, p200-223
43. Lowy, M., *The Politics of Combined and Uneven Development,* Verso, London, 1981, p37
44. Trotsky, L.D., *Results and Prospects,* New Park Publications, London, 1962, p200
45. Trotsky, L.D., *1905,* Vintage Books, New York, 1972, p55
46. Trotsky, L.D., *Results and Prospects,* New Park Publications, London, 1962, p201
47. Trotsky, L.D., *Ibid,* p203
48. Trotsky, L.D., *Ibid,* p203
49. Stalin, J., *The October Revolution and the Tactics of the Russian Communists,* FLPH Peking, 1976, *p 124*
50. Woods, A. and Grant, T., *Lenin and Trotsky:What They Really Stood For,* Wellred Publications, London, 1976, p69

51. Knei-Paz, B., *The Social and Political Thought of Leon Trotsky*, Clarendon Press Oxford, 1978, p21

52. Trotsky, L.D., *Permanent Revolution,* New Park Publications, London, 1962, p63

53. Deutscher, I., *op cit,* p113-114

54. Lowy, M., *The Politics of Combined and Uneven Development*, Verso, London, 1981, p41. Lenin supports this analysis of Parvus' having an essentially reformist perspective in *Revolutionary Democratic Dictatorship of the Proletariat and Peasantry*, March 1905, CW 8:298

55. Trotsky, L.D., *Results and Prospects,* New Park Publications, London, 1962, p236

56. Lenin, V.I., *The Stages, the Trend and the Prospects of the Revolution*, 1905/06, CW 10:89

57. Marx, K., *The Civil War in France*, www.marxists.org/ archive/marx/works/ 1871/civil-war-france/index.htm)

58. Trotsky, L.D., *Results and Prospects,* New Park Publications, London, 1962, p232

59. Trotsky, L.D., *ibid*, p237-247

60. Lenin, V.I., *The Stages, the Trend and the Prospects of the Revolution*, 1905/06, CW 10:89

61. Trotsky, L.D., *Results and Prospects,* New Park Publications, London, 1962, p246

62. Lowy, M., *The Relevance of Permanent Revolution*, International Viewpoint Oct 2000, http:\\internationalviewpoint.org/ article.php3?id_article=353&var_recherche=Lowy

63. Mandel, E., *Trotsky: A Study in the Dynamic of His Thought*, NLB, London, 1979, p12 -14

64. Trotsky, L.D., *Stalin,* Hollis and Carter, London, 1947, p422-423

65. Zinoviev, G., *History of the Bolshevik Party*, New Park Publications, London, 1973

66. Trotsky, L.D., *Results and Prospects,* New Park Publications, London, 1962, p169-177

67. Lenin, V.I., *From a Publicist's Diary*, Aug 1917, CW 25:278-286

68. Trotsky, L.D., *Results and Prospects,* New Park Publications, London, 1962, p195

69. Trotsky, L.D., *Terrorism and Communism,* George Allen & Unwin, London, 1921, p43

70. Thatcher, I. D., *Trotsky,* Routledge, London and New York, 2003, p38

71. Trotsky, L.D., *1905* Vintage Books, New York, 1972, p312

72. Lenin, V.I., *The Proletarian Revolution and the Renegade Kautsky,* Oct-Nov 1918, CW 28:227-325

73. Cliff, T.C., *Lenin: Building the Party, Pluto Press,* 1975, p201- 204

74. Lenin, V.I., *The Aim of the Proletariat in Our Revolution,* March 1909, CW 15:368

75. Quoted in Woods, A. and Grant, T., *Lenin and Trotsky: What They Really Stood For,* Wellred Publications, London, 1976

76. In his July 1905 preface to Lassalle's *Speech before a Jury* Trotsky wrote "the dictatorship of the proletariat supported by the peasantry", quoted in Trotsky, L.D., *1905* Vintage Books, New York, 1972, p310

77. Lenin, V.I., *Two Tactics of Social-Democracy in the Democratic Revolution,* June-July 1905 CW 9:28

78. Trotsky, L.D., *1905* Vintage Books, New York, 1972, p315

79. Lenin, V.I., *The Stages, the Trend and the Prospects of the Revolution,* 1905/06, CW 10:89

80. Trotsky, L.D., *1905* Vintage Books, New York, 1972, p317-318

81. Lenin, V.I., *The Stages, the Trend and the Prospects of the Revolution,* 1905/06, CW 10:92

82. Trotsky, L.D., *1905* Vintage Books, New York, 1972, p319-325

83. Lenin, V.I., *On the Two Lines in the Revolution,* Nov 1915 CW 21:419

84. Trotsky, L.D., *The Lessons of the Great Year*, originally published in New York Jan. 20th 1917, available on www.

85. Lenin, V.I., *On the Two Lines in the Revolution,* Nov 1915 CW 21:419

86. Lenin, V.I., *Ibid,* CW 21:420

87. Lenin, V.I., *Ibid,* CW 21:420

88. Lenin, V.I., *The Discussion on Self-determination Summed Up,* July 1916, CW 22:353-358

89. See New International Vol 1 No 1 pp 149-156

90. Trotsky, L.D., *Lessons of the Events in Dublin*, originally published 4 July 1916, New International, Vol 1, No 1., pp149-151.

91. Mandel, E., *Trotsky: A Study in the Dynamic of his Thought,* NLB, London, 1979, p15.

92. Lenin, V.I. *Development of Capitalism in Russia,* 1899, CW 3:21-607

93. Trotsky, L.D., *Permanent Revolution,* New Park Publications, London, 1962, p40-41

94. Woods, A. and Grant, T., *Lenin and Trotsky: What They Really Stood For,* Wellred Publications, London, 1976,

95. Lenin, V.I., *Report on the Activities of the Council of People's Commissars,* Jan 1918, CW 26:470

96. Lenin, V.I., *Speech on the International Situation*, Nov. 1918, CW 28:151

97. Lenin, V.I., *Speech at a Joint Plenum of the Moscow Soviet of Workers'. Peasants' and Red Army Deputies*, Nov 1920, CW 31:399

Chapter 5
1917 : FROM THE APRIL THESES, TO THE OCTOBER, PROLETARIAN REVOLUTION

5.1   Introduction
5.2   February, the Letters from Afar and the April Theses
5.3   Trotsky in Early 1917
5.4   The April Conferences
5.5   From the April Conferences to the July Days: All Power to the Soviets
5.6   July Days and Consequences
5.7   The Class Character of the October 1917 Revolution and the Nature of the Resulting State
5.8   References

5.1   Introduction

In the period February to October 1917, Lenin's strategic goal for the Russian Revolution passed from the stagist position of the *RDDPP*, as adopted in the 1905 Revolution, to a position that was in all essentials identical with the *ToPR*. Between receiving news of the February Revolution, and his delivery of the April Theses at the Tauride Palace on 4 April (developed into a programme for action at the Petrograd City *RSDLP(B)* Conference on 22-24 April and the Seventh All-Russian Conference of the *RSDLP(B)* of 24-29 April), Lenin moved to a position of publicly calling for the Bolsheviks to lead the Russian socialist revolution.

Just as events in Russia caused Lenin to change his political goal and to consciously work towards establishing, in October 1917, the dictatorship of the proletariat rather than a democratic dictatorship, so those same events caused Trotsky to completely revise and change his position on the party. Throughout the rest of his life, Trotsky readily admitted how wrong he had been on this question, and how on all issues relating to the party, Lenin had been correct.

During the initial period of the so-called dual power, the Bolshevik fraction was in a small minority in the Soviets; barely 13% at the First All-Russian Congress of Soviets, and insignificant at the First All-Russian Congress of Peasant Delegates held on 17 May 1917. From his return in April to the events of 4 July, Lenin and the Bolsheviks campaigned for a peaceful transfer of power to the Soviets, mounting a campaign under the slogans "All Power to the Soviets" and "Down with the Capitalist Ministers". During this period Bolshevik policy was to win a majority in the Soviets by demonstrating that the Mensheviks and SRs were tied to the government presided over by Prince Lvov, and would not carry out policies that were in the interests of either the proletariat or peasantry.

After the July Days, and the repression unleashed by Kerensky's coalition government, Lenin's called for all state power to be in the hands of the proletariat, and for the Bolshevik Party to take that power in an armed uprising. After July, he openly argued that only by the dictatorship of the proletariat, could peace be achieved and the agrarian problem solved.

Lenin, being human, could not see, in advance, how the Russian Revolution would actually unfold. He wrote in April 1917, "The highly remarkable feature of our revolution is that it has brought about a *dual power*. ... Nobody previously thought, or could have thought, of a dual power"[1]. An inability to foresee such an eventuality did not mean that the class struggle confounded his expectations and left him floundering. Lenin's methodological emphasis on reality and concrete events meant that his strategies would be altered or fine-tuned as events unfolded. It was one of his great strengths that he could throw away an old schema if events proved it outmoded, and develop new strategies that would take the movement forward. As we have seen, Lenin, based on his experiences of the revolutionary upheavals of 1903-1906 had changed the orientation of the Bolsheviks towards the peasantry. He would do so again in 1917.

But it is not helpful to talk of Lenin's strategy as though it were a single indivisible unit. Like all real life, Lenin's strategy contained within it contradictory elements, it developed dialectically. Where he erected schema that were based not on actual events but on prognostications, such as the idea of the provisional *RDDPP*, he had, subsequently, to measure these against reality. In 1905-1906, Lenin projected onto the future revolution, his ideas of how the bourgeois-democratic tasks could be achieved to the best advantage of the working class, but events unfolded differently, in a way he did not foresee. Lenin's methodology enabled him to develop a strategy necessary for the success of the Russian Revolution, even though this meant changing party policy during the revolution itself. As a consequence, in 1917, he independently adopted the essence of the *ToPR*. Such an analysis explains his political development, including the changes made to the party programme in 1917, adopted through the support of the newer, rank and file members, and against the opposition of the Old Bolsheviks.

One obvious, and important, reflection of the change to his political line was his dropping of the use of the term "*RDDPP*" to describe the goal for the second Russian Revolution. Lenin later described the post-October regime in Russia in terms to suit the particular audience he was addressing, referring to it as the dictatorship of the proletariat, as a step towards socialism, and even as a Workers' and Peasants' Government. He did so because it was simultaneously each and every one of these, but he never referred to the post-October 1917 regime in Russia as the *RDDPP*. The reason for this was because the post-October regime in Russia, brought to power by the Bolsheviks, was not a democratic (i.e. bourgeois) dictatorship, but a Workers' and Peasants' Government resting on the power of the dictatorship of the proletariat.

Different authors propose different reasons for Lenin's transition from a belief that the Russian Revolution would be in two separate and distinct stages, to the demand that the Bolsheviks take the power in a socialist revolution. Leibman argued that this was due to Lenin's better appreciation of the international context of the Russian Revolution: "Furthermore, and most important of all, it was during the First World War that Leninism and its founder acquired an *international* dimension"[2]. This is a somewhat harsh view of a man who from at least 1905 had proposed that the ultimate success of a thorough-going revolution in Russia depended upon revolution in Western Europe. However, it is undeniable that Lenin's *Imperialism the Highest Stage of Capitalism*[3] gave him a new insight on the integration of the Russian banks, bourgeoisie and landowners with, particularly, French imperialism[4], and the consequent negligible possibilities for the independent capitalist development of Russia. Harding concurs, and places the cause of the transition as due to Lenin having reaching a new stage in his economic analysis, a stage which demonstrated that capitalism had entered its world-encompassing imperialist phase, with no space for new imperialisms, and which required a world-wide socialist response[5]. Both stress the inner consistency of Lenin's socio-political analysis, and date Lenin's move to adopt a socialist goal for the Russian Revolution as beginning with the development of his theory of imperialism. However, Harding believes Lenin was an opponent of the *ToPR* but this opinion appears to be based on his erroneous belief that the *ToPR* meant an attempt to immediately introduce socialism into Russia[6]. Alternatively, Carr argued that the problems of the severe food shortages in the cities of Russia and the dangers of social collapse were the spur that caused Lenin's re-orientation[7].

Of course, any number of reasons may be proposed, but whatever the reasons for the change, Lenin had adopted a new perspective on the goals of the Russian Revolution by the time of his arrival in Russia in April 1917.

5.2 February, the Letters from Afar and the April Theses

The February 1917 Revolution was unplanned and spontaneous. The Tsarist secret police, the *ohkrana,* reported that the Revolution was "a purely spontaneous phenomenon, and not at all the fruit of party agitation"[8]. One relatively honest eye-witness, the Menshevik Sukhanov, recorded that "Not one party was prepared for the great upheaval"[9], confirming Trotsky's account that "no-one, positively no-one - we can assert this categorically on the basis of all the data - then thought that 23 February was to mark the beginning of a decisive drive against absolutism"[10].

The February Revolution was, almost exclusively, the work of the Petrograd working class. Trotsky writes in his *History of the Russian Revolution*, "It would be no exaggeration to say that Petrograd achieved the February Revolution. The rest of the country adhered to it"[11]. The peasantry supported the February Revolution, but they did not make it. The removal of the Tsar was accomplished by the working class which drew behind it the peasants in the form of army delegates to the Soviets. That the Soviets assumed such an overwhelming importance right from the start was not only due to the memories of 1905 but because there was little alternative; state oppression after the commencement of the war closed the trade unions, abolished the socialist press, and arrested and exiled every revolutionary it could catch[12].

From 23-28 February, the revolution was confined to Petrograd, with the Soviet being convened on the afternoon of the 27th. The country went about its business unaware that anything unusual had occurred. The first city to react was Moscow, which had strikes and demonstrations on 28 February and the following day elected a workers' Soviet. On 1 March, meetings took place in several provincial towns, including Tver, Nizhnii, Novgorod, Samara and Saratov. In the course of March there emerged, in all these cities, Soviets modelled on that of Petrograd. The leadership of these Soviets, with a few local exceptions, was Menshevik and *SR*. In early April, the provincial Soviets sent representatives to Petrograd where they formed an All-Russian Soviet. The revolution spread slowly across the country, more or less peacefully, with many villages not hearing the news until four or six weeks later, and little or no resistance was encountered[13]. The earliest reports of agrarian disturbances, such as assaults on private landed property, reached Petrograd in the middle of March, but they assumed mass proportions in April, stimulating the first mass desertions of soldiers who hurried home from fear of being left out[14].

The Russian bourgeoisie, true to expectations, proved to be cowardly and deeply counter-revolutionary. Sukhanov describes in detail, the manoeuvrings of the leaders of the bourgeoisie, whose first inclination was to betray the revolution and maintain the Tsar, and only when this stratagem collapsed did they move onto the riskier path of keeping the revolution in check by accepting the offer of the Mensheviks and *SRs* to become the Provisional Government[15]. Pipes gives a good description of the Provisional Government as a group of individuals who could not **take** the power, but had to have it thrust on them by, essentially, the abdication of leadership by the newly-born Petrograd Soviet which was the only real power in Russia at that moment[16].

In fact, the Provisional Government emerged out of the Duma and initially gave itself a title that clearly revealed its goals: Committee for the Re-establishment of Order and Relations with Public Institutions and Personages. Their first instinct, as Sukhanov explained, was to resort to repression, but as that was impossible, they were compelled to compromise and play for time. The aim of the liberal bourgeoisie was to halt the revolution by making cosmetic changes intended to preserve as much of the old regime as possible, thus they 'gave' to the masses, the liberties and freedoms that the workers and soldiers had already taken. The old regime had been severely battered, bruised and shaken, but was still in existence in the shape of the economic power of the landlords, bankers and big business, and the social and political power of the huge state bureaucracy, the officer caste, the Duma and the monarchy. The liberal bourgeoisie, believing the monarchy was still the firmest bulwark of private property and order, attempted to preserve the Romanovs, and the Provisional Government manoeuvred to replace Tsar Nicholas II with his son or brother. The workers, who had overthrown the Tsar, handed power to the leaders of the Soviets, who, in turn, handed it to the Provisional Government, who, in their turn, offered it back to the Romanovs![17]

In February, the capitalists knew they had no significant armed force at their disposal and, initially, the decrees of the Provisional Government were carried out only to the extent permitted by the Soviets. "The Soviet of Workers' and Soldiers' Deputies ... possesses the most important elements of real power, such as the troops, railroads, posts and telegraph communication. One may say directly that the Provisional Government exists only as long as the Soviet permits this"[18]. Sukhanov was one of those delegated by the Executive of the Petrograd Soviet to explain to the Provisional Government that the Soviet would leave the formation of the government to the bourgeois parties. He held the opinion, "It was clear then *a priori* that if a bourgeois government and the adherence of the bourgeoisie to the revolution were to be counted on ... Power must go to the bourgeoisie"[19]. The Soviet leaders begged the bourgeois leaders to take governmental power, and promised to stop the "excesses" of the masses, and to restrict the actions of the Soviet itself.

This was quite understandable behaviour from the Mensheviks and *SR*s as it flowed naturally from their political and social perspectives for the Russian Revolution. However, it meant that the February Revolution brought to power those who opposed its success - the Cadets and their allies. On 2 March, the Provisional Government was constituted. It was comprised mainly of big landlords and industrialists[20].

The pressure of the petty bourgeois masses played a disproportionate role in the early stages as expressed in the system of elections in the Soviets. Initially, the workers were entitled to one representative for every 1,000 voters but one soldier for every company in Petrograd. This gave an overwhelming preponderance to the soldiers, with 800 workers' deputies compared with 2,000 soldiers (in their vast majority junior officers from the democratic middle class who gravitated naturally to the more moderate Mensheviks and *SR*s). Cliff quotes one of the local Bolshevik leaders, Shlyapnikov, as saying that out of about 1,600 Soviet delegates in February only about 40 were Bolsheviks[21].

The strategy sketched by Lenin in *Two Tactics*, of the Soviet acting to destroy the autocratic state, to take state power through an armed popular militia, to act as the provisional revolutionary democratic dictatorship and resolve the land question, had suffered a severe setback due to the lack of a genuine revolutionary leadership - and here the Old Bolsheviks offered nothing significantly different from the Mensheviks and *SR*s. As in 1905, the Bolshevik 'committee-men' quickly lost their bearings when confronted with a new situation and lagged behind the movement[22]. In the initial phase of the revolution, the party showed itself to be woefully unprepared, the upsurge of the masses caught it off guard. "Lacking a vigorous and clear-sighted leadership," writes Liebman, "the Bolsheviks of the capital had reacted to the first workers' demonstrations with much reserve, and even with a suspiciousness that recalls their attitude in January 1905"[23].

The Petrograd leadership was not alone, even though in 1912-14, the Bolsheviks had succeeded in winning the support of the great majority of the organised workers in Russia, even though during the war the Mensheviks had played hardly any role, "yet in the heady days of February-April, the two factions were again merged into a single organisation in every province except Moscow and Petersburg. Indeed, in many areas, they remained united right up to the October Revolution"[24].

Liebman has no hesitation in saying that even the most radical Bolsheviks had no perspective other than the consolidation of a bourgeois regime. "'The coming revolution must only be a bourgeois revolution,' wrote Olminsky, adding that 'this was an obligatory premise for every member of the party, the official opinion of the party, its continual, and unchanging slogan right up to the February revolution of 1917, and even some time after.'" The same idea was expressed even more crudely in *Pravda* on 7 March, 1917, even before Stalin and Kamenev had arrived from exile in Siberia to give it a yet more right-wing slant: "Of course, there is no question among us of the downfall of the rule of capital, but only the downfall of the rule of the autocracy and feudalism"[25].

For over a decade, Bolshevik Party cadres had been educated in the theory of the provisional *RDDPP* (which included both the proletariat limiting its demands, and a significant delay before the socialist revolution). Did Bolshevik leaders such as Kamenev impose that schema on the reality of the February Revolution with the result that the party tail-ended the Menshevik and *SR*-leadership in the Soviets between February and April? Certainly they found it possible to present the slogan of the *RDDPP* with a reformist face, a possibility that Trotsky had foreseen and warned against.

The first exiles to return (about 12 or 13 March) were those who had been sent to Siberia, Kamenev and Stalin among them. The new arrivals used their seniority to push the party's line further to the right. This was immediately reflected in the pages of the central organ. In an editorial in *Pravda* on 14 March, two days after his return, Kamenev wrote: "What purpose would it serve to speed things up, when things [are] already taking place at such a rapid pace?"[26]. The next day, he wrote another piece commenting on Kerensky's statement that Russia would "proudly defend its freedoms" and would not "retreat before the bayonets of the aggressors". Kamenev enthusiastically agreed, in terms which totally rejected Lenin's policy of opposition to the war: "When army faces army, it would be the most insane policy to suggest to one of those armies to lay down its arms and go home. This would not be a policy of peace, but a policy of slavery, which would be rejected with disgust by a free people"[27].

In the solidly-proletarian Vyborg district of Petersburg which consistently voted for Bolshevik delegates to the Soviet, the local committee, predominantly worker activists, in their manifesto demanded a democratic republic [Constituent Assembly], the 8-hour day, seizure of the landlords' estates and an immediate end to the war[28]. The Vyborg district committee also issued leaflets appealing for the establishment of factory committees which, with the revolutionary soldiers, would immediately elect representatives to a provisional revolutionary government. This would be under the protection of the insurrectionary revolutionary people and army[29]. These proposals were the same as those in *Two Tactics*, with the important addition of the demand for immediate peace, a significant move towards the policy that Lenin would propose in his April Theses[30]. However, the demand by the Bolsheviks of the Vyborg district that power be taken by the Soviet was not in order to move towards socialism, but because the Provisional Government was not moving fast enough against the autocracy and failing to implement the Social Democratic minimum programme, particularly land to the peasant.

The call that the Soviets should take the power was rejected by both the Bolsheviks who had returned from exile and the Soviet leaders, who used Lenin's 1905 argument that the revolution was "bourgeois" and the working class was "not ready" to take power; the rank and file had no answer. The Bolshevik leadership present in Petrograd had adopted an interpretation of the *RDDPP* slogan that offered no alternative to the Menshevik perspective. "The left Bolsheviks, especially the workers, tried with all their force to break through the quarantine. But they did not know how to refute the premise about the bourgeois character of the revolution and the danger of isolation of the working class"[31].

It took Lenin five weeks from hearing of the victory of the February Revolution to reach Petrograd. His writings during this period show the transition in his thinking from the stagist theory of *Two Tactics* to the demands for a Commune-type state based on the Soviets, and the overthrow of capital, as a necessary precondition for the achievement of a democratic peace and land to the peasants. On 4 March, immediately on hearing the news of the Tsar's overthrow, Lenin proposed his *Draft Theses, March 4 1917*[32], emphasising that the February Revolution was by no means a complete victory, and that revolutionary measures against the landlords and capitalists were required, including a "democratic republic and socialism". On 6 March he sent his famous telegram to the Bolsheviks returning from Stockholm and Oslo to Petrograd: "Our tactic: no trust in and no support of the new government; Kerensky is particularly suspect; arming of the proletariat is the only guarantee; immediate elections to the Petrograd City Council; no rapprochement with other parties"[33].

As soon as *Pravda* recommenced publication, Lenin began his *Letters from Afar*[34], the first of which was dated 7 March and contained demands which had been clearly described twelve years previously in *Two Tactics,* and had been the backbone of Bolshevik policy since then; the revolutionary overthrow of the Tsarist autocracy and destruction of the autocratic state to be accomplished by the provisional *RDDPP* which would temporarily exercise state power through the Soviets resting on an armed militia of the proletariat and peasants. Comparing these to the actual policies of the Bolsheviks in Russia, one can see why they so shocked the Central Committee members. Most of the first letter was published, with about one fifth, which included the passages criticising those who supported the Provisional Government, censored[35]. All four subsequent letters were effectively suppressed.

Lenin's *Letters from Afar* show that his ideas were in a state of flux, and his concept of how the second Russian Revolution would develop was changing. The February Revolution had placed the capitalist Provisional Government in power, but neither the Tsarist monarchy nor the autocratic state had been finally destroyed. Lenin began by demanding that the old state machine, the army, the police force and bureaucracy be smashed. But he recognised that this could be achieved only if there was a transfer of political power from the government of the landlords and capitalists to a government based on Soviets of Workers' and Peasants' Deputies. These Soviets had to be extended across all of Russia to include, particularly, soldiers, rural wage-workers and the entire peasant poor. This would be a real *RDDPP,* and would be assured of victory if, from the start, it rested on the armed might of a workers' and peasants' militia, and fought for the confiscation of the landed estates of state, church, nobility and crown[36]. In this Lenin emphasised the radical and revolutionary dimension of the *RDDPP* but he had not moved outside a stagist perspective.

Carr has argued that before leaving Switzerland, Lenin had already come to the conclusion that the problems of the severe food shortages in the cities of Russia could not be solved "unless one renounces bourgeois relationships (and) passes to revolutionary measures"[37]. Correct, but **initially**, Lenin, after demanding that every toiler should see and feel some improvement in his life - bread, milk for children, accommodation - made the point that such measures were not socialist since they concerned only the **distribution** of goods, and that such a situation would constitute only a democratic dictatorship. However, to achieve peace, and provide food for the people, more than just the *RDDPP* was required. Now Lenin called for a workers' government based not on an alliance with the whole of the peasantry, but with farm labourers, poor peasants and revolutionary workers in all countries[38]. With the support of these allies the Russian workers could utilise the peculiarities of their situation to achieve a democratic republic and then proceed to socialism[39].

Once again Lenin is deeply radical, but the idea that the revolution in Russia could spark the socialist revolution in Western Europe, with consequent feedback into Russia, is within the schema laid out in *Two Tactics*. In March, Lenin presented this idea several times: that revolutionary victory in Russia, the capture of power by the proletariat and poorest strata of the population and the elimination of the autocracy, would encourage the development of the socialist revolution in the West, and this would lead the

"the whole of mankind" to "*peace* and *socialism*"[40,41]. However, by 11 March (the third of his *Letters*) Lenin shows that he is reconsidering the role of the *RDDPP*. He refers to the *RDDPP*, but immediately adds the qualification:

"It is not a matter of finding a theoretical classification. We would be committing a great mistake if we attempted to force the complete, urgent, rapidly developing practical tasks of the revolution into the Procrustean bed of narrowly conceived 'theory' instead of regarding theory primarily and predominantly as a *guide to action*"[42]

He was re-thinking his strategy. In the unique and desperate position in which Russia found itself, it was necessary to extend his previous theory to meet the needs of the actual situation. Two weeks later, in his unfinished *Fifth Letter* written on 26 March, the changes had progressed substantially. The title of the *Fifth Letter* is *The Tasks Involved in the Building of the Revolutionary Proletarian State*. To have moved from a workers' **government**, whether or not in alliance with the poorest peasants, to a proletarian **state,** implied a qualitative change in his perspective. He developed this theme by calling for the proletariat and the poorest sections of the peasantry to "take further steps towards *control* of the **production and distribution** of the basic products". These actions, when completed, would mark the first steps in "the *transition to socialism*"[43]. Now the Russian Revolution is posed as a socialist revolution, and as beginning in semi-feudal Russia before Western Europe.

This is a very different perspective from that described in *Two Tactics*. Lenin had changed the goal of the revolution. The first steps towards *socialism* were to be taken in the short term since they were intended to resolve, for example, the food and housing shortages created by the war. True, Lenin in his *Fifth Letter,* in item 6 on the list of "immediate tasks", wrote that only the *RDDPP* organised on a Soviet model and supported by such organs of government as a proletarian militia, would be capable of successfully achieving peace[44]. However, as Lenin simultaneously proposed that this *RDDPP*, based in the proletariat and poorest sections of the peasantry, should take steps towards the **control of production and distribution**, he was proposing that this *RDDPP* take immediate steps in the transition towards socialism, a proposal that in 1905 was described as "anarchist" and "absurd". The *Fifth Letter* is short, only two pages long, and there is no reference to how the *RDDPP* would take these steps. This was the last time Lenin was to pose the *RDDPP* as a goal to be achieved, and should be taken as an example of Lenin's ideas in flux. At the very least, the actions proposed were in marked contrast to the schemas of *Two Tactics*, and may very well have been the first clear step outside that framework.

Lenin arrived at the Finland station on 3 April, and on the afternoon of 4 April presented his ten "April Theses"[45] to two meetings at the Tauride Palace where the Soviet held its sessions. Firstly he spoke to Bolshevik delegates of the Soviet, and then to a joint meeting of Bolshevik and Menshevik delegates.

Lenin stated that a situation of dual power existed in Russia, due only to the insufficient class-consciousness and organisation of the proletariat. It was now time to move to power being "in the hands of the proletariat and the poorest sections of the peasants"[46] with the only possible form of the revolutionary government being the Soviets of Workers' Deputies. While the Bolsheviks were in a minority they would restrict their activities to criticism, exposing the errors of the Mensheviks and SRs, all the time attempting to raise the consciousness of the masses to a level which understood the necessity of transferring the entire state power to the Soviets[47]. It is interesting to note that this policy called, in practice, for a Menshevik-SR Government since these were the majority parties within the Soviets. However, this was a time when the bourgeois government was impotent, the Soviets held all effective power, and were truly democratic, allowing a majority to be won by ideological struggle alone.

The fifth thesis offered the most radically new perspective: **No return to a parliamentary republic,** instead a republic of Soviets of Workers', Agricultural Labourers' and Peasants' Deputies from "top to bottom"[48]; that is a government based on the Soviets, responsible to the Soviets and controlled by the Soviets. The memoirs of Raskolnikov, a sailor Bolshevik stationed at Kronstadt, who was present when Lenin first arrived in Russia, described Lenin's initial presentation at Finland station:

"It laid down a Rubicon between the tactics of yesterday and today. Comrade Lenin ... summoned us away from half-recognition and half-support of the Government to non-recognition and irreconcilable struggle. ... It was not without cause that our Party's tactics did not follow a straight line, but after Lenin's return took a sharp turn to the left"[49].

In the so-called economic theses, Lenin proposes confiscation of the landed estates and nationalisation of all land, immediate amalgamation of all banks into a single national bank under the control of the Soviets. He stated that "It is not our *immediate* task to 'introduce' socialism, but only to bring social production and the distribution of products at once under the control of the Soviets of Workers' Deputies"[50]. His emphasis on '*immediate*' was not lost on his audience. Carr comments, "Lenin's cautious phraseology left room for a certain practical vagueness about the precise moment of the transition to socialism, but none for doubt about this transition as the main goal"[51].

The reaction of his listeners showed that the consequences of this were clear to them. Krupskaya describes the reaction of the Bolshevik delegates: "For the first few minutes our people were taken aback. It seemed to many that Lenin presented the question too bluntly, that it was still too early to speak of **socialist** revolution"[52]. It is recorded that only one person spoke in favour of Lenin's theses - Alexandra Kollantai. That evening the Petrograd Committee rejected the theses by thirteen votes to two with one abstention. Lenin's theses were published in *Pravda* on 7 April. They appeared over his name alone. Kamenev, as editor replied the next day in *Pravda* No. 27;

"As for Comrade Lenin's general scheme, it appears to us unacceptable, inasmuch as it proceeds from the assumption that the bourgeois-democratic revolution is completed, and builds on the immediate transformation of this revolution into a **socialist** revolution"[53,54].

This accurately conveyed the stagist opinions of Kamenev, Stalin and most of the other Old Bolsheviks in the spring of 1917 - in fact it probably conveyed the opinions of the majority of the Bolshevik Party at that time.

This new prospect of a socialist revolution and the dictatorship of the proletariat simply did not fit into the mindset of the Old Bolsheviks. Here, it is necessary to remember that up to the outbreak of the February Revolution, only Trotsky had proposed that the Russian proletariat might win the power in advance of the Western proletariat, and that the revolution would not confine itself within the limits of a democratic dictatorship but would be compelled to undertake initial socialist measures. In this sense it is clear that the April theses of Lenin were "Trotskyist".

Lenin's first and immediate task was to win the Bolshevik Party to his new views. Traditionally, Trotskyists have made much of the differences between Lenin and the Old Bolsheviks in the period February to October 1917, particularly Stalin's role. This is understandable in the context of the faction struggles that took place later, but to concentrate on the mistakes of the Old Bolsheviks would obfuscate the central point being made here. Lenin, even if he had maintained the stagist perspective of the *RDDPP* would have had serious differences with the reformist positions adopted by the Old Bolsheviks. What is important here, is the direction in which Lenin's arguments developed, and his political trajectory in 1917, away from a stagist position to a permanentist perspective.

Lenin's analysis began with the assessment that there was no *objective* reason why the workers did not take governmental power in **February** 1917. Despite actual power being in their hands, the proletariat did not elbow the bourgeoisie aside for no other reason than its unpreparedness, its lack of organisation and its lack of class consciousness[55]. This is most interesting since it gives the lie to those who suggest that between February and October 1917, Lenin considered Russia had made sufficient social, political and/or economic advance to proceed from the bourgeois-democratic stage to the proletarian revolution.

However, one reason for the unpreparedness, lack of organisation and lack of consciousness was, as Lenin went on to explain, the betrayal of the revolution by **all** the so-called workers' and peasants' parties. Without the complicity of the Mensheviks and *SR*s in the Soviets, the Provisional Government could not have lasted long, if at all. But Lenin reserved his most stinging criticisms for those among the Bolshevik leadership who had placed the Bolshevik Party as a prop for the Mensheviks and *SR*s:

> "The person who *now* speaks only of a 'revolutionary-democratic dictatorship of the proletariat and the peasantry' is behind the times, consequently, he has in effect *gone over* to the petty bourgeoisie against the proletarian class struggle; that person should be consigned to the archive of 'Bolshevik' pre-revolutionary antiques (it may be called the archive of 'Old Bolsheviks')"[56].

Lenin explained that one must know how to change schemas when they did not fit the facts:

> "... at this point we hear a clamour of protest from people who readily call themselves 'Old Bolsheviks'. Didn't we always maintain, they say, that the bourgeois-democratic revolution is completed only by the 'revolutionary-democratic dictatorship of the proletariat and the peasantry'? Is the agrarian revolution, which is also a bourgeois-democratic revolution, completed? Is it not a fact, on the contrary, that it has *not even* started?
>
> My answer is: The Bolshevik slogans and ideas *on the whole* have been confirmed by history; but *concretely* things have worked out *differently*; they are more original, more peculiar, more variegated than anyone could have expected.
>
> To ignore or overlook this fact would mean ... reiterating formulas senselessly *learned by rote* instead of *studying* the specific features of the new and living reality." ...
>
> One must know how to adapt schemas to facts, instead of reiterating the now meaningless words about a 'dictatorship of the proletariat and the peasantry' *in general*. ... Is this reality [of dual power] covered by Comrade Kamenev's Old-Bolshevik formula, which says that the 'bourgeois-democratic revolution is not completed'? It is not. *The*

formula is obsolete. It is no good at all. It is dead. And it is no use trying to revive it"[57].

Lenin was clear: the *RDDPP* existed in the form of the Menshevik and *SR*-led Soviets, but the democratic dictatorship was handing power to the Provisional Government, an amalgam of landowners and the big bourgeoisie; this new situation required a dictatorship of the proletariat to establish a Commune-type state, to complete the proletarian revolution. The vehemence with which Lenin attacked the key governmental slogan that the Bolshevik Party had used for over a decade should not be missed, particularly as there now exists a current within world Trotskyism which denies he ever made such a statement[58]. He considered the *RDDPP* as no good at all, as dead, **and that those who still espoused it had gone over to the class enemy**. "On the whole", things might have worked out according to Bolshevik ideas, but on the key questions of whether the socialist revolution could begin in Russia, the class nature of the revolution that would solve the agrarian question, and the necessary governmental slogan, things had worked out "differently".

Lenin, in April 1917, was clear that what was missing was the subjective factor - the level of understanding of the workers (and their allies). As long ago as 1906, all Russian *SDs* had predicted that the revolution would triumph as a workers' revolution or not at all, but only Trotsky had warned that the slogan of the *RDDPP* might assume a counter-revolutionary character in the very moment when the question of power was posed. Now he had been proved correct. The practical interpretation of Lenin's theory by the Bolshevik leaders led to serious mistakes being made at the time of the February Revolution, which were only corrected by Lenin after his return. Zinoviev admits this in his tendentious *History of the Bolshevik Party*:

"This evolution in our views ... proceeded with definite inconsistencies which were to produce amongst us very dangerous differences on the eve of October 1917. Some of us (including myself) for too long upheld the idea that in our peasant country we could not pass straight on to the socialist revolution, but merely hope that if our revolution coincided with the start of the international proletarian one it could become its overture"[59].

Anti-Trotskyists often refer to Lenin's throw-away comment made at the end of his *Concluding Remarks in the Debate Concerning the Report on the Present Situation April 14*. In reviewing alternative political positions to his own he said, "Trotskyism: 'No tsar, but a workers' government.' This is wrong. A petty bourgeoisie exists, and it cannot be dismissed"[60]. This author believes it likely that, as in November 1915 in *On the Two Lines in the*

Revolution (see previous Chapter), there was confusion in Lenin's mind between the opinions of Trotsky and Parvus but that, in any case, Lenin's comment was of purely passing interest as he would soon be defending a Bolshevik-only government. In fact, of course, both men recognised that the support of the petty bourgeois peasantry was required if the revolutionary government was to last for any time. However, one academic has suggested that Lenin's comment was made to protect himself from the charges of "Trotskyism" that some 'Old Bolsheviks' were levelling at him[61]. If this were so, it would not have been surprising as, at that time, Lenin had no idea that Trotsky would soon accept the necessity of the Bolshevik Party and be standing at his side as his major ally in making the October, socialist Revolution. Of note is that Lenin did not differentiate himself from the most radical of Trotsky's proposals, that the Russian socialist Revolution would precede the European.

5.3 Trotsky in Early 1917

Trotsky was expelled from France in the autumn of 1916, made his way to Spain, where he spent several months, and from there to America, arriving in New York in January 1917. A succinct synopsis of Trotsky's writings for the revolutionary newspaper *New World* (part edited by Nikolai Bukharin) during the period January to March, while Trotsky was in the United States, and then again after his return to Russia in early April, has been given by Thatcher[62]. Certainly, until his return to Russia, Trotsky emphasised the international aspect of the world war, and tended to have a perspective in which revolution would break out more-or-less simultaneously in several countries. Lenin, however, saw that the stresses of the war produced uneven responses in the different countries, and correctly deduced that it was much more likely that revolution would break out in one state than do so European-wide.

On his arrival at Petrograd railway station (4 May) Trotsky is reported to have raised the slogans: "Long live an immediate, honest, democratic peace! All power to the Workmen's Councils! All the land to the people!"[63]. The next day he made his first speech to the Petrograd Soviet and argued that the Provisional Government could not, and should not, last for long, because it would not meet the three basic demands of the masses of the Russian people: peace, land to the peasant, and an end to the food shortages[64]. Trotsky saw the aim of the Provisional Government as the preservation of the power of the bankers, the factory owners and the landowners, with every likelihood of a restoration of the autocracy. He believed power should be taken by the newly-emerged Soviets who would form a revolutionary workers' government. In this general perspective he was at one with Lenin and at odds with the Old Bolsheviks.

The unity of thought between Lenin and Trotsky was clear as soon as Trotsky addressed the Petrograd Soviet. Advocating the transferral of all power to the Soviets, while continuing to denounce the war, put Trotsky in Lenin's camp[65]. However, it was Trotsky's new-found recognition of the indispensability of a revolutionary, disciplined party that placed him unequivocally at Lenin's side. Trotsky now understood that without the Bolsheviks the Petrograd Soviet lacked the subjective factor necessary to lead a successful revolution[66].

5.4 The April Conferences

It would be pointless to attempt to find any quotation by Lenin in which he specifically said he had been wrong on the question of the *RDDPP*. Not only was this not the style of the man, as had been shown in the Third (Bolshevik-only) Congress when a radical change towards the peasantry was presented as "nothing"[67], but during 1917 he was too busy with the tasks in hand to spend time on such matters which had, in any case, been decided by the actual revolution. Instead, as would be expected, Lenin took care to emphasise the continuity of the Bolshevik programme.

Even though Lenin played the decisive role in overcoming resistance within the Bolshevik Party to the adoption of an orientation toward the seizure of power and the establishment of a proletarian dictatorship, he was waging a struggle against those who had been his closest allies and who claimed adherence to the political line that he, himself, had introduced into the party and made its major policy for over a decade.

Two conferences were called to determine the party's perspectives and resolve the differences in the leadership. The first was the Petrograd City *RSDLP(B)* Conference of 14-22 April, and the second was the Seventh All-Russia Conference of the *RSDLP(B)* of 24-29 April. Given that all the key players were in Petrograd, the first conference effectively decided the issues, and the All-Russia Conference was more a mopping-up operation and opportunity for re-educating party members. To all appearances, the internal party struggle was over very quickly. The battle was won by the party's rank-and-file, predominantly workers who stood well to the left of the leadership, who ensured that branch after branch adhered to Lenin's theses. Liebman describes how the influx of new members "had the effect of crushing the nucleus of 'Old Bolsheviks' who claimed to be the guardians of Leninist orthodoxy, crushing them under the weight of new members who had been radicalised by the revolutionary events and were not paralysed by the principles of that othodoxy"[68]. Stalin learned this lesson well, the faction fight in the Bolshevik Party after Lenin's death would be largely decided by just such an influx - but in conditions where careerists, pen-pushers and bureaucrats made up the new recruits.

In February the Bolshevik Party had about 2,000 members in Petrograd. At the opening of the April Conference it had 16,000. These new members were politically raw, often very young (the Bolshevik Party was referred to as 'the party of kids' by the Mensheviks), eager for immediate revolutionary action (as the July demonstration would show) and impatient with the Old Bolsheviks[69]. These new rank-and-file members, were mainly working class and had not been through the debate of 1905-1907, had never been educated in the perspective of the *RDDPP*, and instinctively accepted Lenin's new revolutionary theses: "These worker-revolutionists, only lacked the theoretical resources to defend their position. But they were ready to respond to the first clear call. It was on this stratum of workers, decisively risen to their feet during the upward years of 1912-14, that Lenin was now banking"[70].

In his *Report on the Present Situation,* at the City Conference, Lenin was clear that the existing Soviets were the implementation of the democratic dictatorship of the proletariat and the peasantry and were interlocked with the bourgeoisie[71], while 'Old Bolsheviks' were locked into the form of the *RDDPP* at the expense of its revolutionary content.

In his *Speech on the Resolution on the Current Situation* given at the subsequent All-Russian Conference, Lenin again answered the arguments of Old Bolshevism that the Russian workers could not take power because the objective conditions in Russia did not permit it, by arguing that while it was true that the objective conditions for socialism did not exist in Russia, they did exist on a world scale. The Russian Revolution was not an independent act, but part of the world revolution. If the Russian workers had the possibility of assuming power before the German, French and British workers, then they should do so. Russian workers could begin the revolution, take power, start to transform society on socialist lines, and this would give a powerful impulse to the revolution that was already maturing in Europe. This is remarkably similar to Trotsky's *ToPR*. Both men were now arguing that Russia might begin the **socialist** revolution, and with the help of the workers of Germany, France and Britain, would finish the job. True, it might be argued that a similar sequence of events had been mooted in *Two Tactics ...,* but then it had been in terms of the *RDDPP* resulting in a progressive bourgeois regime, whereas now it was in terms of a Russian dictatorship of the proletariat beginning the transition to a socialist regime:

"'This is a bourgeois revolution, it is therefore useless to speak of socialism,' say our opponents. But we say just the opposite: 'Since the bourgeoisie cannot find a way out of the present situation, the revolution is bound to go on.' We must not confine ourselves to democratic phrases; we must make the situation clear to the masses, and indicate a number of practical measures to them, ... When all such measures are carried out, Russia will be standing with one foot in socialism"[72].

Just what were these practical steps that would place Russia with one foot in socialism? Lenin listed: nationalisation of the land, state control over the banks and their amalgamation into a single bank, control over the big capitalist syndicates (sugar, coal and metal), and a progressive income tax[73]. Just as Trotsky had foreseen in 1906, the taking of relatively simple, bourgeois-democratic measures (which included 'land to the peasants') would, in a revolutionary situation, require the dictatorship of the urban workers and could not be separated from the first steps towards socialism.

In 1917 Lenin saw the actual *RDDPP* - admittedly without Bolshevik leadership - first failing to undertake any of the fundamental bourgeois-democratic revolutionary tasks and, later, playing an actively counter-revolutionary role. The key tasks of the *RDDPP*, as described in 1905, were to have been: the calling of a Constituent Assembly, the introduction of a radical land reform programme, the implementation of the *RSDLP* minimum programme, and the end of autocracy. The *RDDPP* had become a reality in 1917, it had been implemented, tested, **and found wanting**.

Lenin considered the *RDDPP* an essential part of his strategy between 1905-1917, but we have the luxury of hindsight. The majority leadership of the Bolshevik Party, instead of using Lenin's Marxist method, took Lenin's schema to justify their plan of action. No matter how vehement Lenin was, in 1905, in defence of his position, it can now be seen that in 1917 the *RDDPP*, as realised in the Soviets between February and July, became actively counter-revolutionary and would have to be replaced by the dictatorship of the proletariat if the essential task of the bourgeois-democratic revolution - the end of feudal relations on the land - was to be carried through. This is, of course, quite the opposite viewpoint from Kamenev and the other Old Bolsheviks, who argued that because the agrarian revolution had hardly begun, the call for a proletarian revolution was impermissible.

In an entry into his *Diary* dated 25 March, 1935, Trotsky wrote:

"Had I not been present in 1917 in Petersburg, the October Revolution would still have taken place - on the condition that Lenin was present and in command. If neither Lenin nor I had been present in Petersburg, there would have been no October Revolution: the leadership of the Bolshevik

Party would have prevented it from occurring - of this I have not the slightest doubt! If Lenin had not been in Petersburg, I doubt whether I could have managed to overcome the resistance of the Bolshevik leaders."[74].

In this passage, Trotsky is referring to the political struggle within the Bolshevik Party. Quite correctly, he takes as his starting point the crucial significance of Lenin's reorientation of the Bolshevik Party in April 1917. Without his overcoming the resistance of Old Bolshevik leaders to a strategic change in the political orientation of the Bolshevik Party, the revolution would not have been successful.

At the Seventh All-Russian Conference the draft of a new party programme was discussed and Lenin later proposed a revised version[75]. Bukharin's comments are illuminating as he made clear that, in 1917, he saw the victory of the revolution could be achieved only through the victory of the working class, the overthrow of the capitalists, and the establishment of working class rule[76]. And how was this overthrow of the capitalists expressed in the changes made to the *RSDLP* programme (of 1903)? The following are two important additions to the original.

First, Lenin sited the Russian Revolution in the context of the world socialist revolution:

"The extremely high level of development which world capitalism in general has attained, ... (has) transformed the present stage of capitalist development into an era of proletarian socialist revolution. ...

Objective conditions make it the urgent task of the day to prepare the proletariat in every way for the conquest of political power in order to carry out the economic and political measures which are the sum and substance of the socialist revolution"[77].

The second change specifically rejected a bourgeois parliamentary democratic republic, the governmental goal of the *RDDPP*:

"The party of the proletariat cannot rest content with a bourgeois parliamentary democratic republic, ...

The party fights for a more democratic workers' and peasants' republic, in which the police and the standing army will be abolished and replaced by the universally armed people, by a people's militia; all officials will be not only elective, but also subject to recall at any time upon the demand of a majority of the electors; all officials, without exception, will be paid at a rate not exceeding the average wage of a competent worker; parliamentary representative institutions will be gradually replaced by Soviets of people's representatives (from various classes and professions, or from various localities), functioning as both legislative and executive bodies"[78].

This second point is doubly important since it was a cornerstone of Lenin's rebuttal of Kautsky's criticisms that he (Lenin) opportunistically opposed the Constituent Assembly in December 1917 and January 1918, only after it became clear that the Bolsheviks did not have a majority. In *The ... Renegade Kautsky,* Lenin states that as soon as he arrived in Russia he "proclaimed the superiority of the Paris Commune-type state over the bourgeois parliamentary republic" and, more than that, directly counter-posed the Commune-type state to bourgeois democracy at the *RSDLP(B)* conferences held in April 1917, which accordingly adopted resolutions to the effect that a proletarian and peasant republic was superior to a bourgeois parliamentary republic, and that the Bolshevik Party would not be satisfied with the latter[79].

5.5 "All Power to the Soviets"

On 10 April, Lenin had unambiguously stated, "This revolution took the first step towards ending the war; but it requires a second step, namely, **the transfer of state power to the proletariat**, to make the end of the war a certainty"[80]. This was the position endorsed at both the Petrograd City Conference and the Seventh All-Russia Conference. The major theme at both conferences had been a fight against the *RDDPP*, a struggle against Old Bolshevism with its attempts to fit reality to Lenin's old schemas. The goal was now a Commune-type state, the strategy was maintenance by the Bolsheviks of complete organisational and political independence, and an action plan based on the slogan "All Power to the Soviets".

The key to Lenin's position, and from which the slogan "All Power to the Soviets" flowed, had been stated in his *Letter on Tactics*: The first task that faced the Bolshevik party in the Soviets was to split off the anti-defencist, internationalist, 'Communist' elements who stood for a transition to a commune-type state, from the *SRs*, Mensheviks and other defencists, who were opposed, and were in favour of supporting the bourgeoisie and the bourgeois government[81].

The strategic task facing the Bolshevik Party in April was not the immediate seizure of power, but overcoming the insufficient class-consciousness and organisation of the proletariat and peasantry, the winning of the masses to a revolutionary perspective. Lenin understood that these lessons must come from experience, but that in a revolutionary situation the working class learns very quickly. Even before the April Conferences, Lenin had reduced the question of taking power to a struggle for influence within the Soviets, and emphasised the need for patient, persistent, explanatory work adapted to the actual needs of the masses[82]. From this flowed the slogan All Power to the Soviets.

To avoid confusion it needs to be made clear that the governmental goal of Lenin (and Trotsky) was a Workers' and Peasants' Government with the broadest possible base. The Petrograd City Conference, in its *Resolution on the Attitude Towards the Provisional Government,* determined that "all state power" should pass to the Soviets of Workers' and Soldiers' Deputies, and to this end prolonged work was necessary to extend the power of the Soviets to all of Russia, and to raise the class consciousness of both urban and rural proletarians, which would be demonstrated by the increased representation of the Bolshevik Party in the Soviets[83]. While Lenin did not directly address this aspect in what he wrote, it was absolutely clear that his entire declared strategy rested on the Bolsheviks gaining the support of the majority of the working people, as reflected in winning the leadership of the Soviets.

The same resolution was passed at the All-Russian Conference and further elaborated in Lenin's *Report on the Current Situation*:

"We are all agreed that power must be wielded by the Soviets of Workers' and Soldiers' Deputies. ... This would be a state of the Paris Commune type. Such power is a dictatorship, i.e. it rests not on law, not on the formal will of the majority, but on direct, open force. ... This form (Soviets of Workers' and Soldiers' Deputies) represents the first steps towards socialism and is inevitable at the beginning of a socialist society. ... The Soviets must take power not for the purpose of building an ordinary bourgeois republic, nor for the purpose of making a direct transition to socialism. This cannot be. What, then, is the purpose? The Soviets must take power in order to make the first concrete steps towards this transition, steps that can and should be made.

... The first measure the Soviets must carry out is the nationalisation of the land. ... The alternative is: either the Soviets develop further, or they die an ignominious death as in the case of the Paris Commune. If it is a bourgeois republic that is needed, this can very well be left to the Cadets"[84].

For Lenin, the route to power was for the Bolsheviks to win the political lead in the Soviets, and place the poor peasants, the agricultural labourers, soldiers, and workers under their leadership. In his speeches and articles in the period April-June, while dual power existed, Lenin repeatedly demanded All Power to the Soviets. In this way the reformist leaders of the Soviets would either end feudal relations on the land or stand exposed before Russia's peasant masses; to either end the war or lose their base among, particularly, the soldiers. The slogan All Power to the Soviets was an educational slogan that was part of Lenin's strategy of patiently explaining to the masses that the Bolsheviks were the only party capable of meeting their needs. It was intended to expose the limitation of the reformist leadership, and help win the masses to Bolshevism. As Trotsky explained:

"The correlation of forces inside the Soviets at the time was such that a Soviet Government would have meant, from a party point of view, the concentration of power in the hands of the SRs and Mensheviks. We were deliberately aiming at such a result, since the constant re-elections to the Soviets provided the necessary machinery for securing a sufficiently faithful reflection of the growing radicalisation of the masses of the workers and soldiers. We foresaw that after the break of the Coalition with the bourgeoisie the radical tendencies would necessarily gain the upper hand on the Soviets. In such conditions the struggle of the proletariat for power would naturally shift to the floor of the Soviet organisations, and would proceed in a painless fashion"[85].

The slogan of all power to the Menshevik and SR-led Soviets was by no means a return to the theory of the RDDPP, since the goal was now not a bourgeois-democratic state, but the first steps towards the beginnings of a socialist transformation of society. The slogan All Power to the Soviets was used to win the mass of the population, who still had confidence in the SR and the Menshevik leaders, away from the democratic dictatorship of the proletariat and the peasantry, and towards the Bolshevik Party and the goal of a Commune-type state, precisely by exposing the refusal of the Mensheviks and SRs to break with the Provisional Government, end the war, and resolve the land question.

5.6 July Days and Consequences

The refusal of the Mensheviks and SR-led Soviets to take power and move the revolution forward allowed the forces of reaction to re-group. The result was the "July Days". While workers and soldiers were demonstrating on the streets demanding peace, the Provisional Government launched a new offensive against the Germans on 1 July. On 3 July, sailors, soldiers and workers of Petrograd, incensed at the moves to send them to the front to be slaughtered, spontaneously poured out onto the streets of the capital, their numbers increasing as the day went on. The demonstration started with a meeting "of several thousand machine gunners"[86] who then took to the streets and drew in the workers and soldiers of Petrograd whose anger had been raised to boiling point by the announcement of the offensive. The Bolshevik Central Committee decided to restrain the movement, as the lessons of 1905 told them, quite rightly, that an uprising in Petrograd at that time would be isolated from the rest of Russia. Comrades were hastily dispatched to the factories and barracks to prevent the masses from coming out onto the streets, but it was too late.

On 4 July, more than half a million thronged the streets of Petrograd with no order, aim or leadership but with the Bolsheviks straining to keep things within limits. The Soviet leaders manoeuvred and gained Kerensky time to bring in reliable troops from the front. The arrival of loyal detachments from the Izmailovsk, Semenovsk and Preobrazhensk regiments was the signal for a counter-revolutionary offensive led by the Soviet leaders. "The Bolsheviks were declared a 'counter-revolutionary party'. Later, when the loyal troops had arrived and disarmed the rebel units, the middle classes gave vent to their fury. ... On the night of July 5, the offices of *Pravda* were wrecked by government forces. The Bolshevik papers were suppressed. Rebel units were sent to the front to be massacred. Suddenly, the pendulum was swinging violently to the right."[87]. On 6 July, the government issued an order for the arrest of Lenin, who immediately went into hiding.

After the events of 4 July, Lenin considered that "power has passed into the hands of the counter-revolution"[88]. That is, the **actual** *RDDPP* had not only failed to accomplish any significant bourgeois-democratic reforms, but had ceded power to the Provisional Government and had, itself, become a counter-revolutionary force. After the July Days, from about mid-July onwards, Lenin determined that a peaceful transition of leadership to the Soviets was no longer possible. From mid-July, beginning with *On Slogans*, up to October, he published a series of articles which explicitly stated "the revolutionary proletariat must **independently** take over state power"[89]. There were several articles along these lines, the two titles which most clearly indicated his thinking being *The Bolsheviks Must Assume Power*[90], and *Can the Bolsheviks Retain State Power?*[91].

After 4 July the emphasis of Lenin's writings shifted from a more general argument that the Soviets take the power, to quite specifically arguing that the Bolshevik Party could and should take the power. Any doubt on this matter is dispelled on reading *Letter to I. T. Smilga*[92], *Advice of An Onlooker*[93] and Lenin's various letters to Bolshevik committees, etc. The following passage shows that quite soon after the July Days, Lenin determined that the proletariat should take both political (governmental) power and state power. Whereas in 1905 the Soviets were to collaborate with the revolutionary bourgeoisie to bring about a progressive bourgeois state, in 1917 such collaboration made the victory of the revolution impossible:

"Now, after the experience of July 1917, it is the revolutionary proletariat that must independently take over state power. Without that the victory of the revolution is *impossible.* The only solution is for power to be in the hands of the proletariat, and for the latter to be supported by the poor peasants or semi-proletarians. And we have already indicated the factors that can enormously accelerate this solution.

Soviets may appear in this new revolution, and indeed are bound to, but *not* the present Soviets, not organs collaborating with the bourgeoisie, but organs of revolutionary struggle against the bourgeoisie."[94].

In saying the revolutionary proletariat must independently take over state power, Lenin had arrived at the same conclusions concerning the direction of the revolution, as Trotsky had in 1906. That is, the alliance of the proletariat and the poor peasantry which would take the bourgeois-democratic revolution to its conclusion could be achieved only through the dictatorship of the proletariat. Trotsky and the Inter-District Group of which he was a leading figure, were formally accepted as members of the Bolshevik Party at the Sixth Party Congress in July-August 1917. Unfortunately, Trotsky was in prison and so missed this important occasion, robbing posterity of his appreciation of the event[95].

By August 1917 Lenin was propagating an openly permanentist line, and argued that there could be no solution to the land question in Russia under bourgeois democracy. On 29 August, 1917, he wrote *From a Publicist's Diary* which clearly and unambiguously places him as a permanentist:

"You do not have to give these demands a lot of thought to see that it is absolutely impossible to realise them *in alliance* with the capitalists, without breaking completely with them, without waging the most determined and ruthless struggle against the capitalist class, without overthrowing its rule.

The Socialist-Revolutionaries are deceiving themselves and the peasants precisely by assuming and spreading the idea that these reforms, or *similar* reforms, are possible without overthrowing capitalist rule, *without all state power being transferred to the proletariat, without the peasant poor supporting the most resolute, revolutionary measures of a proletarian state power against the capitalists. ...*

Indeed, confiscation of all private land means the confiscation of hundreds of millions in capital belonging to the banks to which the greater part of this land is mortgaged. How can any measure like this be taken without the revolutionary class overcoming the capitalists' resistance by revolutionary methods? Moreover, it is here a question of the most highly centralised capital of all, bank capital, which is connected through billions of threads with all the nerve centres of the capitalist economy of a huge country and which can be defeated only by the no less centralised might of the urban proletariat"[96].

This reference to the bourgeois-democratic demand of land to the peasant being realised only after the seizure of power by the armed proletariat, being possible only **after** the overthrow of capitalist rule, is a more radical version of Permanent Revolution than that proposed by Trotsky in 1906. If Lenin was correct in August 1917, then the *RDDPP* could never have been the process whereby the land would be distributed to the peasants. Trotsky started with the specificity of Russia, and it would take the Chinese debacle of 1925-27, before he generalised his *ToPR*. Lenin, on the other hand, would later present the history of the October Revolution to the Communist International, from which all colonial and semi-colonial countries could draw pertinent lessons. In this sense, one could argue that Permanent Revolution as an internationally applicable theory owes more to Lenin than to Trotsky.

Lenin was confident of victory because, as he had already observed, not a single important task of the revolution had been accomplished by the Provisional Government or their reformist allies leading the Soviets. All indications were that events were continuing to accelerate and that the country was fast approaching a situation when the majority of the working people would have to entrust their fate to the revolutionary proletariat. "The revolutionary proletariat will take power and begin a socialist revolution"[97]. Lenin was confident that the proletarian state power would win over the army and the peasants as an estate:

> "What would such a dictatorship mean in practice? It would mean nothing but the fact that the resistance of the Kornilov men would be broken and the democratisation of the army restored and completed. Two days after its creation ninety-nine per cent of the army would be enthusiastic supporters of this dictatorship. This dictatorship would give land to the peasants and full power to the local peasant committees. How can anyone in his right senses doubt that the peasants would support this dictatorship?'[98].

Lenin concluded that only the revolutionary proletariat led by the Bolshevik Party would be able to actually confiscate the land; the *SRs*, the traditional peasant party, had allied itself with the capitalists, and was actively betraying the peasants' interests. Only the workers could, and would, give the peasants what they wanted; only the workers while upholding their own interests could, at the same time, protect the interests of the vast majority of the peasants **against the capitalists**:

"If the land is confiscated, that *means* the domination of the banks has been undermined, if the implements are confiscated, that *means* the domination of capital has been undermined -- and in that case, *provided the proletariat rules centrally*, provided political power is taken over by the proletariat, the rest will come *by itself*, as a result of 'force of example', prompted by experience. The crux of the matter lies in political power passing into the hands of the proletariat"[99].

What Lenin understood from at least July 1917, was that without the leadership of the Bolsheviks, without the proletariat holding governmental and state power - that is the bands of armed men who gave the state its authority being loyal to Bolshevik Soviets - the bourgeois-democratic revolution could not be carried to completion. Of course, the Bolshevik, proletarian dictatorship would initially carry through the very same programme that Lenin had originally proposed for the *RDDPP*. The qualitative difference was that Lenin now argued that this bourgeois-democratic programme could only be carried through once the Bolsheviks held state power, with or without any alliances they might make. But this is the very essence of Trotsky's *ToPR*. The government that emerged from the Soviets might, for a short period, be two-class (see later), but the decisive decisions would be determined by the proletarian elements, and state power would most definitely be in the hands of the proletariat.

After General Kornilov's failed coup attempt, many rank and file *SR*s and Mensheviks switched their loyalties to the Bolsheviks, and in the first week of September, control of the Petrograd Soviet passed to the Bolsheviks. Lenin revived the slogan All Power to the Soviets, but with the clear and publicly-declared aim of the Bolshevik Party alone taking the leadership because, by that time, he considered proletarian revolutionary power and Bolshevik power, one and the same thing.[100] The slogan now meant All Power to the **Bolshevik** Soviets. The party was on the path of armed insurrection in the name of the Soviets, having gained a majority within them peacefully[101].

Actually, during the attempted coup, Lenin offered a united front to the Mensheviks and *SR* parties against Kornilov. At first sight this might be seen as an attempt to revive the slogan All Power to the Soviets and return to the Menshevik and *SR* led *RDDPP* as it existed from February to July. Lenin imposed only two conditions; (i) full freedom of propaganda for the Bolsheviks (which would have included freedom to criticise the vacillations and weakness of Kerensky, freedom to call for arming the Petrograd workers, etc.), and (ii) the Mensheviks and *SR*s would form a government responsible solely and exclusively to the Soviets. Formally, Lenin made the same offer of All Power to the Soviets that he had before July. However, while preserving the same form, now the context and content of the offer were very different. In September Lenin was convinced that the Bolsheviks would obtain a clear majority in the Soviets in the immediate future, and so the emphasis of his proposal was not on 'exposing' the Mensheviks and *SRs*, but pulling them into a government, the programme of which was to be immediate peace, immediate land to the peasants, and the establishment of the dictatorship of the proletariat that would take the first steps towards socialism[102]. This would have helped ensure the most peaceful transition possible to a Workers' and Peasants' Government. However, by Monday 4 September, Lenin concluded, that the opportunity for such a development of the revolution had passed, and the offer was never made.

5.7 The Class Character of the October 1917 Revolution and the Nature of the Resulting State

The acid test of any theory is how well it measures up to reality. It has been seen that in Lenin's 1905 theory of the provisional *RDDPP*, the Russian bourgeois-democratic revolution would take place prior to the solution of the agrarian question, would hopefully inspire a successful socialist revolution in Western Europe which would guarantee the gains of the bourgeois-democratic revolution, and would lead to the Russian socialist revolution. However, in 1917, in the run-up to the October Revolution, Lenin saw the immediate goals of the Bolshevik Party as taking state and governmental power, initiating the dictatorship of the proletariat, taking the first steps towards socialism and solving the agrarian question as a by-product of the proletarian, socialist revolution. Here the 1905 schema is turned on its head and, in accord with the *ToPR*, the Russian socialist revolution precedes the European.

The tactics and methods by which Lenin and the Bolsheviks waged their struggle immediately prior to October 1917, ensured the Bolshevik Party took power, that is, the Bolshevik Party **alone** took power. There was no call for, nor necessity of, an alliance with any other party to carry through the revolution. The bodies of armed men that comprised the power of the resulting state were the Red Guards, and those sailors and regiments within the army supporting the Bolsheviks.

In September, Lenin first demanded that the Bolshevik Party proceed immediately with the insurrection[103]. In October, Lenin insisted that the Revolution be planned, organised and led independently of the Soviets, that to wait for the endorsement of the Congress of Soviets would be both a "disgrace and a betrayal"[104]. In his theses for the Petrograd Conference of 8 October, Lenin wanted the Party to press ahead with the insurrection, that to wait for the Congress of Soviets was to fall prey to constitutional illusions[105]. A direct consequence of Lenin's insistence that the revolution should be directed by the Central Committee of the *RSDLP(B)*, and that the Bolshevik party alone took power, was that the initial government following the October Revolution was a Bolshevik-only government.

However, the Central Committee did not accept the insurrection should be carried out in the name of the party and instead, following Trotsky, linked the insurrection with the forthcoming Second Soviet Congress. This difference of opinion was not a question of principle, but rather a tactical and psychological issue which, almost certainly, reflected the two men's experiences in 1905. Trotsky was determined to gain maximum support and co-operation from the Left *SR*s, the Menshevik Internationalists and non-aligned delegates to the Soviets. Lenin feared that the opportunity for insurrection could be lost, fears that the behaviour of Kamenev and Zinoviev would prove justified. It was Trotsky, proponent of the *ToPR*, who sought to include representatives of the peasant party in the actual struggle for power. It was Lenin who was lukewarm and who, by no stretch of the imagination, indicated the Left *SR*s were essential to either the uprising or the resulting regime.

Lenin's proposals showed that, quite contrary to the spirit of the *RDDPP*, he saw no need for any co-ordination of effort with the peasantry in the armed uprising. The urban working class would take the power alone. It was Trotsky who argued that to organise the insurrection and carry it out under the slogan of defending that Soviet Congress, would have the huge advantage of giving the insurrection a legal cover in the eyes of all the non-Bolsheviks in the Soviets. "... under the slogan of a struggle for the Second Soviet Congress we won over to our side the bayonets of the revolutionary army and consolidated our gains organisationally"[106].

The initial Workers' and Peasants' Government that was formed following the October Revolution was a Bolshevik-only government. The Bolsheviks invited the Left *SR*s to join as junior partners, but the offer was initially refused in the hope of pressurising the Bolsheviks to bring all the socialist parties into a coalition government[107]. The Left *SR*s did join the government, but not until mid-December, and withdrew only three months later - they wished to continue the war, and would not agree to the peace conditions negotiated by the Bolsheviks. During this time there was a two-class government, but it should be noted that the Left *SR*s joined the government after the major bourgeois-democratic task (land to the peasants) had been accomplished and withdrew well before the bourgeois-democratic tasks were completed. [Two small groups split from the Left *SR*s and remained in government with the Bolsheviks.]

Lenin's open letter written in early November 1917 (one month before the Left *SR*s joined the government), makes clear the process by which the Left *SR*s found themselves in the government, the conditions placed on their role in government, and the specific weight Lenin placed on gaining their support:

"The majority at the Second All-Russia Congress of Soviets belonged to the Bolshevik Party. Therefore the only Soviet Government is the one formed by that Party. ... the Central Committee of the Bolshevik Party ... summoned to its session three of the most prominent members of the group of Left Socialist-Revolutionaries, ... and *invited them* to join the new government. We very much regret that the Left Socialist-Revolutionary comrades refused ... We are ready at any moment to include Left Socialist-Revolutionaries in the government, but we declare that, as the majority party at the Second All-Russia Congress of Soviets, we are entitled to form the government, *and it is our duty to the people to do so.*

Everybody knows that the Central Committee of our Party submitted a purely Bolshevik list of People's Commissars to the Second All-Russia Congress of Soviets, and that *the Congress approved this list of a purely Bolshevik government.*

The statements to the effect that the Bolshevik government is not a Soviet Government are therefore pure lies, and come, and can come, only from the enemies of the people, from the enemies of Soviet power. On the contrary, now, after the Second All-Russia Congress of Soviets, and until the Third Congress meets, or until new elections to the Soviets are held, or until a new government is formed by the Central Executive Committee, *only* a Bolshevik government can be regarded as the *Soviet* Government."[108]

The evidence is incontestable - Lenin welcomed support from the Left *SR*s but did not consider it essential in order to form a government. The Bolsheviks took power through an armed uprising and formed a government, both without support of the Left *SR* Party. Whatever the relative numerical strengths of the Bolsheviks and the Left *SR*s, Lenin was in favour of an alliance with them, but not reliance on them. In the same letter, Lenin also described the conditions set on the participation of the Left *SR*s in the government:

"We agreed, and *still agree*, to share power with the minority in the Soviets, provided that minority loyally and honestly undertake to submit to the majority and carry out the programme, *approved by the whole* Second All-Russia Congress of Soviets, for gradual, but firm and undeviating steps towards socialism"[109].

That is: any party could join the government if it agreed to enact core Bolshevik policy as accepted by the Second Soviet Congress. It should be remembered that the fundamental agricultural policy - land to the peasant - was enacted by this Bolshevik-only government some two months before the peasant party joined, making the participation of a peasant party in the Workers' and Peasants' Government desirable, but not essential. The departure of the Left *SR*s from the government had no resonance in the countryside and the news of their departure was received without any recorded dissent amongst the peasant masses.

Radkey describes the Left *SR*s as, largely, a party of the peasant soldiers who, he estimated, comprised two-thirds their support. This was an important factor in the rapid disintegration of the Left *SR*s after their withdrawal from the government in mid-March 1918. Peace now, and land to the peasant were what the soldiers wanted, and it was the Bolsheviks who gave these to them, not the Left *SR* leadership. In fact, Bolshevism better represented the interests of the soldier base of the Left *SR* Party, than did the Left *SR* leadership. "The soldiers and sailors who at first had followed the Left *SR*s now streamed into the Bolshevik fold"[110].

Here is how Trotsky described the Left *SR*s in his *History of the Russian Revolution*,

"... the Left Social Revolutionaries ... split off in the form of an independent party, to inscribe in the book of revolution one of its most fantastic pages. This was the last flare-up of self-sufficient intellectual radicalism, and a few months after October there remained nothing of it but a small heap of ashes"[111].

For Lenin to emphasise the Bolshevik nature of the Workers' and Peasants' Government, and to adopt a certain 'take it or leave it' attitude towards the only peasant party willing to participate, must - given his previous emphasis on the necessity for an alliance between workers and peasants - indicate that he considered the Bolsheviks had enormously increased their influence in the countryside. Here is what Lenin had to say about how the Bolsheviks won the peasantry away from their traditional loyalty to the *SR*s, both Left and Right:

".. the proletariat can, and must, at once, or at all events very quickly, win from the bourgeoisie and from petty-bourgeois democrats *'their' masses*, i.e., the masses which follow them - win them *by satisfying their most urgent economic needs in a revolutionary way by expropriating the landowners and the bourgeoisie. ...*

That is exactly how the Russian proletariat *won the peasantry* from the Socialist-Revolutionaries, and won them literally *a few hours after* achieving state power; a few hours after the victory over the bourgeoisie in Petrograd, the victorious proletariat issued a 'decree on land', and in that decree it entirely, at once, with revolutionary swiftness, energy and devotion, *satisfied* all the most urgent economic needs of the *majority* of the peasants, it expropriated the landowners, entirely and without compensation.

To prove to the peasants that the proletarians did not want to steam-roller them, did not want to boss them, but to help them and be their friends, the victorious Bolsheviks did not put *a single word of their own* into that "decree on land", but copied it, word for word, from the peasant mandates (the most revolutionary of them, of course) which the *Socialist-Revolutionaries* had published in the *Socialist-Revolutionary* newspaper"[112].

While Lenin may have been a little optimistic in writing that the Bolsheviks won the support of the peasantry in just a 'few hours', his analysis is clear - the Bolsheviks won the support of the peasantry, and won it quickly. The Bolsheviks alone could embody the necessary alliance between workers and peasants because only the dictatorship of the proletariat could end feudal relations in agriculture. In March 1918 Lenin reminded delegates to the Soviets that the Left *SR*s had remained in the *SR* Party until the previous October, during the period when it was acting as an agent of imperialism and keeping the war going. He went further, "the party of the Left *SR*s is losing votes, it deserves to, ... (it) is the same soap bubble amongst the peasantry as it proved to be amongst the working class"[113].

Interestingly, the party which received the majority of the peasant vote, 37 out of 43 provinces, and so could be said to be the party representing the peasants in the countryside - the *SR* Party - never offered any serious opposition to the Bolsheviks. With the decree on land the Bolsheviks emasculated the *SR*s. Later, after January 1918, the *SR* Party sealed its demise by calling for the Constituent Assembly to be the government, which the peasants saw as a threat to their occupation of the land. The *SR* Party which had already lost the support of most peasant soldiers in all but the most far-flung armies by the October Revolution [support for which was the cause of the split with the Left *SR*s], subsequently lost the support of the peasants in the villages[114].

In *The Constituent Assembly Elections and the Dictatorship of the Proletariat,* Lenin describes his thinking in the run-up to the October Revolution, and the calculations he made of the forces on which the

Bolsheviks could rely, and those that would be opposed to the armed insurrection. He explains that the Bolsheviks were victorious because they had behind them the vast majority of the proletariat (especially the most class-conscious, energetic and revolutionary sections), the support of the two metropolitan cities, and an overwhelming majority in the armed forces nearest to Moscow and Petrograd. That is, the Bolsheviks had an overwhelming superiority of forces at the decisive points at the decisive moment. He goes on to say that the armies which appeared loyal to the *SR*s, were on the Rumanian and Caucasian fronts, far from the main cities. If the Bolsheviks successfully took governmental power into their hands through armed insurrection, they would have the time and opportunity to win the peasants and the remainder of the army rank and file away from the *SR* Party. He said "the victorious proletariat issued a 'decree on land', and in that decree it entirely, at once, with revolutionary swiftness, energy and devotion, *satisfied* all the most urgent economic needs of the *majority* of the peasants, it expropriated the landowners, entirely and without compensation."[115]. But he was unambiguous, land to the peasant - the key bourgeois-democratic demand - was carried out by a Bolshevik-only government, after the assumption of power by the proletariat, after the victory of the **proletarian, socialist** revolution. His description of actual events bears an uncanny resemblance to Trotsky's predictions made in *Results and Prospects, "The proletariat in power will stand before the peasants as the class which has emancipated it."*

A complete list of the articles in which Lenin referred to the October Revolution as socialist and the state that resulted as the dictatorship of the proletariat, could be useful but there are just too many. Following are six passages selected by the author as typical and an accurate representation of Lenin's assessment.

14 November 1917:

"... the full implementation of all the measures constituting the law on land is possible only if the workers' socialist revolution which began on October 25 is successful, for only the socialist revolution can ensure the transfer of the land to the working peasantry without compensation. ...

A necessary condition for the victory of the socialist revolution, which alone can secure the lasting triumph and full implementation of the law on land, is the close alliance of the working and exploited peasantry with the working class - the proletariat - in all the advanced countries"[116].

13 December 1917:

"There can be no doubt at all that the October Revolution, carried out by the workers, peasants and soldiers, is a socialist one"[117].

10-18 January 1918:

"We are far from having completed even the transitional period from capitalism to socialism. We have never cherished the hope that we could finish it without the aid of the international proletariat. We never had any illusions on that score, and we know how difficult is the road that leads from capitalism to socialism. But it is our duty to say that our Soviet Republic is a socialist republic because we have taken this road"[118].

6-8 March 1918:

"The Revolution of October 25, 1917 in Russia brought about the dictatorship of the proletariat, which has been supported by the poor peasants or semi-proletarians ... confronts the Communist Party in Russia with the task of carrying through to the end, of completing, the expropriation of the landowners and bourgeoisie that has already begun, and the transfer of all factories, railways, banks, the fleet and other means of production and exchange to ownership by the Soviet Republic ..."[119].

April 1919:

"How is it that one of the most backward countries of Europe was the first country to establish the dictatorship of the proletariat, and to organise a Soviet republic?"[120]

7 November 1919:

"We accomplished instantly, at one revolutionary blow, all that can, in general, be accomplished instantly; on the first day of the dictatorship of the proletariat, for instance, on October 26, 1917, the private ownership of land was abolished without compensation for the big landowners - the big landowners were expropriated. Within the space of a few months practically all the big capitalists, owners of factories, joint-stock companies, banks, railways, and so forth, were also expropriated without compensation. The state organisation of large-scale production in industry and the transition from "workers' control" to "workers' management" of factories and railways - this has, by and large, already been accomplished; but in relation to agriculture it has only just begun"[121].

It is possible to go on and on. One looks in vain for Lenin to analyse or describe post-October Russia in terms qualitatively different from those above. Lenin consistently referred to the October Revolution as socialist, with a Workers' and Peasants' Government resting on the dictatorship of the proletariat. Of course, the October Revolution was a democratic revolution in terms of the first tasks it had to carry out, and in that sense, was a great democratic revolution - but the bourgeois-democratic tasks could be completed only because the state power was the dictatorship of the proletariat, supported by the mass of peasants. The strictly bourgeois-democratic tasks, e.g., votes for women, abolition of the autocracy and ending feudal relations on the land, had to be implemented, but now they intermingled with the first steps towards socialism, e.g., workers' control and nationalisation of the banks.

Lenin in his published works, repeated many times that the Bolshevik, proletarian, socialist revolution did not skip the bourgeois-democratic stage of land to the peasant. This was obviously true (private ownership of land was abolished, land became the property of the whole people and passed to those who cultivated it) and was the basis for Bolshevik support amongst the peasantry. Much more importantly, he also claimed that the Bolshevik Revolution was a necessary pre-requirement for carrying through the Russian bourgeois-democratic revolution to its end.

Lenin, with Trotsky, organised the October Revolution and brought into power the first dictatorship of the proletariat. Lenin, Trotsky, and all the Bolshevik leaders agreed that the dictatorship of the proletariat began in Russia with the October Revolution. The Russian Revolution was the beginning of the international revolution and was openly socialist in its objectives right form the start. The issue is not so much the immediate tasks that the Bolsheviks set themselves, but the goals they served. Lenin was convinced that the Bolshevik Party, having seized state and governmental power, had set in motion events that would take the revolution into the countryside, but he knew that real processes took time, and did not even suggest socialist measures in the countryside until the summer of 1918.

5.8 References

1. Lenin, V.I., *The Dual Power*, April 1917, CW 24:38. A review of the reasons why the Bolsheviks could have the support of the majority of the core proletariat but be a small minority in the soviets can be found in Longley, D.A., *Iakovlev's Question*, in *Revolution in Russia*, ed. Frankel E.R., CUP, 1992, pp365-387

2. Leibman, M., *Leninism Under Lenin*, Merlin Press, London, 1975. p114

3. Lenin, V.I., *Imperialism the Highest Stage of Capitalism*, Jan-June 1916, CW 22:85- 304

4. Lenin, V.I., *Ibid*, CW 22:231- 231

5. Harding, N., *Lenin's Political Thought, Vol 1 Theory and Practice of the Democratic Revolution*, Macmillan Press, London, 1977, p6

6. Harding, N., *Lenin's Political Thought, Vol 2 Theory and Practice in the Socialist Revolution*, Macmillan, 1981, p75

7. Carr, E.H., *The Bolshevik Revolution, 1917-1923*, Pelican, 1983. Vol 2 p34

8. Cliff, T.C., *Lenin: All Power to the Soviets,*, Pluto Press, 1975, p82

9. Sukhanov, N.N., *The Russian Revolution 1917 A Personal Record*, Oxford University Press, London, 1955, p5

10. Trotsky, L.D., *History of the Russian Revolution*. Three volumes, Sphere Books Ltd, London, 1967, Vol 1 p122

11. Trotsky, L.D., *Ibid*, Vol 1 p1

12. Harding, N., *Lenin's Political Thought, Vol 2 Theory and Practice of the Socialist Revolution*, Macmillan Press, London, 1981, p11

13. Pipes, R., *The Russian Revolution*, Harvill Press. London, 1997, p340

14. Pipes, R., *Ibid*, p326-327

15. Sukhanov, N.N., *The Russian Revolution 1917 A Personal Record*, Oxford University Press, London, 1955, p18 and p54-55

16. Pipes, R., *op cit*, p287-290

17. Woods, A., *Bolshevism the Road to Revolution*, Wellred Publications, London, 1999, p509 - 511

18. Guchkov, Minister of War quoted in Chamberlin, W.H. *The Russian Revolution,* , Grosset & Dunlap, NY, 1965, Vol 1:435

19. Sukhanov, N.N., *The Russian Revolution 1917 A Personal Record*, Oxford University Press, London, 1955, p 8-9 and 12

20. Lenin, V.I., *The Revolution in Russia and the Tasks of the Workers in all Countries*, March 1917, CW 23:350-354, for details of composition of the Provisional Government

21. Cliff, T.C., *Lenin: All Power to the Soviets,*, Pluto Press, 1975, p97

22. Sukhanov, N.N., *The Russian Revolution 1917 A Personal Record*, Oxford University Press, London, 1955, p43
23. Leibman, M., *Leninism Under Lenin*, Merlin Press, London, 1975, p117
24. Woods, A., *op cit*, p517
25. Both quoted in Liebman, M., *op cit*, p127
26. Quoted in Liebman, M., *op cit*, p123
27. Quoted in Carr, E.H., *The Bolshevik Revolution, 1917-1923*, Pelican, 1983, Vol 1, p75
28. White, J.D. *Lenin The Practice and Theory of Revolution*, Palgrave, 2001. P130-131
29. Longley, D.A., *The Divisions in the Bolshevik Party in March 1917*, Soviet Studies, 1972, 24(2) pp61-76
30. Lenin, V.I., *The Tasks of the Proletariat in the Present Revolution*, April 1917, CW 24:21-26
31. Trotsky, L.D., *History of the Russian Revolution*. Three volumes, Sphere Books Ltd, London, 1967, Vol 1 p273
32. Lenin, V.I., *Draft Theses, March 4 1917*, March 1917, CW 23:287-291
33. Lenin, V.I., *Telegram to the Bolsheviks Leaving for Russia*, March 1917, CW 23:292
34. Lenin, V.I., *Letters from Afar*, March 1917, CW 23:295-342
35. Editors Note 127, CW 23:407
36. Lenin, V.I., *Letters from Afar*, March 1917, CW 23:341
37. Carr, E.H., *The Bolshevik Revolution, 1917-1923*, Pelican, 1983. Vol 2 p34 (Carr is quoting from *Third Letter from Afar*, CW 23:323 March 1917)
38. Lenin, V.I., *Draft Theses, March 4 1917*, March 1917, CW 23:289
39. Lenin, V.I., *Letters from Afar*, March 1917, CW 23:308
40. Lenin, V.I., *Ibid,* CW 23;332
41. Lenin, V.I., *To Our Comrades in Prisoner of War Camps*, March 1917, CW 23:348
42. Lenin, V.I., *Letters from Afar*, March 1917, CW 23;330
43. Lenin, V.I., *ibid*, CW 23:341
44. Lenin, V.I., *ibid*, CW 23:340
45. Lenin, V.I., *The Tasks of the Proletariat in the Present Revolution*, April 1917, CW 24:21-26
46. Lenin, V.I., I*bid,* CW 24:22
47. Lenin, V.I., *Ibid*, CW 24:22-23
48. Lenin, V.I., *Ibid*, CW 24:23
49. Raskolnikov *Kronstadt and Petrograd in 1917,* New Park Publications, London, 1982, p76

50. Lenin, V.I., *The Tasks of the Proletariat in the Present Revolution*, April 1917, CW 24:24

51. Carr, E.H., *The Bolshevik Revolution, 1917-1923*, Pelican, 1983. Vol 1 p91

52. Krupskaya, N., *Memories of Lenin*, Panther History, 1970, p297

53. Quoted in Lenin, V.I., *Letters on Tactics, April 1917*, CW 24:50

54. Quoted in Sukhanov, N.N., *op cit*, p289

55. Lenin, V.I., *Report at a Meeting of Bolshevik delegates to the All-Russian Conference of Soviets of Workers' and Soldiers' Deputies*, April 1917, CW 36:437

56. Lenin, V.I., *Letter on Tactics*, April 1917, CW 24:45

57. Lenin, V.I., *Letter on Tactics*, April 1917, CW 24:44 and 50

58. Barnes, J. *Their Trotsky and Ours: Communist Continuity Today*, Fall 1983, New International, Vol 1, No 1, p 63

59. Zinoviev, G., *History of the Bolshevik Party*, New Park Publications, London, 1973, p177-178

60. Lenin, V.I. *Concluding Remarks in the Debate Concerning the Report on the Present Situation April 14.*, April 1917, CW 24:150

61. Frankel, J., *Lenin's Doctrinal Revolution of April 1917*, Jnl of Contemporary History, 1969, 4(2) pp117-142

62. Thatcher, I. D., *Trotsky,* Routledge, London and New York, 2003, p78-92

63. Trotsky, L.D., *Trotsky on the Platform in Petrograd* www. marxists.org/archive/trotsky/works/1918/ourrevo/index.htm

64. Trotsky, L.D., *Speech in the Soviet Against the Coalition Government* in *The Age of Permanent Revolution: A Trotsky Anthology*, Dell Publishing Co Inc, New York, 1964, p97

65. Nelson, H.W., *Leon Trotsky and the Art of Insurrection*, Frank Cass, England, 1988, p95

66. Knei-Paz, B., *The Social and Political Thought of Leon Trotsky*, Clarendon Press Oxford, 1978, p228

67. Lenin, V.I., *Report on the Resolution on the Support of the Peasant Movement*, April 1905, CW 8:400-404

68. Liebman, M., op cit, p134

69. Woods, A., op cit, p545

70. Trotsky, L.D., *History of the Russian Revolution.* Three volumes, Sphere Books Ltd, London, 1967, Vol 1 p306

71. Lenin, V.I., *Report on the Present Situation*, April 1917, CW 24:142-143

72. Lenin, V.I., *Speech in Favour of the Resolution on the Current Situation*, April 1917, CW 24:308

162

73. Lenin, V.I., *ibid* 24:307
74. Trotsky, L.D., *Diary in Exile,* Atheneum, New York, p46-47
75. Lenin, V.I., *Materials Related to the Revision of the Party Programme*, May 1917, CW 24:459-479
76. Bukharin, N. and Preobrazhensky, E., *ABC of Communism*, University of Michigan Press, 1966, p22
77. Lenin, V.I., *Draft of a Revised Programme*, May 1917, CW 24:469
78. Lenin, V.I., *Ibid*, CW 24:461
79. Lenin, V.I., *The Proletarian Revolution and the Renegade Kautsky,* Oct-Nov 1918, CW 28:265
80. Lenin, V.I., *Tasks of the Proletariat in our Revolution,* May 1917, CW 24:67
81. Lenin, V.I., *Letter on Tactics,* April 1917, CW 24:45
82. Lenin, V.I., *Ibid,* CW 24:49
83. Lenin, V.I., *Resolution on the Attitude Towards the Provisional Government*, April 1917, CW 24:155
84. Lenin, V.I., *Report on the Current Situation*, April 1917, CW 24:242
85. Trotsky, L.D., *The Russian Revolution* in *Essential Trotsky,* London, 1963, p37
86. Trotsky, L.D., *History of the Russian Revolution.* Three volumes, Sphere Books Ltd, London, 1967, Vol 2 p26
87. Woods, A., *op cit*, p563
88. Lenin, V.I., *On Slogans,* July 1917, CW 25:187
89. Lenin, V.I., *Ibid,* CW 25:188
90. Lenin, V.I., *The Bolsheviks Must Assume Power*, September 1917, CW 26:19-21
91. Lenin, V.I., *Can the Bolsheviks Retain State Power*, October 1917, CW 26:87-136
92. Lenin, V.I., *Letter to I. T. Smilga*, September 1917, CW 26:69-73
93. Lenin, V.I., *Advice of An Onlooker*, October 1917, CW 26:179-181
94. Lenin, V.I., *On Slogans,* July 1917, CW 24:191
95. Thatcher, I. D., *op cit,* p87-88
96. Lenin, V.I., *From a Publicists Diary,* August 1917, CW 25:280
97. Lenin, V.I., *The Beginning of Bonapartism*, July 1917, CW 25:226
98. Lenin, V.I., *One of the Fundamental Questions of the Revolution*, September 1917, CW 25:376
99. Lenin, V.I., *From a Publicists Diary,* August 1917, CW 25:285
100. Lenin, V.I. *Advice of an Onlooker*, October 1917, CW 26:179
101. Woods, A., *op cit*, p583
102. Lenin, V.I., *On Compromises,* September 1917, CW 25:309:314
103. Lenin, V.I., *Marxism and Insurrection,* September 1917, CW, 26:27

104. Lenin, V.I., *Letter to the Central Committee, the Moscow and Petrograd Committees and the Bolshevik Members of the Petrograd and Moscow Soviets,* October 1917, CW 26:141

105. Lenin, V.I., *Ibid,* CW 26:144

106. Trotsky, L.D., *Lessons of October* in *The Challenge of the Left Opposition* Pathfinder Press, New York, 1975, p241

107. Daniels, R.V., *Red October,* Secker and Warberg, London, 1967, p202-203

108. Lenin, V.I., *From the Central Committee of the Russian Social-Democratic Labour Party (Bolsheviks),* November 1917, CW 26:303-4

109. Lenin, V.I., *Ibid,* CW 26:307

110. Radkey, O.H., *Sickle Under the Hammer,* Columbia University Press, New York, 1963, p137

111. Trotsky, L.D., *History of the Russian Revolution.* Three volumes, Sphere Books Ltd, London, 1967, Vol. 3, p279-280

112. Lenin, V.I., *The Constituent Assembly Elections and the Dictatorship of the Proletariat,* December 1919, CW 30:264-5

113. Lenin, V.I., *Extraordinary 4th All-Russian Congress of Soviets March 14-16 1918, Reply to the debate on the Report on Ratification of the Peace Treaty,* March 1918, CW 27:193 [Lenin is referring to a passage in the *SR* paper three days after the insurrection "The Bolshevik ... adventure like a soap bubble will burst at the first contact with hard facts" quoted in A. Kopp *Town and Revolution* London 1967, 1-2]

114. Radkey, O.H., The Sickle Under the Hammer, Columbia University Press, 1963, p451

115. Lenin, V.I., *The Constituent Assembly Elections and the Dictatorship of the Proletariat,* December 1919, CW 30:265

116. Lenin, V.I., *Draft Resolution for the All Russian Congress of Peasant Deputies,* November 1917, CW 26:327-8

117. Lenin, V.I., *Speech at the Extraordinary All-Russian Congress of Railwaymen,* December, 1917, CW 26:384,

118. Lenin, V.I., *Third All-Russian Congress of Soviets of Workers', Soldiers' and Peasants' Deputies,* January 1918, CW 26:465

119. Lenin, V.I., *Extraordinary Seventh Congress of the RCP(B),* March 1918, CW 27:139

120. Lenin, V.I., *The Third International and its Place in History,* April 1919, CW 29:307-308

121. Lenin, V.I., *Economics and Politics in the Era of the Dictatorship of the Proletariat,* November 1919, CW 30:109

Chapter 6
LENIN SAID SO HIMSELF

6.1   Introduction
6.2   Contra-Proposals
6.3   Lenin's Considered Opinion
6.4   The Communist International
6.5   References

6.1 Introduction

It has been shown that from July 1917 Lenin was working consciously and deliberately towards a proletarian revolution that would, in October, transfer state power to the proletariat and initiate the first steps towards socialism. The decision that the international socialist revolution could begin in semi-feudal, backward Russia meant Lenin had independently arrived at one of the core conclusions of the *ToPR*. The previous chapter also showed that in the immediate aftermath of the revolution, up to the summer of 1918 at least, Lenin consistently described the October Revolution as a socialist, proletarian revolution with a Workers' and Peasants' Government resting on the dictatorship of the proletariat.

6.2 Contra-Proposals

But is it possible that Lenin, after due reflection, later changed his mind: that the October Revolution was not a socialist revolution and the regime that resulted from it was not the dictatorship of the proletariat? Is it possible, on the basis of Lenin's published works, to maintain that he held, or later returned to, his 1905-06 schema of the *RDDPP* as accurately describing the events in Russia 1917-1918? Or could it be, that Lenin simply failed to see that his governmental strategy from 1905 for at least a decade had been realised, and was just plain wrong in the many speeches, pamphlets and articles, where he analysed and described the October Revolution as a socialist, proletarian revolution and the Soviet state immediately following it as a dictatorship of the proletariat? The suggestion would be that Lenin, at the height of his intellectual powers, did not understand the class nature of the revolution he had campaigned for, organised and led.

Nevertheless, a number of authors have attempted to square this particular circle, and in this chapter we discuss four more recent examples. The core of the argument, is proposed by, for example, Jenness[1,2] and rests on the observations that:

(i) the Bolshevik Party adopted a policy which, at least initially, mobilised the peasantry as a whole in its support,

(ii) the participation of a peasant party (the Left *SRs*) alongside the Bolsheviks in the government, from mid-December 1917 to early March 1918, gave that government a two-class character,

(iii) the proletarian revolution did not extend to the rural districts before the summer of 1918. So, from October 1917 to that time, the Russian state rested predominantly on bourgeois and petty bourgeois property relations, and

(iv) the Workers' and Peasants' Government, while it included the Left *SRs*, largely limited itself to carrying through the bourgeois-democratic revolution and did not begin to systematically overthrow the capitalist economy until the summer of 1918, after the peasant party had quit the government.

From these observations Jenness has concluded that from October 1917 to the summer of 1918 the Soviet regime was the *RDDPP* foreseen by Lenin in *Two Tactics*. Jenness' arguments lack rigour because they do not contain a sufficient criterion to allow us to differentiate between the three schemas as proposed by Lenin pre-1917 in the *RDDPP*, Lenin post-July 1917 after he had adopted a permanentist perspective, and Trotsky in the *ToPR* in 1906.

(i) Common to the stated positions of Lenin in 1905 and 1917 was the proposition that the proletariat - by resolutely endorsing a consistently revolutionary solution of the agrarian problem - would obtain the support of the peasantry as a whole for the completion of the bourgeois-democratic tasks of the revolution. It has already been shown that Trotsky in 1906 was convinced that a the Workers' and Peasants' Government, by ratifying the peasants' seizure of the land, would gain the support of the peasantry as a whole. Of course, because they were writing about likely future events, neither Lenin nor Trotsky could even hint in 1905 or 1906 that the mechanics of gaining the support of the peasants as a whole for the proletarian revolution, would require the *RSDLP(B)* to borrow without alteration the land programme of the *SRs*, and then implement it against the wishes of that party. All three schemas were clear that governmental endorsement of the revolutionary seizure of the land by the peasants and its distribution by the peasants to the peasants, would win for that government the support of the peasantry as a whole, at least in its early stages. Peasant support for the government is not the issue, what is in question is the class nature of the government and state required to have the will to nationalise the land without compensation, and 'give' it to the peasants.

(ii) Did the inclusion of the Left *SR*s in the government, offer a way of differentiating between Lenin's position in 1905, his position post-July 1917, and Trotsky's *ToPR*? Is it possible to argue sensibly that the participation of the Left *SR*s was essential for the government to successfully carry through the bourgeois-democratic tasks of the revolution? And, if essential, did such a requirement determine the nature of the state on which the government rested? The answer to these questions is "No".

- The necessary condition for entry and participation of the Left *SR*s in the Workers' and Peasants' Government was acceptance of the core Bolshevik programme, which openly included the goal of socialism and taking the first steps towards it[3]. This alone effectively excluded the possibility of the Left *SR*s playing the determining role in the nature of that government.

- That the presence of the Left *SR*s did not make the Workers' and Peasants' Government the *RDDPP* was unequivocally demonstrated when the Left *SR*s accepted the dissolution and dispersion of the Constituent Assembly - the governmental goal of the *RDDPP*.

- The key bourgeois-democratic task, and the one of paramount importance to the peasants - nationalisation of the land - was carried out by the Bolsheviks **alone**, before the Left *SR*s joined the Government. We have already seen that Lenin claimed it was this action that won for the Bolsheviks the support of the peasants as a whole (support that had previously gone to the *SR*s), and won it quickly.

- Neither the *SR*s joining nor leaving the government marked any significant change in that government's direction or momentum. The Left *SR*s were participants for only three of the nine months for which Jenness claims the Workers' and Peasants' Government was, in fact, the *RDDPP*. The issue on which the Left *SR*s quit the government, was not the steps taken towards socialism, but the terms for peace with Germany. Such transitory participation (as junior partners who determined not one major item of policy), cannot be taken to mean that the inclusion of the Left *SR*s determined the class character of the regime.

The conditions imposed on the Left *SR*s were not accidental, they were the result of lengthy and acrimonious discussions within the Bolshevik Central Committee with Lenin, Sverdlov and Trotsky at one extreme, and the erstwhile supporters of the *RDDPP*, Kamenev, Rykov and Zinoviev at the other. The issue was the ultimatum of the Union of Railway Workers to bring the country to a halt by strike action unless the Bolsheviks agreed to a coalition government of leading members of all the socialist parties with the exception of Lenin and Trotsky[4]. Opposition within the Central Committee to

Lenin's view was founded on the belief that a Bolshevik-only government did not have the support required to carry through the necessary tasks, and that a coalition government of all the so-called socialist parties was required. Lenin's response was to move a resolution at the Central Committee on 2 November denouncing any such coalition. Here Lenin was arguing against a core concept of the *RDDPP*: "The CC affirms that the purely Bolshevik government cannot be renounced without betraying the slogan of Soviet power"[5]. Compare this to Lenin's writings of 1905, when a revolutionary dictatorship with a Social Democratic majority was not only undesirable, it was ... "impossible".

We have already visited Trotsky's position regarding peasant representation in the Workers' and Peasants' Government, and seen that the only condition he imposed was that the proletariat wielded hegemony in the government, and through it in the country[6] Although written twelve years earlier, it was identical in principle with Lenin's stated position of 1917.

While participation of the Left *SR*s in the government may have been desirable, it did not alter the essential nature of that government, and does not offer a rigorous basis on which to challenge Lenin's opinion that this period was the dictatorship of the proletariat.

(iii) Jenness' third observation is that the proletarian revolution did not extend to the rural districts before the summer of 1918, with the establishment of the Poor Peasants' Committees (*kombedy*). Thus, during the intervening nine months, the Russian state rested predominantly on bourgeois and petty bourgeois property relations. From this Jenness draws the conclusion that because, in his opinion, a state can never have a distinctly different class character from its economic base, a state resting on a petty bourgeois economic base could not be the dictatorship of the proletariat. It then followed quite naturally, that the dictatorship of the proletariat did not become the state power in Russia until the summer of 1918, at the earliest, and thus the Workers' and Peasants' Government over the preceding period must have been a **transitional** regime leading to the dictatorship of the proletariat, that is it must have been the *RDDPP*.

What Lenin would have made of such formalism, it is only possible to imagine, for such an argument fails to recognise that any real process takes time. In Russia, in 1917-18, with its antiquated communication systems and its vast distances, the revolution may have been completed quickly in the major towns, but it took months for it to extend into the countryside, and then only after the working class consolidated its hold on power in the towns. Lenin developed the argument that Trotsky had first proposed thirteen years earlier, and explained "the proletariat must first overthrow the bourgeoisie and win *for itself* state power, and then use that state power, that is, the dictatorship of the proletariat, as an instrument of its class for the purpose of winning the sympathy of the majority of the working people"[7].

Trotsky addressed the question of the dictatorship of the proletariat during the transition from capitalist economy to workers' state thus:

"During the first few months of the Soviet regime the proletariat administered a bourgeois economy. As regards agriculture the dictatorship of the proletariat supported itself upon a petty bourgeois economy ... But what is the meaning of this kind of temporary contradiction between state and economy? It means *revolution* or *counter-revolution*. The victory of one class over another is gained precisely in order to transform the economy in the interests of the victor. But such a dual state of affairs is a necessary moment of every social revolution ... it was accomplished, to use Marx's words, in the form of the *dictatorship of the proletariat supported by the peasant war*. ...

The proletariat took power together with the peasantry in October, says Lenin. By that alone, the revolution was a bourgeois revolution. Is that right? In a certain sense, yes. But this means that the *true* democratic dictatorship of the proletariat and the peasantry, that is, the one which actually destroyed the regime of autocracy and serfdom and snatched the land from the feudalists, was accomplished not *before* October but only *after* October; it was accomplished, to use Marx's words, in the form of the *dictatorship of the proletariat supported by the peasant war* - and then, a few months later, began growing into a socialist dictatorship. Is *this* really hard to understand? Can differences of opinion prevail on this point *today*?"[8].

Lenin wrote *State and Revolution* in August and September 1917. He hadn't finished when he was interrupted by the October Revolution, so we can take this pamphlet as representing his final thoughts on the nature of the transitional state as he analysed and planned what he later consistently referred to as a socialist revolution. Lenin was breaking new ground, so the pamphlet was primarily concerned with defining principles and the necessary strategic activities of the proletariat during their seizure of power. If Jenness were correct that the class nature of the regime was directly determined by its economic base, even during its initial transitional period, then he should have found something here to cite in his favour.

However, it turns out that *State and Revolution* was surprisingly unconcerned with the economic base of society during and immediately after the workers' socialist revolution. Instead Lenin was absorbed with the question of the "power of the state", the chief instruments of which were the special bodies of armed men having prisons, etc., at their disposal, and so he placed great emphasis on the role of the army, police and bureaucracy[9]. In this respect Lenin understood that the immediate and crucial issue was **governmental** power. A party that gained governmental power thereby gained the possibility of smashing the old state structure and overturning capitalism.

Lenin argued that when (i) the proletariat had taken political power, (ii) the army and police had been smashed by the armed workers, and (iii) the bureaucratic **machine** smashed, then the dictatorship of the proletariat had been realised. Whilst the smashing of the standing army and police were essential **pre-requisites,** it was wishful thinking to expect to complete the abolition of the Tsarist bureaucracy overnight. What had to be achieved was the smashing of the old bureaucratic machine and **to begin at once to construct** a new one under workers' control that would, in time, enable the abolition of all bureaucracy[10].

Specific measures Lenin recommended for the abolition of the bureaucratic **machine** included the well-known, simple and direct[11];

1. All officials, without exception, elected and subject to recall *at any time*, and
2. Salaries of all 'servants of the state' reduced to the level of ordinary workmen's wages,

These simple and 'self-evident' **democratic** measures would, under a Workers' and Peasants' Government, serve as a bridge leading from capitalism to socialism, and implementing these measures would show clearly the end of the state as a special force for the suppression of the majority, and its transition into a force composed of the majority of the people - the workers and the peasants - for the suppression of the minority. The economic condition Lenin set was that the 'expropriation of the expropriators' was **in preparation**[12], i.e., the first steps of the transformation of capitalist private ownership of the means of production into social ownership had been taken. From this last point it is clear that Lenin considered that the dictatorship of the proletariat would require time to carry through the expropriation of the expropriators and, in its early days would be limited only to planning that expropriation. But what else could the situation have been in a Russia, where the predominant, small-scale, peasant economy formed an insurmountable barrier to the introduction of socialism without the aid of socialist revolution in the West? As an aside it is worth mentioning that nowhere in *State and Revolution* did Lenin propose any interim state forms such as the *RDDPP*.

A second serious flaw in Jenness' argument that the dictatorship of the proletariat could not be the state power in Russia until the summer of 1918, due to the class nature of its economic base is that, to be self-consistent, he should defer classifying the post-October 1917 Russian state as the dictatorship of the proletariat until the end of the New Economic Policy (NEP). The NEP, which was introduced in the middle of 1921 to increase food production, emphasised private enterprise, particularly private agriculture, and did not end until about 1929[13]. Here Jenness is at odds not only with Lenin, but virtually every member of the Bolshevik Party. The very moment that Jenness chooses to switch from claiming the regime was the *RDDPP* to confirming the existence of the dictatorship of the proletariat, is just the moment when - for the first time - rank and file Bolsheviks raised the question of whether the free market in agricultural produce would undermine the dictatorship of the proletariat.

Contradictorily, the October Revolution greatly strengthened the petty bourgeois nature of agriculture in Russia. Bukharin in his *ABC of Communism*[14], describes how the outcome of the land revolution throughout Great Russia was that virtually all the large estates passed into hands of those who had previously worked them, and were now farmed as small-holdings. The state had retained for Soviet agriculture less than 5% of the lands seized, and most of this was unsuitable for cultivation. In fact, both the number and proportion of poor peasants and agricultural labourers, on which state power was notionally resting, fell substantially. Indeed, as early as 1907, Lenin had foreseen that land distribution would transform the poor peasants into middle peasants, and this was one of the core reasons why, in the *RDDPP*, he had predicted the peasantry would desert the revolution, and an interim period of decades would be necessary between the completion of the bourgeois-democratic revolution and the beginning of the socialist[15]. Simultaneously, the number of rich peasants significantly decreased and landlordism was eliminated, so class antagonisms in the countryside were substantially reduced as a result of the October revolution.

On the first anniversary of the October Revolution, Lenin discussed the processes of expanding the revolution into the countryside. Having consistently defined the October Revolution as socialist, he makes the point that there was a deliberate delay in extending this socialist revolution from the towns into the countryside. The Bolsheviks saw themselves as, initially, limiting their rural activities to the democratic as a stratagem to protect the socialist, urban revolution and lay the ground for the expansion of that revolution into a socialist rural revolution:

" ... it was only in the summer and autumn of 1918 that the urban October Revolution became a real rural October Revolution. The Petrograd workers and the Petrograd garrison soldiers fully realised when they took power that great difficulties would crop up in rural organisational work, and our progress there would have to be more gradual ... We therefore confined ourselves to what was absolutely essential in the interests of promoting the revolution ... In October we confined ourselves to sweeping away at one blow the age-old enemy of the peasants, the feudal landowner, the big landed proprietor. This was a struggle in which all the peasants joined. ...

The law we then passed was based on general democratic principles, on that which unites the rich kulak peasant with the poor peasant - hatred for the landowner. ... We left the road open for agriculture to develop along socialist lines, knowing perfectly well that at that time, October 1917, it was not yet ready for it"[16].

The use of the adjective 'transitional' to describe the Workers' and Peasants' Government does not determine its class nature. Both Lenin and Trotsky saw the Workers' and Peasants' Government in Russia resting on the dictatorship of the proletariat. What was in transition was the nature of the economic base of the state. In the periods between revolutions, when progress is more gradual and linear, it is quite correct to say that the state power cannot have a different class character from its economic base. In the last analysis the economic base and political superstructure must correspond, but in the highly turbulent and non-linear situations that constitute a revolution, it is perfectly possible, for a short period in historical terms (months or even years), for the class that has seized power and destroyed the old state machine, to hold state power while it re-orders the economic base to its own requirements.

(iv) Neither Lenin pre or post-July 1917, nor Trotsky in 1906, suggested that every economic element of capitalism would be overthrown immediately, although both insisted that the initial tasks necessary for the introduction of socialism would begin at once. However, Lenin was keen for it to be widely understood that the Soviet regime moved ahead as fast as it could and accomplished "at one revolutionary blow, all that can, in general, be accomplished instantly"[17]. Lenin was fond of pointing out that not only was private ownership of land immediately abolished without compensation, but that within the space of a few months practically all the big capitalists, owners of factories, joint-stock companies, banks, railways, and so forth, were also expropriated without compensation. The pace of events may have been largely determined by the **practical** problems facing the Soviet regime due to the civil war, but Lenin never suggested there was a qualitative change in the class nature of the dictatorship, from democratic to a proletarian, some time after October 1917. Is Jenness suggesting he just didn't notice it?

(v) Jenness has challenged the statement that Lenin adopted a permanentist approach. However, his arguments ignore one of the most fundamental facts of all: that the Bolsheviks, under Lenin's leadership, began the world socialist revolution in backward, semi-feudal Russia.

6.3 Lenin's Considered Opinion

How then did Lenin describe the process of the October Revolution in subsequent years? The following will show his analysis was consistent, and demonstrate that Lenin never deviated from considering the October Revolution a proletarian, socialist revolution and the immediately consequent regime, the dictatorship of the proletariat. In March 1918, as part of the discussion on the Bolshevik Party's programme, Lenin had this to say:

"The Revolution of October 25, 1917 in Russia brought about the dictatorship of the proletariat ... the sole type of state corresponding, on the basis of the experience of the Paris Commune of 1871 and equally of the experience of the Russian revolutions of 1905 and 1917-18, to the transitional period between capitalism and socialism"[18].

It must be made clear, however, that during this period Lenin saw the Russian Revolution as an integral part of the international revolutionary upsurge and without this perspective - which flowed naturally from his economic analysis laid out in *Imperialism*[19] - his socialist perspective for Russia cannot be fully appreciated. In December 1917 he wrote: "We have now reached the stage of world economy that is the immediate stepping stone to socialism. The socialist revolution that has begun in Russia is, therefore, only the beginning of the world socialist revolution"[20]. The schema of 1905, where the more advanced workers of Western Europe would show "how to do it" is turned on its head, and a permanentist perspective accepted as a guide to action.

Lenin, as has been shown, was always keen to stress the continuity in his ideas and analyses. After October, he refers many times to the correctness of elements contained in *Two Tactics* including; the necessity of destroying the absolutist state, the leadership role of the proletariat in the revolution, the need for a worker-peasant alliance, the expected support of the peasantry as a whole for the end to feudalism, the subsequent differentiation of the peasantry, and opposition of the well-to-do peasants. It has been shown that these elements were common with both his position post-July 1917, and the *ToPR* as developed in 1906. However, should one wish, it is quite possible to select passages in Lenin's writings that stress this continuity, and avoid any reference to the issues which qualitatively separated the 1905 theory of the

RDDPP from the post-July 1917 Lenin. Such passages, taken out of context, are open to misinterpretation and might be seen to contradict the argument that he adopted a permanentist position. When reading such extracts it is necessary to determine whether the item was written before or after Lenin went through the experience of 1917 and re-assessed his 1905 schema, to check the source and read the extract in context, and always to bear in mind the multitude of speeches, articles and pamphlets in which Lenin, repeatedly stressed the socialist nature of the October Revolution and the proletarian nature of the resulting state power.

The method used by Jenness and others to support their argument that the Russian state between October 1917 and the summer of 1918 was the *RDDPP*, is to present selected extracts from Lenin's writings in an attempt to demonstrate that more or less everything else Lenin wrote about the October Revolution was wrong. The authority of Lenin is used in an attempt to show he was wrong in his analysis of the most important event in his life.

Attempts are made to mislead the reader by taking certain of Lenin's articles and speeches where he discussed the dynamics of the revolution in the Russian countryside (which had two distinct stages in the period being discussed - the bourgeois-democratic land to the peasant and, subsequently, the introduction of the *kombedy* and War Communism), and presenting the selected quotations as though they referred to the urban, proletarian revolution, giving the impression that the latter was also a two-stage affair. Typically, all that Lenin wrote which demonstrated that initial stage of land to the peasant could not have been realised without the October, socialist Revolution, is ignored.

One of Lenin's most important pamphlets on the theory and history of the Russian dictatorship of the proletariat was his November 1918 reply to Kautsky who had accused the Bolsheviks of opportunistically changing their policy towards the Constituent Assembly and, as part of his reply, Lenin naturally emphasised the continuity of Bolshevik ideas. It is possible to find a number of passages in this pamphlet which, in isolation, could give the impression that Lenin considered the bourgeois and socialist revolutions as quite separate and that it was necessary to complete the former before undertaking the latter: "It was the Bolsheviks who strictly differentiated between the bourgeois-democratic revolution and the socialist revolution: by carrying the former to its end, they opened the door for the transition to the latter. This was the only policy that was revolutionary and Marxian".

The passage above was, indeed, used by Jenness[21] to give the false impression that the solution of the agrarian question took place before, not after the proletarian, socialist revolution. Here is the original passage, in context, with the extract given by Jenness highlighted:

"It was the Bolsheviks who strictly differentiated between the bourgeois-democratic revolution and the socialist revolution: by carrying the former to its end, they opened the door for the transition to the latter. This was the only policy that was revolutionary and Marxian.

... On October 26, 1917, i.e., on the very first day of the proletarian, socialist revolution, private ownership of land was abolished in Russia.

This laid the foundation, the most perfect from the point of view of the development of capitalism ... and at the same time created an agrarian system which is the *most flexible* from the point of view of the transition to Socialism. From the bourgeois-democratic point of view, the revolutionary peasantry in Russia *could go no further* ... than the nationalisation of the land and equal land tenure. It was the Bolsheviks, and only the Bolsheviks, who, thanks only to the victory of the *proletarian* revolution, helped the peasantry to carry the bourgeois-democratic revolution really to its conclusion. And only in this way did they do the utmost to facilitate and accelerate the transition to the socialist revolution"[22].

There can be no doubt, after reading the section from which the quotation was torn, that Lenin was the discussing the revolution in the countryside and making the case that the **proletarian, socialist** revolution was necessary **before** nationalisation of the land and equal land tenure was, or could have been, enacted in Russia. That is, the socialist, October Revolution was necessary in the urban centres **before** the bourgeois-democratic revolution could be carried through in the countryside, and that the latter was undertaken to best facilitate the **future** (unrealised in 1918) socialist revolution on the land.

A second example of an attempt, using selected quotations from *The .... Renegade Kautsky*, to present the government that emerged in October 1917 as the *RDDPP*, is by Mavrakis. The argument is little different from that of Jenness, it simply uses another quotation. The argument is that the government of Bolsheviks and Left *SR*s carried through democratic tasks and thereby opened the door to the workers to form an alliance with the rural poor in the struggle against the bourgeoisie. That is, the government was a **transitional** government and, because it was followed by the dictatorship of the proletariat, must have been the *RDDPP*. Mavrakis, with no sense of irony, gives this scenario the name "uninterrupted revolution by stages"[23]!

Here the quoted extract is again given (in bold) with its two immediately preceding paragraphs. It can be seen that, again, Lenin is referring to the revolution in the countryside, and relates his argument to what he said in

1905 and how this changed in April 1917. It is obvious, when in context, that the quotation is claiming that elements in *Two Tactics* which were common to the *ToPR*, i.e. the necessary support of the peasantry for the proletarian revolution, plus the **changes** Lenin made in April 1917 have been confirmed by the course of the revolution:

"The question which Kautsky has so tangled up was fully explained by the Bolsheviks as far back as 1905. Yes, our revolution is a bourgeois revolution *so long* as we march *with* the peasantry *as a whole*. This has been as clear as clear can be to us, we have said it hundreds and thousands of times since 1905, and we have never attempted to skip this necessary stage of the historical process or abolish it by decrees. ...

But beginning with *April* 1917, long before the October Revolution, that is, long before we assumed power, we publicly declared and explained to the people: the revolution cannot now stop at this stage, for the country has marched forward, capitalism has advanced, ruin has reached unprecedented dimensions, which (whether one likes it or not) will *demand* steps forward, *to Socialism*. For there is *no* other way of advancing, of saving the country which is exhausted by war, and of *alleviating* the sufferings of the toilers and exploited.

Things have turned out just as we said they would. The course taken by the revolution has confirmed the correctness of our reasoning. *First*, with the "whole" of the peasantry against the monarchy, against the landlords, against the medieval regime (and to that extent, the revolution remains bourgeois, bourgeois-democratic). *Then*, with the poor peasants, with the semi-proletarians, with all the exploited, *against capitalism*, including the rural rich, the kulaks, the profiteers, and to that extent the revolution becomes a *socialist* one. To attempt to raise an artificial Chinese Wall between the first and second, to separate them by anything else *than* the degree of preparedness of the proletariat and the degree of its unity with the poor peasants, means monstrously to distort Marxism, to vulgarise it, to substitute liberalism in its place. It means smuggling in a reactionary defence of the bourgeoisie against the socialist proletariat by means of quasi-scientific references to the progressive character of the bourgeoisie as compared with medievalism"[24].

In so far as Lenin was describing the two stages of the revolution in the countryside there is nothing here to challenge the view that Lenin adopted a permanentist approach in 1917. Rather the reverse, Lenin is saying that there was a qualitative change in his analysis of the Russian Revolution in 1917, it could no longer stop at the stage of the bourgeois revolution. The Bolshevik, proletarian, socialist revolution did not skip the bourgeois-democratic stage of (primarily) land to the peasant and was, in fact, a necessary pre-requirement in Russia for carrying through the bourgeois-democratic revolution to its end.

Carr's interpretation of the above passage, was the precise opposite of Mavrakis, that Lenin was "reviving after a long interval, Marx's idea (though not the phrase itself) of 'permanent' or 'uninterrupted' revolution."[25] This links back directly to *Two Tactics*, but as its antithesis, since in *Two Tactics* Lenin had taken great pains to explain that the degree of consciousness of the working class then existing, and the constraints needed to maintain unity with the peasantry, made it impossible to proceed to the socialist stage of the revolution without an interim period of at least several decades.

In the period from 1905, while he was still working towards the *RDDPP*, Lenin maintained that the alliance between the proletariat and the peasants would be with the peasantry as a whole, within a bourgeois-democratic state. But in 1917 his position changed, the land question could not be solved without all state power being transferred to the proletariat[26], without the peasant poor being organised separately from the better-off peasants to protect their own interests, and to support the most resolute, revolutionary measures of a proletarian state power against the capitalists[27]. Lenin's move to a permanentist perspective is epitomised by his change of perspective for the revolution, from a democratic dictatorship of the workers and peasants as a whole, to a dictatorship of the proletariat and poor peasants[28].

Jenness and Mavrakis were highly selective in the quotations they took from *The ... Renegade Kautsky*, and ignore all those passages where Lenin left no doubt that the central bourgeois-democratic task of land to the peasant was carried out as the result of the proletarian, socialist revolution:

"... the vast majority of the peasants in Russia, members of village communities as well as individual peasant proprietors, were in favour of the nationalisation of all the land. The Revolution of 1917 confirmed this, and after the assumption of power by the proletariat this was done. The Bolsheviks remained loyal to Marxism and never tried ... to "skip" the bourgeois-democratic revolution. ... **On October 26, 1917, i.e., on the very first day of the proletarian, socialist revolution,** private ownership of land was abolished in Russia."[29].

We now turn our attention to the second article, from which Jenness quotes in his attempt to show the period from October 1917 to the summer of 1918 was the *RDDPP*, Lenin's *Report of the Central Committee* at the Eighth Congress of the RCP(B), on 18 March 1919:

"our revolution was largely a bourgeois revolution until the Poor Peasants' Committees were set up, i.e., until the summer and even the autumn of 1918. We are not afraid to admit that. We accomplished the October Revolution so easily because the peasants as a whole supported us and fought the landowners for they saw that as far as they were concerned we would go the limit, ... But from the moment the Poor Peasants' Committees began to be organised, our revolution became a *proletarian* revolution"[30].

But Jenness' interpretation is soon seen to be unacceptable:

- It is clear that Lenin is describing the extension of the urban revolution into the countryside, and that "our revolution" with which Jenness' quotation begins, refers to the revolution in the countryside.

- Jenness omits a section of the first sentence from the quotation: "In a country where the proletariat could only assume power with the aid of the peasantry, where **the proletariat had to serve as the agent of a petty bourgeois revolution**, our revolution was largely a bourgeois revolution ... ". Lenin is describing the revolutionary processes in the countryside, but the words excised by Jenness (innocently I've no doubt) confirm that it would not have occurred at all without the urban, socialist revolution.

- At the commencement of his report Lenin situated the party's work in the countryside in its revolutionary context. The first and principal task of the revolution had been to "transfer power to the working class, to secure its dictatorship, to overthrow the bourgeoisie"[31]. Now the regime wanted to win the support of the middle peasants. Lenin's Report made no pretence of presenting a systematic summary of the experiences of the previous year but instead presented that history "only in the light of what is required for our policy tomorrow and the day after"[32].

- At the same Congress, Lenin confirmed that the struggle for power had passed through two main phases, the first of which was the seizure of power in the cities and the establishment of the Soviet form of government. In the countryside the parallel phase had the support of the peasants as a whole since the measures taken had a bourgeois character[33].

- With the food crisis threatening to engulf the regime, a major theme of the Eighth Congress was how to win the confidence and support of, or at least neutralise, the middle peasants. It should be noted that while authors such as Jenness stress the importance of the founding of the *kombedy*, they make no claims of significant economic or social changes in the countryside as a result of their existence. This is most strange if these committees spearheaded the **socialist** revolution into the countryside, and were a key factor in the transition from a revolutionary democratic dictatorship to the dictatorship of the proletariat. In fact, these committees failed in the major task set for them - finding food for the starving towns - and were "consolidated" after about six months (the promised Soviets of rural workers and poor peasants failed to appear), and their functions returned to the local Soviets most of which were dominated by middle peasants[34,35,36]. It was precisely because of the failure of such initiatives as the Poor Peasants' Committees that the NEP was launched. War Communism, of which these committees were an initial step, was a stop-gap measure, necessary to sustain the regime during the civil war but - despite the hopes of many Bolsheviks - without a socialist revolution in the West proved a dead end[37]. That Lenin could describe the Poor Peasants' Committees as representing the extension of the October Revolution into the countryside despite there being no consequent qualitative or substantial social changes, demonstrated he was consistent in the criteria he used for determining the October Revolution as socialist from the start. One searches in vain through Lenin's writings of 1917 for any attempt to justify the socialist nature of the revolutionary dictatorship of the proletariat in economic terms. Instead, Lenin's emphasis was on who held state power and the nature of the new state; arguing that it was sufficient that a Workers' and Peasants' government (led, of course, by a party dedicated to the socialist transformation of Russia) was taking, or preparing to take, the first steps to socialism, and was implementing measures which demonstrated that state power was serving the interests of the great majority of the people. The socialist nature of the revolution was guaranteed by the presence of the Bolshevik party of Lenin and Trotsky, and its leadership role in the soviets and the government.

On the fourth anniversary of the October Revolution, Lenin was explicit that the bourgeois-democratic revolution was a by-product of the Bolsheviks' main proletarian, revolutionary, socialist activities:

"The direct and immediate object of the revolution in Russia was a bourgeois-democratic one, namely, to destroy the survivals of medievalism and sweep them away completely, to purge Russia of this barbarism, of this shame, and to remove this immense obstacle to all culture and progress in our country.

... The last four years have proved to the hilt that our interpretation of Marxism on this point, and our estimate of the experience of former revolutions were correct. We have *consummated* the bourgeois-democratic revolution as nobody had done before. ... the social relations (system, institutions) of the country are purged of medievalism, serfdom, feudalism.

... We solved the problems of the bourgeois-democratic revolution in passing, as a 'by-product' of our main and genuinely *proletarian - revolutionary*, socialist activities. .... The Soviet system is one of the most vivid proofs, or manifestations, of how the one revolution develops into the other[38].

This last sentence is a wonderful statement, describing precisely the actuality of the *ToPR* in 1917.

A slightly more sophisticated method of attempting to ascribe to Lenin, post-July 1917, anti-permanentist views, is to take selected passages written before and after 1917 and present them as a continuous thread. Johnstone took an abridged quotation from *Two Tactics* and followed it with a passage from *The ... Renegade Kautsky*. This is a particularly good example of this method of juxtaposition, as Johnstone does not date the passages and refers to an unspecified edition of Lenin's **Selected** Works where the volume numbers give no indication of the dates on which the passages were written, so there is little to indicate that the selected quotations are separated by thirteen years and the October Revolution:

"In concrete historical circumstances, the elements of the past get mixed ... Surely we all draw a distinction between bourgeois revolution and socialist revolution, we all absolutely insist on the necessity of drawing a most strict line between them; but can it be denied that in history certain particular elements of both revolutions become interwoven ? ... Will not the future socialist revolution in Europe still have to do a very great deal that has been left undone in the field of democracy?"

"To attempt to raise an artificial Chinese Wall between the first and second, to separate them by anything else *than* the degree of preparedness of the proletariat and the degree of its unity with the poor peasants, means monstrously to distort Marxism, to vulgarise it, to substitute liberalism in its place"[39].

The first extract is from *Two Tactics,* from a passage in which Lenin was arguing against exactly the point that Johnstone wishes to make. Lenin explained that it was necessary to insist on the absolute necessity of strictly distinguishing between the democratic and socialist revolutions; but that nevertheless in the course of history there would occur certain specific situations where individual, particular elements of the two revolutions (bourgeois and socialist) would become interwoven. Lenin cites the example that the future socialist revolution in Europe will still have to complete a great deal left undone by the earlier democratic revolutions - in the UK he might have had in mind votes for women, or abolition of the House of Lords.

But he was absolutely clear that to raise socialist demands in the struggle for the democratic revolution "would be tantamount to forgetting the logical and historical difference between a democratic revolution and a socialist revolution. To forget this would be tantamount to forgetting the character of the democratic revolution as one *of the whole people*: ... Beyond the bounds of democracy there can be no question of the proletariat and the peasant bourgeoisie having a single will"[40]. Because of its nature, the socialist revolution can solve outstanding problems remaining from the bourgeois-democratic revolution, *en-passant*. The opposite is most certainly not the case. The latter extract from *The ... Renegade Kautsky*, has already been discussed.

The latest example of taking quotations from different stages in Lenin's development, combining them a-historically and using them to claim support for the idea that the regime in Russia after October 1917 was the *RDDPP*, has raised the method to new heights. It appears in an 80-page pamphlet by Lorimer[41] which attempts a critique of Trotsky's *ToPR* from 1905 to 1940. In this book, concern is limited to his analysis and treatment of the Russian Revolution.

In common with Jenness, Johnstone, and Mavrakis, Lorimer studiously ignores the multitude of references by Lenin describing the October Revolution as socialist and proletarian, and the Bolshevik-only government resulting from it being a Workers' and Peasants' Government, resting on the dictatorship of the proletariat. What is novel about Lorimer's approach is a certain determined casualness in the interpretation of what Lenin wrote in 1905-07. Such an approach may have been adopted because the passages in Lenin's writings that can be made suitable for his purposes are limited, and to increase their number, interpretation had to be widened. Lorimer starts as he means to go on. On p13-16 of his pamphlet he lays out the core of his thesis. Passages from three pamphlets by Lenin, one written in 1905, one in 1907 and one from 1918 are strung together and interpreted in a manner that allows the former to be presented as prescient of events in 1917-18.

Lorimer first quotes from Lenin's *Speech on Attitudes Towards Bourgeois Parties* given at the Fifth Congress of the RSDLP in May 1907. "In all the embryonic organs of revolutionary power (the Soviets of Workers' Deputies, the Soviets of Peasants' and Soldiers' Deputies, etc.) representatives of the proletariat were the main participants, followed by the most advanced of the insurgent peasantry"[42]. This is followed by an extract from the 1905 article *Social-Democracy's Attitude Towards the Peasant Movement* to the effect that the Bolsheviks stood "for uninterrupted revolution", and would "not stop half-way"[43]. To complete the argument there is the now familiar quotation from *The ... Renegade Kautsky* to the effect that "Things have turned out as we said they would". (What a wonderful sentence that is! "Things have turned out just as we said they would". A possible litmus test for the lack of rigour and depth in any analysis of Lenin's works could be the presence of this sentence.) From this amalgam it is concluded that Lenin argued in 1905-07 that the revolution would organise state power through the Soviets, would pass uninterruptedly to the socialist revolution, and in 1918 things had worked out just as predicted.

Unfortunately for Lorimer's argument, the 1907 speech from which his first quotation is taken has, as a major theme, Lenin maintaining unequivocally that the forthcoming revolution in its social and economic content would be a bourgeois revolution. That the aims of the revolution then taking place in Russia did not exceed the bounds of bourgeois society:

> "even the fullest possible victory of the present revolution -- in other words, the achievement of the most democratic republic possible, and the confiscation of all landed estates by the peasantry -- would not in any way affect the foundations of the bourgeois social system. Private ownership of the means of production (or private farming on the land, irrespective of its juridical owner) and commodity economy will remain"[44].

In this very pamphlet Lenin was at pains to point out that the basic question of the revolution was whether it would secure the development of capitalism through the landowners' victory over the peasants or through the peasants' victory over the landowners[45]. That is, whether the **future** bourgeois development would take place in the "Prussian" or "American" way.

The reference to Soviets is equally problematic for Lorimer's argument. In the aftermath of the First Russian Revolution, Lenin's attitude to the Soviets was quite different from that implied by Lorimer. In his article defining the Bolshevik attitude to the Soviets, *Our Tasks and the Soviet of Workers' Deputies,* Lenin does indeed expect them to be "a strong nucleus" for the *RDDPP*, but not with the content or form that Lorimer suggests[46]. Lenin argued that representation in the Soviets was far too narrow, and should be extended to include the "revolutionary bourgeois intelligentsia" including the Union of Unions, the better to achieve an alliance with the "revolutionary democrats". The programme of the alliance was bourgeois-democratic; the workers' demands would be limited to the 8-hour day and measures to curb the worst excesses of capitalist exploitation. The political goal of the revolution was, "a freely convened constituent assembly of the whole people" to which "every class of the population" would turn. In 1905 Lenin considered the Union of Unions - led by the liberal professor P Miliukov - later to become Foreign Minister in Prince Lvov's Provisional Government -

"really revolutionary", and would "really support" the proletariat[47]. But what happened in October 1917? The revolution was openly socialist, and the Russian middle classes acted accordingly. The social groups which comprised the Union of Unions formed the core of the middle class strike wave against the Bolshevik government. Did Lenin completely misunderstand dynamics of the middle classes in 1905? No. In 1905 he expected the middle classes to support the revolution because at that time the Bolsheviks limited the revolution to bourgeois-democratic tasks. Lorimer has failed to understand that in 1905 Lenin proposed quite different goals for the Soviets than he did in 1917.

In 1905-07, Lenin presented the Soviets as the key element of the state and governmental structures during the provisional *RDDPP*, but there was never any suggestion that the Soviets would seek to overthrow the bourgeois economic base, no suggestions of the Soviets immediately taking the first steps towards socialism. In fact, there was no suggestion that the Soviets would continue their existence after the convening of the Constituent Assembly. Such a scenario would have been a form of dual power which, as we know, Lenin had never conceived of before 1917, and had rejected as unacceptable in a stable state structure[48].

Lorimer then adds a passage taken from the article *Social-Democracy's Attitude Towards the Peasant Movement* (published 1 September 1905). Lenin is discussing the class struggle during and after the revolutionary dictatorship:

" ... from the democratic revolution we shall at once, and precisely in accordance with the measure of our strength, the strength of the class-conscious and organised proletariat, begin to pass to the socialist revolution. We stand for uninterrupted revolution. We shall not stop half-way. ...

... we shall bend every effort to help the entire peasantry achieve the democratic revolution, in order thereby to make it easier for us, the party of the proletariat, to pass on as quickly as possible to the new and higher task - the socialist revolution"[49].

Of course the Bolsheviks stood for "uninterrupted revolution", of course the Bolsheviks would not stop half-way, of course the Bolsheviks would strive at once, as quickly as possible for a new (socialist) revolution. Of course the Bolsheviks were unafraid to carry the democratic revolution to its furthest limits, and even try to take it beyond those limits[50]. But Lenin imposed a severe constraint on this "uninterrupted revolution". The limiting factor would be "the measure of our strength, the strength of the class-conscious and organised proletariat", and we know from his other writings at the time, particularly *Two Tactics*, that the alliance with the peasants would impose limitations on the revolution, and the success of the bourgeois revolution would remove the peasantry (as a whole) from the revolutionary alliance. There would then be a period of the development of urban capitalism, the raising of the class consciousness in the proletariat, and class differentiation in the countryside, before the Russian socialist revolution (unless the Western socialist revolution came to its aid). Class-antagonisms in the countryside would develop after the democratic revolution with the rural and urban proletariat as allies against the peasant bourgeoisie within a democratic - that is bourgeois - state.

It must be said that Lenin's use of the phrase "uninterrupted revolution" in September 1905 was a one-off, and rather out of character. It is possible, of course, that Lenin, in the early stages of developing a new theory (the *RDDPP*), did indeed briefly consider a permanentist approach but, atypically for Lenin, whose style was to reinforce his views by repetition, presenting them in a number of different ways, each with an altered emphasis, there is no repetition of these views on "uninterrupted revolution". There is neither any development of this idea, nor anything resembling any further endorsement of "uninterrupted revolution" in Lenin's writings from 1905 to 1917, quite the reverse, as has already been shown in Chapter 3. However, Lenin, himself, cleared up any possible ambiguity on this point when, at the Fifth Congress of the *RSDLP*, held in April-May 1907, after Trotsky had spoken and proposed his new theory, Lenin replied: "Quite apart from the question of 'uninterrupted revolution', we have here solidarity on fundamental points in the question of the attitude towards bourgeois parties"[51]. That is, Lenin declared himself no supporter of "uninterrupted revolution" in the sense of the revolution flowing directly from the bourgeois-democratic into the socialist, proletarian revolution.

Later in *The ... Renegade Kautsky*, Lenin justified the October 1917 socialist revolution arguing that "Struggle, and struggle alone, decides how far the second succeeds in outgrowing the first"[52]. This, of course, was simply another way of expressing his famous dictum "Concrete political aims must be set in concrete circumstances. All things are relative, all things flow and all things change. ... There is no such thing as abstract truth. Truth is always concrete"[53]. This emphasis on objective events gave him sufficient insight and flexibility of mind that he could drop a dead slogan - no matter how important it had been in its day - and formulate a new one to match the given circumstances[54], as happened in 1917. It was one of Lenin's great strengths that he could throw away schema if events proved them outmoded, and develop new strategies that would take the movement forward.

Finally, Lorimer refers to the obligatory passage from *The ... Renegade Kautsky:* "Things have turned out just as we said they would. ... ". This has been discussed above to show that it refers to the changes made in 1917 and not the 1905 schema projected onto the revolution.

Lorimer's pamphlet also contains a systematic attempt to misrepresent Lenin:

> "Lenin argued [in 1905] that the completion of the bourgeois-democratic revolution by an alliance of the workers and peasants, led by the Marxist Party, would then enable the working class, in alliance with the poor, semi-proletarian majority of the peasantry, to pass uninterruptedly to the socialist revolution"[55].

But Lenin, in 1905, as we have seen in Chapter 3, was of the opinion that it was precisely the *RSDLP* that would restrict the proletarian demands to the minimum programme, and that the possibility of a socialist revolution would be eliminated by the Marxist Party itself. Lenin had addressed this question directly in *Social Democracy and the Provisional Revolutionary Government* when he criticised Parvus for declaring that the revolutionary provisional government in Russia would be a Social Democratic government. Lenin was at pains to show that he considered such a scenario impossible[56].

Lorimer also ignores completely two key elements in Lenin's writings of 1905 *et seq:* (i) that the rightist backlash against the democratic revolution would be defeated only with the support of workers in Western Europe, and (ii) the socialist revolution in Russia would occur only as a subsidiary part of an international socialist revolution led by the Western proletariat.

Finally, Lorimer gives his own, very personal, interpretation of Lenin's 1905 schema, which has absolutely nothing to do with Lenin's actual strategy during the first Russian Revolution:

> "A revolutionary worker-peasant dictatorship, or state power, could only come into being if the workers in the cities overthrew and replaced the state institutions of the tsarist landlord-capitalist state with their own organs of state power. The workers would use the state power they had conquered to rally the peasantry as a whole to consummate the bourgeois-democratic revolution and then, once the poor peasants came into conflict with the peasant bourgeoisie, to rally the poor peasants in the struggle for the transition to socialism. The proletarian-peasant dictatorship would therefore be the first stage of the proletarian dictatorship in Russia, ... "[57].

Lorimer has attempted to backdate onto Lenin his (Lorimer's) interpretation of what happened in 1917. It is extremely telling that in doing so he is forced to project onto Lenin a schema that was far closer to Trotsky's *ToPR* than to Lenin's own *RDDPP*!

To bolster his argument that the regime immediately following the October Revolution was the *RDDPP* (and, incidentally, to attempt to prove that Trotsky under-estimated the importance of the peasantry in the bourgeois-democratic revolution), Lorimer is reduced to, somewhat foolishly, describing the Left *SR*s as an independent revolutionary peasant party capable of expressing the interests of the peasants in general and - with the support of the proletariat - capable of conquering power[58]. This is clearly nonsense. The 'soap bubble' that was the Left *SR*s was defined by:

(i) the conditions whereby it came into existence. The Left *SR* Party formally emerged from a split in the *SR*s as a result of the October Revolution. In a sense, the Left *SR* Party was an incidental and accidental creation of the socialist revolution. The Left *SR* Party initially defined itself by its support for the proletarian revolution led by the Bolsheviks and, in doing so, irrevocably condemned itself to a secondary role, and

(ii) the essential condition to which the Left *SR*s agreed as part of their joining the Bolshevik government, was that they would support all key Soviet decisions. When they could no longer agree with government policy they withdrew, with no significant change in direction or tempo of the revolution.

Until the Bolsheviks led the October Revolution the Left *SR*s were part of the *SR* Party, a party which, while it held de facto power in the Soviets, did its best to hold back the peasant masses and stop them from enacting the *SR*s' very own land programme. The Left *SR* Party came into existence just as the mass of their supporters in the army and towns participated in the seizure of power, mostly under the leadership of Bolsheviks. Simultaneously, the Land Decree issued by the Bolshevik-only government effectively removed their peasant support. The Left *SR*s played no independent revolutionary role representing either the interests of the peasants in general or of major sections of the peasantry. Nor were the Left *SR*s, with or without, the support of the proletariat, ever capable of conquering power. The lack of any response amongst the peasantry either to the Left *SR*s leaving the government or the subsequent moves to ban the party, show it had little or no real independent mass base.

The great majority of Lenin's writings which define the post-October regime as socialist, as a dictatorship of the proletariat, and which directly contradict Lorimer's core argument, are simply ignored in the pamphlet. Thus, Lorimer fails to even note, let alone address, a major division between the Lenin of 1905 and the Lenin of 1917, whether or not a workers' revolution was necessary before the agrarian problem in Russia could be solved in the interests of the peasants. Instead, emphasis is placed on Trotsky supposedly under-estimating the revolutionary role of the peasantry in the bourgeois-democratic revolution in his book *Results and Prospects*.

Lorimer writes:

"Trotsky argued in *Results and Prospects* that immediately on coming to power, the 'proletariat will find itself compelled to carry the class struggle into the villages and in this manner destroy that community of interest which is undoubtedly to be found among all peasants, although within comparatively narrow limits. From the very first moment after its taking power, the proletariat will have to find support in the antagonisms between the village poor and village rich, between the agricultural proletariat and the agricultural bourgeoisie'"[59].

On referring to the actual text, we find that Lorimer has dramatically shortened the time-scale with the introduction of "immediately". The impression given is that an impatient, ultra-left Trotsky had no interest in any alliance with the peasantry as a whole and was hell bent on prematurely introducing class differentiation into the villages. In fact, Trotsky believed that if the revolutionary workers' government - which would include influential revolutionary leaders of the peasantry - abolished feudalism, recognised and legitimised all revolutionary expropriations of land carried out by the peasants, then it would have the support of the "*entire* peasantry" in the first and most difficult period of the revolution[60]. It should be noted that in the real, October Revolution, Lenin believed the class division in the countryside had taken place so rapidly that after only nine months the "rural October Revolution" could occur, and the class struggle be extended into the countryside. Its difficult to see how it could have happened more quickly, and one wonders why this was not too "immediate" for Lorimer.

6.4 The Communist International

It would be expected that the theories that led to the success of the Russian Revolution would be seen in the subsequent policies of the Third (Communist) International (*CI*). Unfortunately, there were a number of factors which complicated the issue.

Firstly, explicit references to the *ToPR* should not be expected as Trotsky arrived at the original theory from a study of the specific conditions in Russia and, until about 1925, until the revolutionary upsurge in China, did not extend his theory to beyond Russia. During the first years of the Third International Trotsky was engaged on such crucial domestic tasks as the building of the Red Army, and internationally was concerned primarily with the situation in the French CP[61]. Where the *ToPR* appeared in the documents relating to the *CI*, it was in the form of Lenin's more fundamental formulations, such as his descriptions of the overthrow in Russia of the landlords, and how realising land to the peasants, was not possible "without overthrowing capitalist rule, without all state power being transferred to the proletariat, without the peasant poor supporting the most resolute, revolutionary measures of a proletarian state power against the capitalists"[62].

Secondly, Lenin suffered a severe stroke at the end of May 1922, which totally incapacitated him for some four months and he did not return to active work until 2 October, only a few weeks before the Fourth Congress (November - December 1922). His state of health restricted his participation to a single report on the first five years of the Russian Revolution, given on 13 November. Thus, Lenin's relevant writings are largely restricted to those for the Second Congress of the *CI*, from about the end of 1919 to mid-1920. The National and Colonial Question (including reference to Turkey, India and China) was discussed at the Fourth Congress of the *CI*, but Lenin's contribution was minimal.

Thirdly, key figures in the *CI*, especially Zinoviev (President of the *CI*), had important deeply-rooted political differences with Trotsky over domestic matters, such as the question of the role of trade unions during the dictatorship of the proletariat. Typically, Trotsky had insulted Zinoviev before several thousand party members at a debate held at the Bolshoi Theatre in late December 1920, calling him "an apologist, defender, advocate and proponent of what is purely unproductive"[63].

However, Zinoviev, as President, dominated much of the Third International and was not above using his presentations to justify his political position of 1917; "The Mensheviks ... were quarter-Bolsheviks. ... Objectively the Menshevik government was best adapted to make a hash of capitalism by making its position impossible. ... they made steps which are objectively against the bourgeois state"[64]. By the Fourth Congress the triumvirate of Kamenev, Stalin and Zinoviev had begun to prepare for their battle with Trotsky, and the ground chosen was the *ToPR*: in 1923, Zinoviev published his *History of the Bolshevik Party*[65], which sought to downplay Trotsky's role in the 1905 Petrograd Soviet and the October Revolution, and vilify the *ToPR*. Trotsky replied at the beginning of 1924 by writing *Lessons of October* as an introduction to Volume Three of his collected works, containing his writings of 1917[66]. By the time of Lenin's death, the *Troika*'s faction struggle against Trotsky (and Lenin) was well developed, and the fight that subsequently took place for the continuity of Leninism was couched in terms of Permanent Revolution against socialism in one country.

Fourthly, the Soviet government was initially much more interested in Europe than in Asia as, simultaneously, both the main danger to it (war with one or more of the major capitalist countries), and its main opportunity (revolution in Germany), came from the centre of world capitalism[67].

Some seven to eight months before the Second Congress of the *CI*, Lenin addressed the Second All-Russian Congress of Communist Organisations of the Peoples of the East where, after describing the majority of the Eastern peoples as exploited peasants and victims of feudalism, he explained the process by which the October Revolution overthrew such conditions in Russia. "The Russian revolution showed how the proletarians, **after defeating capitalism** and uniting with the vast diffuse mass of working peasants, rose up victoriously against medieval oppression"[68]. That is, medieval oppression was ended in Russia **after** the proletarian revolution overthrew the bourgeoisie. Lenin returned to this theme in June 1920, just one month prior to the Second Congress, in his *Draft Theses on the Agrarian Question*[69]. Here, he articulated the form of the alliance between the proletariat and the peasantry that led to the success of the Russian Revolution. The similarity with Trotsky's position as described in 1906 "*The proletariat in power will stand before the peasants as the class which has emancipated it.*"[70] is, once again, striking:

" ... a truth which has been fully proved by Marxist theory and fully corroborated by the experience of the proletarian revolution in Russia, namely, that .... the rural population - who are incredibly downtrodden, disunited, crushed, and doomed to semi-barbarous conditions of existence in all countries, even the most advanced - are economically, socially, and culturally interested in the victory of socialism, they are capable of giving resolute support to the revolutionary proletariat only *after* the latter has won political power, only *after* it has resolutely dealt with the big landowners and capitalists, and only *after* these downtrodden people see *in practice* that they have an organised leader and champion, strong and firm enough to assist and lead them and to show them the right path"[71].

That this analysis was presented to both the *CI* and Communist Organisations of the East is significant. It analysed the process of the revolution in Russia, a backward capitalist, semi-colonial country, a country of which Lenin had said in *Democracy and Narodnism in China*: "In very many and very essential respects, Russia is undoubtedly an Asian country and, what is more, one of the most benighted, medieval and shamefully backward of Asian countries"[72]. There can be little doubt, that Lenin meant his analysis to be taken seriously as a guide to action in, e.g., China, and as a basis for the *CI*'s strategic orientation towards the peasant masses in the semi-colonial countries. The analysis is unapologetically permanentist. The proletariat **first** took state and governmental power, overthrew capitalism **and then** won the support of the peasantry as a whole by dispossessing the landlords. This confirmed exactly the analysis proposed by Lenin in August 1917, in *From a Publicist's Diary*[73], where he said the solution of the land question was not possible without all state power being transferred to the proletariat (and the poor peasants). There is no question here but that the proletariat took power relying on the support of the semi-proletarians in the countryside (though, in fact, enacting the *SR* land programme gained the support of the peasantry as a whole). In Lenin's description we see the proletariat standing before the peasantry as its liberator. There is no suggestion in this analysis of a *RDDPP* type solution to the agrarian problem, engendering a subsequent class differentiation in the countryside, and then the overthrow of the capitalist class and seizure of state power by the proletariat.

In the immediate term, Lenin's appraisal strongly suggested that the emerging communist parties in the colonial countries had to establish relations with the peasants using the same fundamental slogan as won the Russian peasants to the October Revolution: an end to feudal relations on the land, expropriation of the land and its division amongst the peasants by the peasants themselves. This was to be achieved by peasant Soviets set up in opposition to the local bourgeoisie and landlords who were tied to imperialism and would not support the necessary radical land reforms.

The Bolsheviks in Russia had used all manner of means to conduct their campaigns including participation in elections to the autocratic Duma, day-to-day-work in police-organised trade unions, etc., so it was to be expected that the *CI* recommended work in, and with, the bourgeois national revolutionary movement, provided it was a genuinely revolutionary movement against imperialism, which allowed the communists to organise and educate the workers and peasants separately[74].

However, the material and human base for socialism - a developed industry, high productivity of labour and a working class conscious of its own interests, simply did not exist in the backward and colonial countries. What perspective did the *CI* offer? In an important passage in his *Report of the Commission on the National and Colonial Question*, Lenin confirmed that he considered there was a non-capitalist road to socialism:

"The question was posed as follows: are we to consider as correct the assertion that the capitalist stage of economic development is inevitable for backward nations now on the road to emancipation and among whom a certain advance towards progress is to be seen since the war? We replied in the negative. If the victorious revolutionary proletariat conducts systematic propaganda among them, and the Soviet governments come to their aid with all the means at their disposal - in that event it will be mistaken to assume that the backward peoples must inevitably go through the capitalist stage of development. Not only should we create independent contingents of fighters and party organisations in the colonies and the backward countries, not only at once launch propaganda for the organisation of peasants' Soviets and strive to adapt them to the pre-capitalist conditions, but the Communist International should advance the proposition, with the appropriate theoretical grounding, that with the aid of the proletariat of the advanced countries, backward countries can go over to the Soviet system and, through certain stages of development, to communism, without having to pass through the capitalist stage"[75].

It is noticeable that Lenin never recommended the *RDDPP* either as a strategy or goal for the revolutionary movements in the colonial world. There was one occasion on which Lenin did refer to the *RDDPP* in passing (quoted by both Jenness and Lorimer[76]). Lenin was arguing that due to the semi-feudal nature of Russian society the agrarian revolution and the proletarian revolution had merged, and it was this that made the initial success of the October 1917 Revolution so easy. He then refers to the *RDDPP* to demonstrate that the Bolshevik's recognised the importance of allying the proletarian revolution with the goals of the peasantry, an element which *Two Tactics* has in common with the *ToPR* and Lenin's own post-July 1917 goals:

"As long ago as 1856, Marx spoke, in reference to Prussia, of the possibility of a peculiar combination of proletarian revolution and peasant war. From the beginning of 1905 the Bolsheviks advocated the idea of a revolutionary-democratic dictatorship of the proletariat and the peasantry"[77].

Lenin did not elaborate his point, he simply used it to demonstrate that the Bolsheviks recognised the importance of the worker-peasant alliance in a semi-feudal country, at least as far back as 1905. There was no suggestion that the *RDDPP* itself was being recommended as a correct strategy for the *CI*. A search of Lenin's Collected Works reveals this to be the one and only reference to the *RDDPP* in his writings for the *CI*, and this is taken as confirmation that he considered the formula - as a guide to action - obsolete, no good at all, as dead, and that it was no use trying to revive it[78].

What alliances a Communist Party adopted on the way to the overthrow of capitalism, and how it worked with the national bourgeois movements, were matters that, as Lenin put it, must be based on a concrete appraisal of actual national and international conditions. The point is that Lenin was quite clear that the national bourgeois-democratic revolution in Russia was carried through to success with the overthrow of capitalism and its replacement by a Soviet system. Hybrid state forms such as the *RDDPP*, or transitional stages, are significant by their absence, an omission that is all the more significant when we consider that Lenin was including in this discussion, countries with an even more overwhelmingly peasant population than Russia.

In April 1919, Lenin made the point,

"How is it that one of the most backward countries of Europe was the first country to establish the dictatorship of the proletariat, and to organise a Soviet republic? We shall hardly be wrong if we say that it is this contradiction between the backwardness of Russia and the 'leap' she has made over bourgeois democracy to the highest form of democracy, to Soviet, or proletarian, democracy ..."[79].

Lenin, then, considered that in Russia, bourgeois democracy had been leapt over. It is obvious that he is talking about governmental and state forms and not such bourgeois-democratic tasks as the abolition of the monarchy, or the right to civil marriage and divorce, but this again confirms Lenin's view that the bourgeois-democratic revolution was carried through under the Soviet regime, the dictatorship of the proletariat.

Lenin, with Trotsky, organised the Bolshevik, October Revolution and brought into power the first dictatorship of the proletariat. Lenin, Trotsky, and all the Bolshevik leaders agreed that the dictatorship of the proletariat (also referred to as the Workers' and Peasants' Government) began in Russia with the October Revolution. A review of Lenin's post-October 1917 publications, speeches and reports, demonstrate he was consistent and never changed his opinion on the character of the October Revolution. The failure of Lenin to recommend, after 1917, the *RDDPP* as a strategy at any time, in any way, and the wealth of material where he stated unambiguously that the dictatorship of the proletariat was initiated in Russia by the October Revolution, confirm that Lenin dropped a dead slogan and embraced a permanentist perspective.

It should be noted that the arguments of Jennes, Johnstone, Mavrakis, and Lorimer, do not challenge the undeniable fact that the international socialist revolution began in backward, semi-feudal Russia. They merely argue over how it was implemented. Their differences are not with the essence of Trotsky's idea but the manner in which Lenin carried it out.

After 1917, and during Lenin's leadership, Trotsky's writings such as *1905* and *Results and Prospects* were republished, in many languages, making the *ToPR* an authoritative statement of Communist doctrine.

During and after the October 1917 Revolution, the Bolshevik leaders had more to do than analyse past errors. However, there is a footnote that appeared in Lenin's Collected Works Moscow 1921, that makes more than a nod in this direction: "Before the Revolution of 1905 he (Trotsky) advanced his own unique and now completely celebrated theory of permanent revolution, asserting that the bourgeois revolution of 1905 would pass directly to a socialist revolution which would prove the first of a series of national revolutions"[80]. As this statement appeared in his officially published Collected Works, one can assume that, at the very least, Lenin was aware of it and raised no objections.

6.5 References

1. Jenness, D., *How Lenin Saw the Russian Revolution.* International Socialist Review November 1981
2. Jenness, D., *Our Political Continuity with Bolshevism,* International Socialist Review June 1982
   [both above references available in *Bolshevism and the Russian Revolution,* published in 1985 by Education for Socialists, Pathfinder Press, 410 West St., N.Y. 10014, USA]
3. Lenin, V.I., *From the Central Committee of the Russian Social-Democratic Labour Party (Bolsheviks),* Nov 1917, CW 26:303-307
4. Cliff, T.C., *Lenin: Revolution Besieged,* Pluto Press, 1975, p22-29
5. Lenin, V.I., *Resolution of the CC,* November 1917, CW 26:277
6. Trotsky, L.D., *Results and Prospects,* New Park Publications, London, 1962, p202
7. Lenin, V.I., *The Constituent Assembly Elections and the Dictatorship of the Proletariat,* December 1919, CW 30:263
8. Trotsky, L.D., *The USSR; non-Proletarian and non-Bourgeois State?* W.I.R. Publications, London. 1946
9. Lenin, V.I., *State and Revolution,* Aug-Sept 1917, CW 25:394
10. Lenin, V.I., *State and Revolution,* Aug-Sept 1917, CW 25:430
11. Lenin, V.I., *State and Revolution,* Aug-Sept 1917, CW 25:426
12. Lenin, V.I., *State and Revolution,* Aug-Sept 1917, CW 25:426
13. Knei-Paz, B., *The Social and Political Thought of Leon Trotsky,* Clarendon Press, Oxford, 1978, p262
14. Bukharin, N. and Preobrazhensky, E., *ABC of Communism,* University of Michigan Press, 1966, p296-297
15. Lenin, V.I., *Third International and its Place in History,* April 1919, CW 29:310
16. Lenin, V.I., *Extraordinary 6ᵗʰ All Russia Congress of Soviets of Workers', Peasants', Cossacks' and Red Army Deputies: Speech on the Anniversary of the Revolution November 6,* November 1918, CW 28:141-142
17. Lenin, V.I., *Third International and its Place in History,* April 1919, CW 29:307-308
18. Lenin, V.I., *Extraordinary 7ᵗʰ Congress of the RCP(B): Rough Outline of the Draft Programme,* March 1918, CW 27:153
19. Lenin, V.I., *Imperialism the Highest Stage of Capitalism* CW 22:185-304, Jan-June 1916
20. Lenin, V.I., *For Bread and Peace,* December 1917, CW 26:386

194

21. Jenness, D., *Our Political Continuity with Bolshevism*, International Socialist Review, June 1982, p23

22. Lenin, V.I., *The Proletarian Revolution and the Renegade Kautsky,* November 1918, CW 28:311 and 313. (Quoted in *Our Political Continuity with Bolshevism*, Doug Jenness, International Socialist Review, June 1982, p23)

23. Mavrakis, K., *On Trotskyism Problems of Theory and History*, Routledge & Keegan Paul, London, 1976, p34

24. Lenin, V.I., *The Proletarian Revolution and Renegade Kautsky,* November 1918, CW 28:299-300, (Quoted in Kostas Mavrakis *On Trotskyism Problems of Theory and History,* Routledge & Keegan Paul, London, 1976, p22)

25. Carr, E.H., *The Bolshevik Revolution, 1917-1923*. In 3 volumes. Pelican, 1983, Vol 1 p312

26. Lenin, V.I., *From a Publicists Diary*, August 1917, CW 25:280

27. Lenin, V.I., *First All-Russian Congress of Peasant Deputies*, May-June 1917, CW 24:501

28. Lenin, V.I., *April Theses*, April 7 1917, CW 24:21

29. Lenin, V.I., *The Proletarian Revolution and Renegade Kautsky,* November 1918, CW 28:313

30. Lenin, V.I., *Report of the Central Committee,* March 1919, CW 29:157

31. Lenin, V.I. *Report on Work in the Countryside,* March 23 1919, CW 29:198

32. Lenin, V.I., *Report of the Central Committee,* March 1919, CW 29:151

33. Lenin, V.I., *Report on Work in the Countryside,* March 1919, CW 29:203

34. Harding, N., *Lenin's Political Thought*, in 2 Volumes, Macmillan, 1981, Vol 2 p217,

35. Carr, E.H., *The Bolshevik Revolution, 1917-1923*. In 3 volumes. Pelican, 1983, Vol 2 p162

36. Willets, H., *Lenin and Marxism*, in Schapiro, L, and Reddaway, P. (eds), *Lenin, the Man, the Theorist, the Leader, a Reappraisal*, Pall Mall Press, London, 1967, p225

37. Trotsky, L.D., *The First Five Years of the Comintern* (Vol 2) Pioneer Publishers, New York, 1945, pp227-231.

38. Lenin, V.I., *Fourth Anniversary of the October Revolution*, October 1921, CW 33:51-59

39. Johnstone, M., *Trotsky - His Ideas*, Cogito, Journal of the Young Communist League, No 5, 1968 (Juxtaposed quotations from CW 9:85 and CW 28:299-300)

40. Lenin, V.I., *The Two Tactics of Social Democracy in the Democratic Revolution,* June-July 1905, CW 9:84

41. Lorimer, D., *Trotsky's Theory of Permanent Revolution: A Leninist Critique*, Resistance Books NSW, 1998

42. Lenin, V.I., *Speech on Attitudes Towards Bourgeois Parties,* May 1907, CW 12:459

43. Lenin, V.I., *Social-Democracy's Attitude Towards the Peasant Movement,* Sept 1905, CW 9:236

44. Lenin, V. I., *Speech on Attitudes Towards Bourgeois Parties.* May 1907 CW 12:457

45. Lenin, V. I., *Ibid,* CW 12:465

46. Lenin, V.I., *Our Tasks and the Soviet of Workers' Deputies*, Nov 1905, CW 10:19-28

47. Lenin, V.I., *Our Tasks in the Soviet of Workers' Deputies*, Nov 1905, CW 10:24

48. Lenin, V.I., *The Dual Power*, April 1917, CW 24:38. See also *Report on the Present Situation*, April 1917, CW24:145

49. Lenin, V.I., *Social-Democracy's Attitude Towards the Peasant Movement,* Sept 1905, CW 9:236-237

50. Lenin, V.I., *Two Tactics of Social Democracy in the Democratic Revolution,* July 1905, CW 9:124

51. Lenin, V.I., *The Fifth Congress of the RSDLP*, April-May 1907, CW 12:470

52. Lenin, V.I., *The Proletarian Revolution and the Renegade Kautsky,* November 1918, CW 28:237-238

53. Lenin, V.I., *Two Tactics of Social Democracy in the Democratic Revolution,* July 1905, CW 9:92

54. Rees, J.C., *Lenin and Marxism*, in Schapiro, L, and Reddaway, P. (eds), *Lenin, the Man, the Theorist, the Leader, a Reappraisal*, Pall Mall Press, London, 1967, p97

55. Lorimer, D., *Trotsky's Theory of Permanent Revolution: A Leninist Critique*, Resistance Books NSW 1998, p13

56. Lenin, V.I., *Social-Democracy and the Provisional Revolutionary Government*, April 1905, CW 8:291

57. Lorimer, D., *op cit,* p41

58. Lorimer, D., *op cit,* p75

59. Lorimer, D., *op cit,* p19

60. Trotsky, L.D., *Permanent Revolution and Results and Prospects,* New Park Publications, 1962, the quotations are from p208, 201 and 203, respectively.

61. Thatcher, I. D., *Trotsky,* Routledge, London and New York, 2003, p110

196

62. Lenin, V.I., *From a Publicist's Diary*, August 1918, CW 25:278-286
63. Quoted in Thatcher, *op cit,* p109
64. Zonoviev, G., Theses on Tactics, Minutes Fourth Congress C.I. November 1922
65. Zinoviev, G., *History of the Bolshevik Party*, New Park Publications, London, 1973
66. Thatcher, I. D., *op cit,* p6
67. Trotsky, L., *The First Five Years of the Communist International*, New Park Publications, London, 1973
68. Lenin, V.I., *Address to the Second All-Russia Congress of Communist Organisations of Peoples of the East*, November 1919, CW 30:161
69. Lenin, V.I., *Draft Theses on the Agrarian Question*, June 1920, CW 31:152-164
70. Trotsky, L.D., *Results and Prospects,* New Park Publications, London, 1962, p203
71. Lenin, V.I., *Draft Theses on the Agrarian Question*, June 1920, CW 35:155-6
72. Lenin, V.I., *Democracy and Narodnism in China*, July 1912, CW 18:164
73. Lenin, V.I., *From a Publicist's Diary,* August 1917, CW 25:278-286
74. Lenin, V.I., *Report of the Commission on the National and Colonial Question,* July 1920, CW 31:240-5
75. Lenin, V.I., *Ibid*, CW 31:244
76. Lorimer, D., *op cit,* p6
77. Lenin, V.I., *Third International and its Place in History*, April 1919, CW 29:310
78. Lenin, V.I., *Letter on Tactics*, April 1917, CW 24:50
79. Lenin, V.I., *Third International and its Place in History*, April 1919, CW 29:307-308
80. Quoted in *Lenin and Trotsky: What They Really Stood For,* by Woods, A. and Grant, T., Wellred Publications, London, 1976, p78 - (Lenin, V.I. Moscow 1921, CW 14 (Part 2):481-2)

Chapter 7
CONSTITUENT ASSEMBLY OR COMMUNE-TYPE STATE?

7.1   Introduction
7.2   The Slogan of the Constituent Assembly, 1903 to February 1917
7.3   The Constituent Assembly - the Goal of the Revolution?
7.4   Lenin, the October Revolution and the Constituent Assembly,
7.5   The Workers, the Red Guard, and the Power of the State
7.6   Town and Country
7.7   References

7.1 Introduction

The demand for a democratic (bourgeois) republic governed by a Constituent Assembly was one of the main planks of Russian Social Democracy from its foundation, and considered by Lenin as one of the 'three pillars of Bolshevism' until at least 1915 (see, for example, *On Two Lines in the Revolution*[1]). But what happened in 1917-18? A Bolshevik-only Government solved the agrarian question, the key task of the bourgeois-democratic revolution, immediately on establishing the dictatorship of the (urban) proletariat and, rather than empower the popular Constituent Assembly, dispersed it at bayonet point. What does that tell us about Lenin's transition to a permanentist position?

In 1917 the development and change of Bolshevik attitudes towards the Constituent Assembly was complex and contradictory. The call for All Power to the Soviets, and the preparations by the Bolshevik Central Committee for an armed uprising to take state power in the name of the Soviets was, in reality, completely at odds with the simultaneous call for convocation of the Constituent Assembly. In their public statements, the Bolsheviks demanded elections for the Assembly be held immediately, and repeatedly argued that the best way to ensure the convocation of the Assembly was to give all power to the Soviets.   At the same time the Bolsheviks were organising for a Commune-type state based on soviets from top to bottom, in which all power would be with the proletariat (and poor peasants).

How could Lenin, usually so clear on political matters have allowed such confusion? The answer appears sixfold: (i) the call for the Constituent Assembly had enormous popular appeal, and the Bolsheviks were keen to accept the popular will - as in the Land Decree - if it took the revolution forward, as the call for the Constituent Assembly initially appeared to do, (ii) demands for the convocation of the Assembly revealed the non-democratic nature of the Provisional Government, (iii) a significant section of the Bolshevik leadership simply failed to see the contradiction between a Commune-type state and a Constituent Assembly - even after the October Revolution, (iv) Trotsky, at least among the Bolshevik leaders, saw the Assembly as a possible fall-back if the planned uprising failed, (v) some in the Bolshevik leadership believed that after more than a decade of calling for a Constituent Assembly the masses needed the educational experience of seeing the actual Assembly in action before it could be jettisoned, and (vi) Lenin, himself, until almost the last moment, appeared to have had an open mind on whether or not to convene the Assembly - as late as 27 September he saw a bloc with the Left SRs as a possible means of achieving a majority in the Assembly, giving an essential coherence between the Assembly and Soviet power, and stability in the country.

7.2 The Slogan of the Constituent Assembly, 1903 to February 1917

From May 1903, when the League of Russian Revolutionary Social Democracy Abroad published Lenin's pamphlet *To the Rural Poor - An Explanation for the Peasants of What the Social-Democrats Want*[2], the bourgeois-democratic Constituent Assembly was the *RSDLP's* declared governmental goal in the Russian Revolution. *To the Rural Poor* stated that the key to ending the poverty and brutality of peasant life, lay in three demands, the first of which was the convocation of a national Assembly to establish an elected government in place of the Tsarist autocracy. The second was freedom of political expression, and the third was abolition of all forms of serf bondage and for the equality of the peasantry with the other social estates[3].

The development of the Bolsheviks' governmental slogan is an object lesson of how to consistently apply Marxist theory to real life. By early 1905, following the peasant revolts of the previous two years and the upsurge in the towns after Bloody Sunday, *SD* was faced with how free and fair election of deputies to the Constituent Assembly could be assured. If the purpose of the Constituent Assembly was to get rid of the autocracy, could officials responsible to the Tsar be trusted to convene the Assembly on the basis of universal, direct, and equal suffrage by secret ballot, and ensure real and complete freedom of expression during the elections? Of course not. Lenin concluded that only an interim government that originated from within the revolutionary forces determined to overthrow the autocracy, and committed to the success of the Assembly, could be trusted[4].

The demand for a Constituent Assembly may have been a key part of the Bolshevik programme but, as Lenin pointed out, even the Cadet Party, representing the liberal bourgeoisie, was publicly calling for an elected Constituent Assembly, but with a Tsar, and a two-tier governmental structure with an non-elected upper house, somewhat on the English model. The Cadets proposed that the officials of the autocratic state, with the Tsar Nicholas II still in power, would organise and monitor the elections, and convene the Assembly. Such an expectation, in Lenin's view, made the Cadets brazen charlatans or hopeless fools.

At the Third (Bolshevik-only) Congress of the *RSDLP*, April 1905, Lenin emphasised that the Russian proletariat needed a period of the fullest possible political freedom if it was to achieve its ultimate aim of the socialist revolution, and this would require the replacement of the autocracy by a democratic republic[5] to allow (amongst other things) the *RSDLP* to transform itself into a mass movement of the working class. This republic would be founded in an armed uprising of the people which would overthrow the Tsar and establish a provisional revolutionary government which, in turn, would organise the election of a Constituent Assembly.

The Congress resolved that in the event of a victorious uprising, the *RSDLP* would participate in any resulting provisional revolutionary government subject to a number of conditions: party control over its representatives, the party would defend, consolidate, and extend the gains of the revolution in the interests of the working class, the party would be irreconcilably opposed to the bourgeois parties, the party would continue to strive for the socialist revolution, etc[6]. However, it was clear that such conditions could be met, and were intended to be met, within the limits of bourgeois democracy.

To preserve the revolutionary content of the demand for a Constituent Assembly, Lenin now emphasised the associated demands which would give the Assembly its power and authority: the Tsar had to be overthrown by the armed people who would create a provisional revolutionary government whose duty it was to repel the counter-revolution and convene the Assembly. The Bolsheviks were clear that only a provisional revolutionary government based on a victorious popular insurrection could secure free elections and subsequently convene an Assembly that would genuinely express the will of **all** the people. Only in this way would a democratic republic place supreme authority in the hands of the people. Without this, Russia would have an Assembly that would be little more than a mechanism for allowing the big bourgeoisie to bargain with the Tsar[7,8].

Lenin's major work of this period *Two Tactics*[9], reinforced and extended the arguments put forward in the Third Congress concerning the responsibilities of the *RDDPP*. One point in particular was repeated: "Its formal purpose must be to serve as the instrument for convening a popular constituent assembly"[10].

To avoid confusion on the aims of the *RDDPP*, and dispel any "absurd, semi-anarchist ideas" that it might attempt to put into effect the maximum programme of the *RSDLP*, Lenin was quick to emphasise that the tasks of the provisional revolutionary dictatorship would be limited to the *RSDLP* **minimum** programme[11]. To confirm that the provisional revolutionary government and the Constituent Assembly would not necessarily have a proletarian character, Lenin pointed out that the armed workers led by the *RSDLP* would exercise pressure on the provisional revolutionary government, not to overthrow it but to ensure it extended the gains of the revolution until they fulfilled the whole of the *RSDLP* **minimum** programme[12].

Of particular interest here, in June 1905, was Lenin's rejection of the Paris Commune as a model for the forthcoming Russian Revolution, precisely because it had combined the tasks of fighting for a democratic (i.e. bourgeois) republic with those of fighting for socialism. Lowy has correctly pointed out that since Marx's *Civil War in France*, May 1871, the Paris Commune had been understood as the first example of the dictatorship of the proletariat, and thus when Lenin wrote in *Two Tactics* that the Commune was an example **not** to be emulated, he was clearly limiting the extent of the activities of the provisional revolutionary dictatorship[13]. The Paris Commune was: "a workers' government that was unable to, and could not at that time, distinguish between the elements of a democratic revolution and those of a socialist revolution, that confused the tasks of fighting for a republic with the tasks of fighting for Socialism, ... it was a government *such as ours should not be*"[14].

Trotsky took a different, more sympathetic view. The lessons to be derived from the Commune were directly relevant to the Russian working class because he believed the objective development of the class struggle in Russia confronted the proletariat with the possibility of taking state power and the first steps towards socialism[15].

In late April and early May 1906, with the experience of 1905 behind him, Lenin attended the Fourth (Unity) Congress of the *RSDLP* in Stockholm. On the Constituent Assembly and the *RDDPP* Lenin spelled it out - the urgent task confronting the party was to join with the revolutionary democrats and unite the insurrection by helping to form a provisional revolutionary government. Only in this way could a victorious insurrection completely crush the resistance of the autocracy and its supporters, ensure electoral freedom, convene a Constituent Assembly capable of really establishing the sovereignty **of the whole people**, and put into effect the minimum social and economic demands of the proletariat. The Soviets of Workers' Deputies were institutions on which the provisional revolutionary government could be based, and so they must possess their own military forces[16].

Not only were the Soviets to seek to extend their membership to the revolutionary elements of the urban petty bourgeoisie, but Lenin proposed that the *RSDLP* should enter into temporary fighting agreements with those revolutionary democratic parties which consistently fought for democracy, recognised the armed uprising as a legitimate means of struggle, and were actually trying to bring it about. The major such organisation was the *SR* Party which closely represented the interests and views of the masses of the peasantry by strongly opposing landlordism and the semi-feudal state. The objective of such temporary fighting agreements was to secure the convocation of a Constituent Assembly by revolutionary means[17], and an essential condition for such unity was a parallel struggle by the *RSDLP* to ideologically expose the pseudo-socialist character of its allies.

At the Unity Congress, Lenin repeated his view that, irrespective of whether or not the *RSDLP* was included in the provisional revolutionary government, an armed proletariat led by the *RSDLP* would bring constant **"pressure"** to bear upon the provisional government, to protect, consolidate and enlarge the gains of the revolution[18]. In principle, then, even if the *RSDLP* were excluded from the provisional revolutionary government, the armed proletariat would not seek to overthrow a bourgeois or petty bourgeois government, but limit itself to exerting "pressure" on it.

In the light of the 1905 Revolution, Lenin redrafted the agrarian programme of the *RSDLP*. He stressed the necessity of the complete victory of the peasant uprising since, without such a victory it would be impossible for the peasants to expropriate all church, monastery, crown and state lands, and the landlords' estates, and freely divide these amongst themselves. The Constituent Assembly would fulfil the peasants' dreams by legitimising the land seizures[19], repealing all laws that restricted the peasants selling or renting their land, authorising the reduction of exorbitant rents and annulling all contracts entailing an element of bondage[20].

Lenin's attitude to the Constituent Assembly remained more or less constant until 1917 as, for example, in 1911 when he wrote:

"As before, the aim of our struggle is to overthrow Tsarism and bring about the conquest of power by the proletariat relying on the revolutionary sections of the peasantry and accomplishing the bourgeois-democratic revolution by means of the convening of a popular constituent assembly and the establishment of a democratic republic"[21].

Similarly in October 1915, when he wrote for the *Sotsial-Demokrat* his *Several Theses Proposed by the Editors*[22], he repeated the slogan of a Constituent Assembly, and re-emphasised that it could not stand alone. The war had made the question of who would convene the assembly even more relevant, but his core message was the same; the *RDDPP* would be victorious only if it overthrew the autocracy, the nobility and the feudal landowners in an insurrection, with the Soviets of Workers' Deputies the major organs of the insurrection and revolutionary rule until the Constituent Assembly was in place.

7.3 The Constituent Assembly - the Goal of the Revolution?

After the news of the 1917 February Revolution reached him, and before his return to Russia, Lenin wrote his *Letters from Afar*. We note the beginning of a new attitude towards the Paris Commune, which had now become an example to be emulated. In the *Third Letter* he said:

"Following the path indicated by the experience of the Paris Commune of 1871 and the Russian Revolution of 1905, the proletariat must organise and arm *all* the poor, exploited sections of the population in order that they *themselves* should take the organs of state power directly into their own hands, in order that *they themselves should constitute* these organs of state power"[23].

By calling for the proletariat, the poor and exploited sections of the population to control the organs of state power, Lenin was implicitly placing a question mark over the role of a Constituent Assembly. Whether, at that time, Lenin foresaw that an elected Assembly composed mainly of peasant representatives, would block attempts to introduce the Bolshevik programme is not clear[24]. However, in his rebuttal of Kautsky's criticism that he (Lenin) opposed the Constituent Assembly in December 1917 and January 1918, only after it became clear that the Bolsheviks did not have a majority, Lenin claimed that as soon as he arrived in Russia he "proclaimed the superiority of the Paris Commune-type state over the bourgeois parliamentary republic" and, more than that, directly counter-posed the Commune-type state to bourgeois democracy:

"the conference of the Bolshevik Party held at the end of April 1917 adopted a resolution to the effect that a proletarian and peasant republic was superior to a bourgeois parliamentary republic, **that our Party would not be satisfied with the latter,** and that the program of the Party should be modified accordingly"[25].

During the crucial Petrograd City Conference (April), Lenin refers to the Paris Commune in his *Report on the Present Situation* in a very different manner from *Two Tactics,* effectively reversing his previous opinion of the Commune as "a government *such as ours should not be*":

"The Paris Commune furnished an example of a state of the Soviet type, an example of direct power wielded by the organised and armed workers, an example of the dictatorship of workers and peasants. ... There can be no dual power in a state. The Soviets are a type of state where the existence of a police is impossible. Here the people are their own rulers, and there can be no return to the monarchy. ... To safeguard freedom, all the people to a man must be armed. This is the essence of the commune. ... Events have led to the dictatorship of the proletariat and peasantry being interlocked with the dictatorship of the bourgeoisie. **The next stage is the dictatorship of the proletariat**"[26].

Also in April, in his *Letters on Tactics* Lenin wrote: "The Commune, unfortunately, was too slow in introducing socialism"[27]. The qualitative difference between his assessment of the Commune as made in 1905, and in early 1917, shows that Lenin had revised his assessment of the class nature of the state that would result from the revolution and thus, implicitly at least, the role of the Constituent Assembly. If "the next stage" were achieved, the need for a bourgeois-democratic Assembly fell.

During the spring of 1917, Lenin and the Bolsheviks showed no open opposition to the Constituent Assembly, but at the Bolshevik Seventh All-Russian Conference Lenin demanded that undivided power rested with Soviets "from the bottom up" all over the country. In his *Report on the Current Situation,* (24 April) he said:

"We are all agreed that power must be wielded by the Soviets of Workers' and Soldiers' Deputies. ... This would be a state of the Paris Commune type. ... The Soviets must take power not for the purpose of building an ordinary bourgeois republic, nor for the purpose of making a direct transition to socialism. This cannot be. What, then, is the purpose? The Soviets must take power in order to make the first concrete steps towards this transition"[28].

Simultaneously with the Conference Lenin published a short series of articles in the newspaper *Volna*[29], in which he answered the question: should a Constituent Assembly be convened?, with an unambiguous 'Yes'. Not only that, but he called for it to be convened as soon as possible, and the best way of ensuring that was to increase the number and strength of the Soviets, and to organise the arming of the working-class masses.

However, the perspective of establishing a commune-type state meant a bourgeois Constituent Assembly could no longer be the governmental goal of a Soviet power. Despite the public statements, the resolution passed at the Seventh All-Russia Conference resolved that the Bolshevik Party should take the necessary steps to "the successful transfer of the entire state power into the hands of the Soviets of Workers' and Soldiers' Deputies or other organs directly expressing the will of the majority of the people (organs of local self-government, the Constituent Assembly, etc.)"[30]. This marked a definitive and qualitative change in the party's formal position on the Assembly.

The emphasis here is quite different from Lenin's declared aims pre-1917. Now "the entire state power" is to be transferred to the Soviets of Workers' and Soldiers' Deputies, and the Constituent Assembly - the goal of the Soviets before 1917 - is relegated to an also-ran of "other organs" and put on a par with local self-government. In practice, the Bolsheviks were everywhere applying their energy to extending the Soviets to include the maximum number of people in revolutionary activity in order to raise their political consciousness, with the aim of the Soviets taking power and making the first steps towards socialism.

In July 1917, Lenin outlined the six-month history of the demand for the convocation of a Constituent Assembly in *Constitutional Illusions*[31]. He described how the Provisional Government, aware that any Constituent Assembly would have a majority of peasants who were well to the left of the *SR*s, had continuously postponed the calling of elections because, with such a Constituent Assembly, it would have been virtually impossible to protect the interests of the landowners. In Russia, where the bourgeoisie was closely intertwined with the landowners and the nobility, the seizure of the land without compensation, could have been achieved only by carrying through the most ruthless revolutionary measures against capital. Lenin and the Bolsheviks proclaimed that only the strength and authority of the Soviets could guarantee the successful election and convocation of such a Constituent Assembly, giving the impression that the Constituent Assembly remained an acceptable goal for the party.

Thus, while the general direction the party was taking on the question of the Constituent Assembly was clear, there remained considerable ambiguity in the individual published statements of Lenin and others on the precise relationship between the Soviet regime and the Constituent Assembly. Nevertheless, it had become clear that the role of the Assembly would be determined by the outcome of the class struggle between the bourgeoisie and the proletariat. With the victory of the proletariat and its allies, the Assembly would become subordinate to the organs which best represented the interests of the victors, the Soviets. In this inversion of the importance of the proletarian and bourgeois-democratic institutions, lay a qualitative difference between 1905 and 1917.

Trotsky gave an insight into the relative strengths, and contradictory relations, of the Soviets and the bourgeois-democratic institutions which allows a better understanding the fate of the Constituent Assembly, when he reported on the outcomes of the May elections to the local councils (dumas and zemstvos). These were democratically-elected bodies, based on a wide franchise, with one vote per person over the age of 21 and, in theory, they had responsibility for such important functions as municipal transport and food supplies. In fact, however, in many country districts the peasants tended to see these bodies as a means of preserving the landlords' hold on the land, and it was often necessary to use force to overcome peasant opposition, and allow the elections to proceed[32]. Generally, the *SR*s gained the largest single vote, typically at least one third of the votes cast. Thus, a combination of *SR*s and Mensheviks shared leadership and nominal control of both the local councils and the local Soviets[33]. This leadership had, as its common perspective, the goal of a democratically-elected Constituent Assembly, making it all the more surprising that the functions of the local councils were subsumed into the Soviets and not the other way round. Trotsky explains this as being due to the class nature of the two institutions: "... at critical moments, when the interference of the masses was defining the further direction of events, these governments simply exploded into the air, their constituent elements appearing on different sides of a barricade"[34].

Lenin returned to the lessons to be learned from the Commune in *State and Revolution,* written while in hiding in August and September 1917. He pointed out that the most significant change to the *Communist Manifesto* was made by Marx and Engels on the basis of the experience of the Paris Commune and quoted: "*One thing especially was proved by the Commune, viz., that 'the working class cannot simply lay hold of the ready-made state machinery, and wield it for its own purposes.'*"[35]. Lenin would continue to extol the Commune as an inspiration until the end of his life[36,37], but he was keen to emphasise that one of the reasons for its defeat was that it did not act with sufficient vigour. He drew the lesson that in Russia it was necessary to smash the bureaucratic-military machine **as a pre-condition** for an alliance between the peasants and the workers. This could "be achieved only by the proletariat; and by achieving it, the proletariat at the same time takes a step towards the socialist reconstruction of the state"[38]. The progression is that the workers first destroy the military bureaucratic machine and simultaneously take the initial steps towards socialism, as the pre-condition for the alliance with the peasantry! This is a radical version of Trotsky's *ToPR*!

Lenin's attitude to the Provisional Government was clear, overthrow it by armed insurrection and replace it with Soviet power. How did the Constituent Assembly fit into this? Lenin replied that the Commune, or Soviet, substituted the parliamentarism of bourgeois society with institutions in which the elected representatives themselves had to account for their actions directly and immediately to their constituents. Representative democracy remained without a parliament. The arguments advanced by Lenin in *State and Revolution* were a drawing together of his ideas, as developed over the previous seven months, and left little space in the proletarian state for the presence of a Constituent Assembly. Lenin and Trotsky may have been flexible on governmental form and structure, but they would have found it impossible to have accepted the existence of a Constituent Assembly which was, in principle, in fundamental contradiction with core Bolshevik perspectives.

In 1905, Lenin had disputed with the Mensheviks on whether or not it was permissible for the Social Democrats to participate in the transitional revolutionary government. Only Trotsky unequivocally foresaw "the participation of the proletariat in a government ... as a *dominating and leading participation*"[39]. How far and how fast Lenin moved in Trotsky's direction on this point is indicated by an event that happened on 4 June 1917. During a speech, the Menshevik Tsereteli, then a Minister of the Provisional Government, said that there was no political party which was prepared to take full power in Russia. Lenin interrupted and shouted "There is!" Later in his own speech from the rostrum, Lenin declared that the Bolshevik Party was "ready to take over full power at any moment"[40].

By mid-September, the Bolsheviks had obtained a majority in the Soviets of Workers' and Soldiers' Deputies of both Moscow and Petrograd, and Lenin had reached the conclusion that they could and should, take state power through armed insurrection. Lenin wrote to the Bolshevik Central Committee and argued that by immediately 'giving' the land to the peasants and by establishing democratic institutions and liberties, the Bolshevik Party would form a government which nobody would be able to overthrow[41]. However, even at this stage Lenin could say "Our Party alone, on taking power, can secure the Constituent Assembly's convocation"[42]. Lenin was now talking in terms of the Bolsheviks alone taking power, establishing the dictatorship of the proletariat and convening a bourgeois Constituent Assembly!

Thus, in September, the convocation of the Assembly, after full and free elections, was seen as requiring the success of the revolutionary forces, but no clash of interests between the two was indicated. Why was the door to the convening of the Constituent Assembly being kept open even at this late stage? One possible reason for this apparently ambiguous policy was given by Trotsky; "the Bolsheviks .... had not yet renounced the idea of the Constituent Assembly. Moreover, they could not do this without abandoning revolutionary realism. Whether the future course of events would create the conditions for a complete victory of the proletariat, could not with absolute certainty be foreseen"[43]. In other words, the Constituent Assembly was seen as a possible safety net. At the beginning of October, Lenin wrote *Can the Bolsheviks Retain State Power?*[44], in which he argued that the Bolshevik Party alone had sufficient base in revolutionary Russia to take power and hold onto it. The Constituent Assembly is referred to, but only to draw attention to the failure of Kerensky's government to convene it, and the widespread intimidation of peasants through arrests and military measures to rig the outcomes of the elections.

7.4 Lenin, the October Revolution and the Constituent Assembly

After the October Revolution the Bolsheviks still did not close the door on the Constituent Assembly. The promise to allow elections was kept; partly because the cancellation of the elections could have alienated a section of the peasantry, partly because it did not have sufficient authority in all areas and districts to stop the elections going ahead, partly because the Bolsheviks would have found it difficult to say no after having called for the election of an Assembly since February, but also because the majority of the Bolshevik leadership was committed to the elections[45]. A section of the leadership (Kamenev and Zinoviev) actually had as its goal, the establishment of a dual-power in Russia - the Constituent Assembly with the Bolsheviks a strong minority within it, and the Soviets with the Bolsheviks a strong majority. Their trajectory over this period - support for the war, against the October Revolution, for a coalition government - was parallel to that of the Left *SRs*[46], possibly giving the latter hope of determining governmental policy.

Trotsky described the internal situation within the Bolshevik leadership: Lenin was not opposed in principle to the election of a Constituent Assembly, but wanted to postpone it to avoid an Assembly with a Menshevik and *SR* majority which could pose serious problems for the revolution[47]. Trotsky was to later claim that Lenin had decided that if the Bolsheviks had a majority in the Assembly they would have formally dissolved it and handed all power to the Soviets. Indeed, the democratically elected Petrograd Town Council which had a substantial Bolshevik majority did just that[78].

The first decree, on peace, drafted by Lenin was issued the day after the insurrection, 26 October 1917. On the same day, the decree abolishing private ownership of the land, also drafted by Lenin, was issued. On taking power, and without waiting for the Constituent Assembly, the Soviets introduced a number of measures to destroy the old state, and take the first steps in the construction of the new:

2 November:	Right of the peoples of Russia to self-determination and secession.
10 November:	Castes and civil hierarchy abolished.
14 November:	Decree for workers' control in industry. Nationalisation of the banking and credit institutions.
21 November:	Right of recall established as a necessary condition for any truly democratic and really representative body.
22 November:	Decree passed to replace all serving judges who were, henceforth, to be elected.
9 December:	Brest-Litovsk peace talks commence.
11 December:	Education taken out of the hands of the church.
14 December:	Decree making banking a state monopoly.
16 December:	Ranks in the army abolished, Russo-Belgium Metals Company confiscated.
17 December:	Market in living accommodation abolished in the cities, 1886 Electric Company confiscated.
18 December:	Civil marriage instituted.
19 December:	Divorce instituted.
21 December:	Code for revolutionary courts decreed.
24 December:	Putilov factories confiscated.
3 January:	Russian Federation of Soviet Republics proclaimed, Decree issued for the constitution and organisation of the Socialist Red Army[48,49].

These decisions and decrees were being implemented in parallel with the elections to, and convening of, the Constituent Assembly. The decisions taken by the Bolshevik-dominated Soviets determined policy on all the important issues of the day, particularly the two most pressing questions facing Russia: the end to the war and agrarian policy. Simultaneously, the power of the state in the period of the disintegration of the armed forces, was the Red Guard, sailors and army units loyal to the Bolsheviks. In such a situation, the Constituent Assembly could not, realistically, exert any state or governmental authority which did not accord with the policies of the Soviets.

However, it could become the focus for the campaign against the Soviet regime, and lend legitimacy to anti-Soviet forces. Is it too obvious to point out that the Assembly did become a rallying cry for the so-called democratic forces, all of whom ceded real power to the counter-revolution.

Much of the following material on the elections to, and convening of, the Constituent Assembly is drawn from *The Sickle Under the Hammer*[50], and *Russia Goes to the Polls*[51], both by Oliver Henry Radkey. The elections for the Constituent Assembly were held between 12-14 November. The *SR* Party gained the largest single number of votes, over 22,000,000 from a total of about 42,000,000, and obtained approximately 438 of the 703 seats declared. However, the candidates who made up this block were predominantly middle class intellectuals and army officers who had been selected by a system that effectively excluded the left wing of the party, which would soon break away to become the party of the Left *SR*s. The split would be over whether to support the October Revolution and, in many areas, the Left *SR*s constituted the majority of the party membership.

The vote for the Constituent Assembly included all sectors of the population, in or outside the Soviets. The results showed that at the time of the elections, in the west of Russia, from the army front lines through Minsk and across to Smolensk, the solid majority of all peasants supported the Bolsheviks rather than the *SR*s. The Bolsheviks also held all the major towns and the majority of the soldiers within them. Radkey concludes that this was an under-estimation of Bolshevik support as the dynamic of the revolution was everywhere strongly in favour of the Bolsheviks, even in the *SR* rural heartlands[52]

Immediately after the elections, in preparation for the first meeting of the Constituent Assembly, the Centre/Right *SR*s met in Petrograd. By the time they met, the delegates were aware of the enormous number of votes cast by the peasants for *SR* candidates but were also well aware that nearly all their strength in the urban centres and many barracks had evaporated, going either directly to the Bolsheviks or to the Left *SR*s. The programme and policies they decided would provide the basis of the *SR* challenge to the Bolsheviks for power. Four major issues confronted them, the *SR's* attitude to the Soviets, peace, land, and the national question[53].

The complete divorce of the Centre/Right *SR* leadership from reality is best represented by the policy adopted on the agrarian question. Meeting in the face of the Bolshevik land decree which enacted *SR* policy, they rejected this as far too radical, even though it was clearly what their remaining electoral base - the peasant masses - wanted. Instead they decided that the Constituent Assembly would plan for land socialisation to take place at some, unspecified, future date. In the given situation such prevarication was political suicide. How to explain it? Radkey notes that of all the monies paid into the *SR* treasury, only 3% came from party organisations, and 97% came from the banks in the form of loans! He suggests that this dependence of a party that called itself socialist and revolutionary, upon the institutions of finance capitalism "may explain more than one puzzling circumstance in the conduct of the party in 1917"[54].

The leadership of the Centre/Right *SR*s rightly saw the decision of the Bolsheviks to convene the Third Soviet Congress only three days after the opening of the Constituent Assembly, as preparation for closing down the latter, and concluded that they would have to defend the Assembly militarily. The real strength of the *SR* Party was now revealed; it managed to gather only a few dozen militants who were simply brushed aside by the Red Guards and sailors assigned by the Bolsheviks to "guard" the Assembly. The *SR* Party failed to mobilise peasants for this venture because they saw the Assembly as a distraction from the seizure and re-distribution of the land. The rapidly-declining number of soldiers still loyal to the *SR*s were too far away on, for example, the Rumanian front, to help.

Faced with the results of the elections, Lenin published nineteen theses in *Pravda* on 26 December, which offered serious practical reasons why the Constituent Assembly did not really represent the true opinions of the electorate: the lists of candidates presented did not reflect the split in the *SR* Party, and those representing possibly the majority of members were a small minority of the candidates; the elections had taken place before the news of the October Revolution had spread to many areas, and certainly before its significance for the land question was realised by the overwhelming majority of the peasants; achieving an end to the war could be attempted only as a result of the October Revolution and this was not yet widely appreciated; there was no right of recall of deputies to correct these imbalances[55].

Lenin half-heartedly justified the Bolshevik demand for the convocation of the Constituent Assembly prior to the October Revolution (it was the highest form of bourgeois democracy), but the situation had changed. Now a government best capable of achieving a painless transition from a bourgeois to a socialist system was required, and a republic of Soviets was most suitable. Of course, this was the direction in which the Bolsheviks had been heading since April 1917, and it is, perhaps, surprising that it took Lenin so long to spell it out. The situation was laid bare in Thesis 14:

"Only the complete victory of the workers and peasants over the bourgeois and landowner ... can really safeguard the proletarian-peasant revolution. The course of events and the development of the class struggle in the revolution have resulted in the slogan 'All Power to the Constituent Assembly!' - which disregards the gains of the workers' and peasants' revolution, which disregards Soviet power, which disregards the decisions of the Second All-Russia Congress of Soviets of Workers' and Soldiers' Deputies, of the Second All-Russia Congress of Peasants' Deputies, etc., - *becoming in fact* the slogan of the Cadets and the Kaledinites and of their helpers. The entire people are now fully aware that the Constituent Assembly, if it parted ways with Soviet power, would inevitably be doomed to political extinction"[56].

All the preparation for the Constituent Assembly came to nothing. The Assembly met on 5 January 1918, but of the 800 elected representatives, fewer than 500 attended, and further credibility was lost when it became known that with the withdrawal of the 150 Bolsheviks and Left *SR* delegates, fewer than 40% of the elected delegates remained. Sverdlov, for the Bolsheviks, proposed that the Constituent Assembly endorsed the *Declaration of the Rights of the Labouring and Exploited Masses* drafted by Lenin and adopted by the All-Russian Soviet Executive. The Centre/Right *SR*s and their allies re-ordered the business of the day by 237 votes to 146 and by-passed the Soviet declaration[57]. In this way the Assembly issued a direct challenge to the Soviet regime by showing itself not prepared to accept the fundamentals of Soviet policy. The Bolsheviks caucused with the Left *SR*s and then withdrew from the Assembly on their own, to be followed by the Left *SR*s some time after midnight, after unresolveable differences emerged between them and the Centre/Right *SR*s over whether to support Soviet peace negotiations.

In the remaining two hours and ten minutes of the Assembly's existence, Red Guards and sailors gradually took over the empty seats, forming a hostile ring around the remaining delegates. At 4.40 am on the 6th, the session was declared closed[58]. The dispersal of the Assembly caused remarkably little response. Only Kharkov City Soviet in all of Russia is known to have passed a resolution condemning the dissolution, although this was later reversed by a meeting of the local provincial Soviet[59]. In the spring the Centre/Right *SR*s made some half-hearted attempts to revive the Constituent Assembly in Kiev, but this came to nothing.

Before the first meeting of the Constituent Assembly, both the Centre/Right *SR*s and Left *SR*s had decided to mobilise their respective peasant support by each convening a Third All-Russian Peasants' Congress separately from one another. The Centre/Right *SR* Third Congress of Peasant Soviets opened on 10 January, the Left *SR* Third All-Russian Congress of Peasant Soviets opened on the 14th, and the Bolshevik Third All-Russian Congress of Workers' and Soldiers' Soviets also opened on 10 January. The Third All-Russian Congress called by the Centre/Right *SR*s had over 300 delegates. It never properly met because a contingent of sailors and Red Guards dispersed it during the opening ceremonies. That the Centre/Right *SR*s were already a rump organisation by this time was confirmed by the fact that there was no recorded dissent to the dispersal of this Congress, not even in the *SR*s' strongest areas such as Saratov province. The Congress was the *SR*s' last national action before political extinction[60]. Events had confirmed Lenin's opinion that the results of the Constituent Assembly elections did not reflect the reality of the Russian Revolution.

Was the entry of the Left *SR*s into the government in December a manoeuvre by Lenin to forestall the Constituent Assembly?[61] Of course, timing is important in a revolution, and it may well have been that having the Left *SR*s in the government bought the Bolsheviks valuable time in which to build up and consolidate their support amongst the peasantry, particularly through the masses of soldiers who had shifted their allegiance from the *SR* Party to the Bolsheviks and were returning home. However, after July but before October, the Left *SR*s were gaining rapidly at the expense of Centre/Right of the Party, but were meeting with much less success in holding their lines against Bolshevism. "The picture varied little from one part of the country to another - everywhere the Bolsheviks were going forward and the Left *SR*'s fighting just to hold their own"[62]. After the Bolshevik government's Land Decree this process underwent a step change, and the *SR*s, Left, Right and Centre, never regained their former mass support amongst the peasantry. Prior to the elections Lenin genuinely believed that an alliance with the Left SRs could benefit the revolutionary transition in Russia, but after the elections the argument for such an alliance lost much of its force.

All that Radkey says confirms Lenin's analysis that;

"... the Russian proletariat *won the peasantry* from the Socialist-Revolutionaries, and won them literally *a few hours* **after achieving state power**; a few hours after the victory over the bourgeoisie in Petrograd, the **victorious proletariat** issued a 'decree on land', and in that decree it entirely, at once, with revolutionary swiftness, energy and devotion, *satisfied* all the most urgent economic needs of the *majority* of the peasants, it expropriated the landowners, entirely and without compensation"[63].

With the decision of the Third All-Russian Congress of Peasant Soviets convened by the Left *SR*s to merge with the Third All-Russian Congress of Workers' and Soldiers' Deputies, to form the All-Russian Congress of Workers', Soldiers' and Peasants' Deputies, the Bolsheviks could legitimately claim that the Soviets represented the vast majority of the working population.

7.5 The Workers, the Red Guard, and the Power of the State

On 28 January 1917 (prior to the Mensheviks and *SR*s voicing their opposition), the Petrograd Soviet sent a directive to each factory to organise a workers' militia. This gave the green light to local activities and received an enthusiastic response, typifying direct proletarian self-assertion. By the end of February, workers militias had sprung up in most of the factories, and by the start of March some 20,000 militia men were under arms in Petrograd alone[64].

The longstanding, formal position of the Bolsheviks (though only the grass roots acted on it in early 1917) was to support the creation of workers' militias and Red Guards, and when both the Mensheviks and *SR*s counterposed a militia loyal to the city dumas they *de facto* ensured that the bands of armed men that would form the power of the Soviet state remained firmly in Bolshevik hands alone. The Bolsheviks formed Soviet militias under their control in all provinces and towns with a proletarian element, including those areas where the Left *SR*s had their strongholds[65]. Arming the workers had been explicit Bolshevik policy from 1905, so the existence of an armed workers' militia does not offer a criterion by which to judge whether the goal of the 1917 Revolution was a Constituent Assembly or Commune-type state, a *RDDPP*, or a dictatorship of the proletariat - however, the actions taken by the Red Guards after the October Revolution do.

In *Can the Bolsheviks Retain State Power*[66], the state order that followed the revolution would be based on the activities of the Red Guards, and Lenin gives examples of how it would be the workers' militia that would determine day-to-day decision-making in the new state. This makes the activities of the Red Guard very important - would the armed might of the workers remain outside the factory gates, or would it flow into the factory? In fact, the spontaneous actions of the workers' militia confirmed Trotsky's central prediction that if the armed workers held the power outside the factory gate, that authority would naturally spill over into a direct challenge to the management and ownership of the enterprises. Dune described how, as soon as the news of the revolution reached his factory, the workers disarmed the owners' factory guard, took their weapons (revolvers and sabres) and formed a "revolutionary defence force"[67]. He went on to say that the factory committee elected by all the workers took over day-to-day running of the factory, but that none of the Mensheviks in the factory joined the Red Guard and left it to the Bolsheviks[68].

Given the geographic and social distribution of Russian society - the workers had to live close to their factories, public transport was a luxury they could not afford - the workers' militias and Red Guard units were, of necessity, factory-based, since there was no realistic alternative. Such a structure posed a serious practical problem for the theory of the *RDDPP*, but lent great strength to the *ToPR*. As Wade reported:

"For the factory workers and their factory committees, then, the presence of factory-based armed units gave emphasis to their demands. ... Indeed, the coercive relationship between the management and workers was reversed. Now the workers had arms ... whereas management had lost its factory guards and the ultimate threat of government police and troops"[69].

Just as Trotsky had predicted, based on his experience of 1905, the workers saw no reason to keep the Red Guards outside the factory gate, quite the opposite, Red Guards provided the muscle to support workers' demands for a larger voice in the factories and, even, workers' seizure of the factories[70]. After October, the Red Guards right across Russia, gradually extended their control beyond the environs of the factories and took responsibility for security within the cities and larger towns, exercising political control by breaking up opponents' demonstrations and meetings, arresting participants and seizing their weapons.

Wade reported that up to the October Revolution, workers were in the majority in the Red Guard units across Russia, typically at least 60%, rising to about 80% in the industrial centres and over 90% in Petrograd[71]. He showed that while the Bolsheviks were initially a minority of the rank and file of the Red Guard, as 1917 progressed they assumed an increasingly important role in leadership, and by October held nearly all the senior positions[72], at which time Wade estimates there were between 100,000 and 200,000 Red Guards in Russia, a key force because - unlike the peasant soldiers in the army - they were prepared to fight (and die) for the revolution[73].

Carr confirms that the leaders of the Bolshevik Party had no further plans for socialisation of the economy after the nationalisation of the banking and credit institutions and the decree for workers' control of industry on 14 November, but:

"... the innumerable economic conflicts that had gone on before October now multiplied, and indeed became more serious as the combativity of the contestants was everywhere greater. The initiative for acts of expropriation, undertaken as necessities of struggle rather than according to any design for socialism, came from the masses rather than the government. It was only eight months later, in June 1918, that the government adopted the great decrees of nationalisation, under the pressure of foreign intervention. ...

The liquidation of the political defences of their capitalist exploiters launched a spontaneous movement among the workers to take over the means of production. Since they were perfectly able to take control of the factories and workshops, why should they abstain? The employers sabotage of production entailed expropriation as an act of reprisal. When the boss brought work to a halt, the workers themselves, on their own responsibility, got the establishment going again. [Council of Peoples' Commissars had to decree the nationalisation of Russo-Belgian Metal Company's factories, the Putilov works, the Smirnov spinning-mills and the power station belonging to the 1886 Electrical Company.]"[74].

7.6 Town and Country

In *Pravda* in December 1917, Lenin had presented nineteen theses explaining why the Constituent Assembly elections were not truly representative of the balance of forces in Russia. In his 1918 dispute with Kautsky, and later in his 1919 review of the elections to the Constituent Assembly, Lenin added another argument to his list, one that was little more than an elaboration of Trotsky's dictum: "The history of capitalism is the history of the subordination of the country to the town"[75], one of the foundation stones of Permanent Revolution:

"The country cannot be equal to the town under the historical conditions of this epoch. The town inevitably *leads* the country. The country inevitably *follows the town*. The only question is *which class*, of the "urban" classes, will succeed in leading the country, will cope with this task, and what forms will *leadership by the town* assume? ....

Capitals, or, in general, big commercial and industrial centres ... , to a considerable degree decide the political fate of a nation, provided, of course, the centres are supported by sufficient local, rural forces, even if that support does not come immediately"[76].

Trotsky had argued in the *ToPR* that the proletariat, having taken political and state power in the bourgeois-democratic revolution, would immediately approve all revolutionary expropriations carried out by the peasants. By this it would effectively rob the Constituent Assembly of its most important prop, and thus, in the initial stages of the revolution, the Russian peasant would have a vested interest in maintaining the proletarian regime, not a Constituent Assembly. Lenin developed this idea of Trotsky's, fleshing it out not only with the practical details of the actual Russian Revolution, but also in terms of Marxist theory:

"But these conditions [Bolshevik domination of the towns and capital] could have ensured only a very short-lived and unstable victory had the Bolsheviks been unable to win to their side the majority of the *non*-proletarian working masses, ... *state power in the hands of one class, the proletariat, can and must become an instrument for winning to the side of the proletariat the non-proletarian working masses, an instrument for winning those masses from the bourgeoisie and from the petty-bourgeois parties.*

The proletariat must (after mustering sufficiently strong political and military "striking forces") overthrow the bourgeoisie, take state power from it in order to use that *instrument* for *its* class aims. .... the proletariat must first overthrow the bourgeoisie and win *for itself* state power, and then use that state power, that is, the dictatorship of the proletariat, as an instrument of its class for the purpose of winning the sympathy of the majority of the working people.

... the proletariat can, and must, at once, or at all events very quickly, win from the bourgeoisie and from petty-bourgeois democrats *"their"* masses, i.e., the masses which follow them -- win them *by satisfying their most urgent economic needs in a revolutionary way by expropriating the landowners and the bourgeoisie. ...* "[77].

A review of Lenin's attitude towards the Constituent Assembly and the Commune-type state shows that until 1917 his goal for the Russian Revolution was a Constituent Assembly elected by free and universal suffrage of all the people, heading a bourgeois state. During 1917/18, the Constituent Assembly was first demoted to assume second place to Soviet power, and then disbanded when it threatened that power. Lenin's attitude to the Constituent Assembly is clearly paralleled in his references to the Paris Commune which, initially rejected in 1905, had by early 1917, become a model that the Soviets were to emulate. The study of Lenin's attitude towards the Constituent Assembly clearly demonstrates his transition from a stagist to a permanentist position, culminating in the socialist October Revolution 1917 and the dissolution of the Constituent Assembly.

7.7 References

1. Lenin, V.I., *On Two Lines in the Revolution*. November 1915, CW 21:418
2. Lenin, V.I., *To the Rural Poor - An Explanation for the Peasants of What the Social-Democrats Want*, March 1903, CW 6:361-432
3. Lenin, V.I., *Ibid*, CW 6:427
4. Lenin, V.I., *The Revolutionary-Democratic Dictatorship of the Proletariat and Peasantry*, April 12 1905, *CW* 8:293-303
5. Lenin, V. I., *Draft Resolution on the Provisional Revolutionary Government*, April 1905, CW8:397
6. Lenin, V.I., *The Third Congress of the RSDLP*, April 1905, CW 8:396-397
7. Lenin, V.I., *The Democratic Tasks of the Revolutionary Proletariat*, June 1905, CW 8: 513-4 and 517
8. Lenin, V.I., *Two Tactics of Social Democracy in the Democratic Revolution*, June 1905, CW 9:26
9. Lenin, V.I., *Ibid*, CW 9:15-140
10. Lenin, V.I., *Ibid*, CW 9:28
11. Lenin, V.I., *Ibid*, CW 9:28
12. Lenin, V.I., *Ibid*, CW 9:29
13. Lowy, M., *Combined and Uneven Development*, Verso, London, 1981, p61
14. Lenin, V.I., *Two Tactics of Social Democracy in the Democratic Revolution*, June 1905, CW 9:80
15. Trotsky, L.D., *Results and Prospects*, New Park Publications, London, 1962, p232
16. Lenin, V.I., *A Tactical Platform for the Unity Congress of the RSDLP, March 1906*, CW 10:155-157
17. Lenin, V.I., *Ibid*, CW 10:158-159
18. Lenin, V.I., *Ibid*, CW 10:156
19. Lenin, V.I., *Revision of the Agrarian Programme of the Workers' Party*, April 1906, CW 10:189-190
20. Lenin, V.I., *Ibid*, CW 10:194
21. Lenin, V.I., *"The Peasant Reform" and the Proletarian - Peasant Revolution*, March 1911, CW 17:128
22. Lenin, V.I., *Several Theses Proposed by the Editors*, October 1915, CW 21:401-404
23. Lenin, V.I., *Letters From Afar,* March 1917, CW 23:325-326
24. White, J.D. *Lenin The Practice and Theory of Revolution*, Palgrave, 2001, p156-157

25. Lenin, V.I., *The Proletarian Revolution and the Renegade Kautsky,* Oct-Nov 1918, CW 28:265

26. Lenin, V.I., *Report on the Present Situation* April 1917, CW 24:145

27. Lenin, V.I., *Letters on Tactics,* April 1917, CW 24:53

28. Lenin, V.I., *Report on the Current Situation,* April 1917, CW 24:239-241

29. Lenin, V.I., *The Political Parties in Russia and the Tasks of the Proletariat,* April 1917, CW 24:99

30. Lenin, V.I., *The Seventh (April) All-Russia Conference of the R.S.D.L.P.(B.),* April 1917, CW 24:275

31. Lenin, V.I., *Constitutional Illusions,* July 1917, CW 25:194-207

32. Trotsky, L.D., *History of the Russian Revolution.* Three volumes, Sphere Books Ltd, London, 1967, Vol 3 p32

33. Sukhanov, N.N., *The Russian Revolution 1917 A Personal Record,* Oxford University Press, London, 1955, p496-497

34. Trotsky, L.D., *History of the Russian Revolution.* Three volumes, Sphere Books Ltd, London, 1967, Vol 1 p345

35. Marx, K. and Engels, F., *Manifesto of the Communist Party,* Selected Works, Moscow, 1951, 1:22

36. Lenin, V. I., *How to Organise Competition,* Dec 1917, CW 26:413

37. Lenin, V. I., *Extraordinary 7th Congress of the RCP(B),* March 1918, CW 27:133

38. Lenin, V. I., *The State and Revolution,* Aug-Sept 1917, CW 25:422 and 426

39. Trotsky, L.D., *Results and Prospects,* New Park Publications, London, 1962, p202

40. Daniels, R.V., *Red October,* Secker and Warburg, London, 1967, p17

41. Lenin, V.I., *The Bolsheviks Must Assume Power: A Letter to the Central Committee and the Petrograd and Moscow Committees of the RSDLP(B),* September 1917, CW 26:19

42. Lenin, V.I., *Ibid* CW 26:19

43. Trotsky, L.D., *History of the Russian Revolution.* Three volumes, Sphere Books Ltd, London, 1967, 2:328

44. Lenin, V.I., *Can the Bolsheviks Retain State Power?* October 1917, CW 26:87-136

45. Thatcher, I. D., *Trotsky,* Routledge, London and New York, 2003, p94

46. Carr, E.H., The Bolshevik Revolution, 1917-1923. Three Volumes. Pelican, 1983, 1:118

47. Trotsky, L.D., *On Lenin* George Harrap and Co., London, 1971, 105-106

48. Serge, V., *Year One of the Russian Revolution*, Pluto Press, London, 1992, p122,

49. Cliff, T.C., *Lenin: Revolution Besieged,* Pluto Press, 1975, p8-11

50. Radkey, O.H., *The Sickle Under the Hammer*, Columbia University Press, New York, 1963

51. Radkey, O.H., *Russia Goes to the Polls,* Cornell University Press, Ithaca, 1989

52. Radkey, O.H., *The Sickle Under the Hammer*, Columbia University Press, New York, 1963, p280-301

53. Radkey, O. H., *Ibid,* p179-200

54. Radkey, O. H., *Ibid ,* p200

55. Lenin, V.I., *Theses On The Constituent Assembly*, December 1917, CW 26:380-382

56. Lenin, V.I., *Ibid,* CW 26:381

57. Radkey, O.H., *The Sickle Under the Hammer*, Columbia University Press, New York, 1963, p396

58. Radkey, O.H., *Ibid,* p413-414

59. Radkey, O.H., *Ibid,* p431

60. Radkey, O.H., *Ibid,* p440-444

61. Carr, E.H., The Bolshevik Revolution, 1917-1923. Three Volumes. Pelican, 1983, 1:121

62. Radkey, O.H., *The Sickle Under the Hammer*, Columbia University Press, New York, 1963, p154

63. Lenin, V.I., *The Constituent Assembly Elections and the Dictatorship of the Proletariat*, December 1919, CW 30:264

64. Wade, R. A., *Red Guards and Workers' Militias in the Russian Revolution,* Stanford University Press, Stanford, 1984, p59-60

65. Wade, R. A., *op cit*, p219-221

66. Lenin, V.I., *Can the Bolsheviks Retain State Power*, October 1917, CW 26:112

67. Dune, E. M., *Notes of a Red Guard*, University of Illinois Press, Chicago, 1993, p36

68. Dune, E. M., *Ibid*, p38

69. Wade, R. A., *op cit*, p67

70. Wade, R. A., *op cit*, p299

71. Wade, R. A., *op cit*, p279, Table 3 et seq.

72. Wade, R. A., *op cit*, p285

73. Wade, R. A., *op cit*, p294-295

74. Carr, E.H., The Bolshevik Revolution, 1917-1923. Three Volumes. Pelican, 1983, 1:135-138
75. Trotsky, L.D., *Results and Prospects,* New Park Publications, London, 1962, p204-205
76. Lenin, V. I., *The Constituent Assembly Elections and the Dictatorship of the Proletariat*, December 1919, CW 30:253-75
77. Lenin, V. I., *Ibid*, CW 30:264
78. Trotsky, L.D., *Terrorism and Communism*, George Allen & Unwin, 1921, pp43 and 76

Chapter 8
CONCLUSIONS

8.1 Conclusions

8.1 Conclusions

This book began by introducing Lenin and Trotsky, the major personalities in the debate on the most appropriate strategy for carrying through the bourgeois-democratic revolution in backward, semi-feudal Russia. The most important problem that revolution had to solve was the land question because the vast mass of the population were semi-literate, oppressed, land-hungry peasants.

The personal hostility between the two men (before 1917) might have given their disagreements a particular colouring, but during that time there were real political differences between them on the class nature of the state that would result from the forthcoming Russian Revolution.

Lenin and Trotsky agreed that the Russian bourgeoisie had arrived late on the scene, as an absolutely conservative force, lacking both the will to provide the leadership necessary to overthrow the autocracy, and the capacity to carry thorough the destruction of feudalism. Both agreed that the successful overthrow of the Tsarist, autocratic state would be achieved under the revolutionary leadership of the proletariat, even though it was politically inexperienced and relatively small in numbers. The very much larger, but geographically dispersed and socially-heterogeneous peasantry was incapable of independent action on a national scale but could be won to a revolutionary perspective, to form an alliance with, and follow the leadership of, the industrial proletariat, provided the proletarian party when in government was determined to abolish serfdom and endorsed the revolutionary expropriation of all lands and estates by the peasantry. Both men agreed the regime following the revolution would be a dictatorship because without it, it would have been impossible to break the resistance of the landlords, big business and Tsarism, and repel their counter-revolutionary attempts.

From about 1905 to about 1917, Lenin saw the alliance with the peasantry as imposing strict democratic, bourgeois limits on the revolution since the peasantry would lose its revolutionary zeal once it had achieved its goal of seizing the land for itself, and could not immediately be won to a socialist perspective. Whilst the proletariat would push the revolution forward with all its might to gain as much as possible for itself, the necessity of maintaining the alliance would impose objective limits on what tasks the revolution could successfully complete, as would the level of class consciousness of the proletariat and the degree of Russia's economic development. Although the more advanced sections of the industrial workers would demand socialist measures, the revolutionary party itself would ensure that these were postponed to some unspecified, future, date - at least several decades away. The governmental form of the alliance of workers and peasants during the transitional period from semi-feudal to bourgeois state, would be the *RDDPP*, founded on Soviets, in which the revolutionary party would participate, but there was no question of an *SD*-only dictatorship, or even of an *SD* majority in the government. The outcome of the transitional period would be an elected Assembly representing the whole people, resting on a bourgeois-democratic state.

Trotsky, as Lenin, saw the alliance as originating from the self-interests of both the proletariat and the peasantry. However, before 1917, Trotsky more than Lenin, stressed that the peasantry would follow the towns and, if won to a revolutionary perspective, would follow the leadership of the industrial proletariat. This would be achieved if the proletariat, having taken power in the towns in the first stage of the bourgeois-democratic revolution, legitimised the peasants' seizure of the land and led the destruction of serfdom. The actions taken by the workers in destroying the Tsarist state would, in the real world, overlap with their first collectivist measures, and the workers, carried by their own dynamic, would enact measures that would be the first steps towards socialism. The workers would have the determining say in the government, and the state form following the revolution would be the dictatorship of the proletariat, not least because during the crucial initial period, the bands of armed men that gave the state its authority would be largely working class, led almost exclusively by *SDs* and loyal to the urban Social Democratic Soviets.

Lenin's own writings, as they appear in his *Collected Works*, show that he made a substantial and qualitative change to his assessment of the nature of the Russian Revolution as 1917 progressed. Beginning with his *Letters from Afar* and the *April Theses,* he posed the socialist revolution as being the new Bolshevik goal. After winning the party to his position in the April conferences, he proceeded to develop a more rounded version of what was, in reality, the *ToPR*, and in August 1917, was propagating an openly permanentist line: the international socialist revolution could begin in backward Russia, there could be no solution to the land question in Russia under bourgeois democracy. *From a Publicist's Diary*, which he wrote at the end of August, places him unambiguously as a permanentist. Importantly, Lenin more than Trotsky, emphasised the need for the workers to seize state power in a proletarian, socialist revolution **before** feudal relations on the land could be abolished and the land question solved.

After the October Revolution, Lenin relentlessly, and without self-contradiction, referred to it as socialist and the state that immediately resulted from it as the dictatorship of the proletariat. In this he was consistent until his death.

It was expected that the theories that led to the success of the Russian Revolution would be seen in the policies of the Third (Communist) International. For a number of specific reasons it was Lenin, not Trotsky, who proposed a permanentist analysis: that medieval oppression was ended in Russia **after** the proletariat took state power for itself in an armed revolution. In July 1920, just one month prior to the Second Congress of the CI, Lenin spelled out that the peasantry were capable of giving resolute support to the revolutionary proletariat only **after** the workers won power, only **after** the peasants saw in practice that they had a leader and champion. Such an analysis was more than just a re-wording of Trotsky's position: "*The proletariat in power will stand before the peasants as the class which has emancipated it*". Trotsky's theory was based on analysis of specifically Russian conditions and history (even if the international context was an essential and important element), and observation of the behaviour of the Russian proletariat in a revolutionary situation. Once the Russian bourgeois-democratic revolution had begun, the workers would come to the fore as the revolutionary dynamo and, after solving the crucial land question, would take the first steps towards socialism.

Lenin's made two significant changes in emphasis to the *ToPR*. Firstly, he stressed that the solution of the all-important agrarian question was not possible unless the workers **first** took state power, established their dictatorship and used it for their own ends. Secondly, by presenting his permanentist analysis to the *CI* and the Communist Parties of the East, he generalised the *ToPR* and gave it an international dimension.

The opinions of certain authors who have attempted, in a partial and one-sided way to present Lenin's ideas on the Russian Revolution as following a single uni-directional trajectory have been considered. The method used was that of the amalgam: unrelated quotations are torn out of context and strung together in a manner that "proved" whatever the author wished. It is shown that by siting the quotations supplied by these authors in their original context, that Lenin did not intend to convey the meaning ascribed to him. The essential weakness of their arguments can be seen in the fact that none of them addressed the key questions of how it was that the first stage of the international socialist revolution took place in backward Russia, or why Lenin consistently referred to the Russian state from October 1917 as a dictatorship of the proletariat, and the October Revolution as socialist and proletarian, or why he never referred to the post-October regime as the *RDDPP*, nor ever suggested that the *RDDPP* was a strategy for any section of the *CI*.

The book ends by considering how the role of the Constituent Assembly in the Russian Revolution, as perceived by Lenin and the Bolshevik Party, changed qualitatively from the declared goal of the revolution (1905-1915), to a counter-revolutionary force that had to be overthrown (1918). In parallel, Lenin's *volte face* on the Paris Commune from something the Russian Revolution should not emulate (1905), to the call for a Commune-type state (1917) is noted. Both changes are taken as alternative expressions of Lenin's transition to a permanentist perspective.

We are now in the position of being able to formulate a number of questions concerning the two theories which test how well they stood up to events:

1. Did the socialist revolution in semi-feudal Russia take place before the socialist revolution in Western Europe?
2. Did Lenin, from April in 1917 argue that Russia faced a revolution that must take the first steps towards socialism?
3. Did Lenin, from at least August 1917, argue that the proletariat must hold state power (the dictatorship of the proletariat) to fully liberate Russia from Tsarism?
4. Was the 1917 October Revolution organised with the clear aim of the (urban) proletariat taking state power?
5. Was the 1917 October Revolution organised by the Bolsheviks alone without any alliance with peasant parties?
6. Did the Bolsheviks achieve the "impossible" and constitute the majority of the Workers' and Peasants' Government? Were the representatives of the working class the dominant and leading participants? Was the revolutionary dictatorship led initially, a Bolshevik-only government?
7. Was Lenin correct, in 1917, when he said the dictatorship of the proletariat was required before the agrarian problem could be solved in the interests of the peasantry?
8. Did Lenin consistently describe the 1917 October Revolution as a 'socialist' revolution, and the state that resulted from it the 'dictatorship of the proletariat'?
9. Was the post-October regime a Commune-type state, or was the goal of the revolution a bourgeois Constituent Assembly?
10. After the October Revolution did Lenin ever refer to the Bolshevik regime as the *RDDPP*?

Political theory should be a guide to action. A political schema should give a correct indication of the general development of the class struggle and help to orient both the individual and his/her political party to the actual course of events. It is argued that in this sense, it is impossible not to recognise that the *ToPR* passed the test of subsequent events much better than the *RDDPP*; that Lenin himself recognised this and, from at least August 1917, changed his revolutionary strategy accordingly.

BIBLIOGRAPHY

1. Adler, A., (Ed) *Theses, Resolutions and Manifestos of the First Four Congresses of the Third International.* Pluto Press, London, 1980
2. Barnes, J., *Their Trotsky and Ours: Communist Continuity Today.* New International Vol 1 No 1 pp 9-90, Pathfinder Press, New York, 1983
3. Bone, A., *The Bolsheviks and the October Revolution.* Minutes of the RSDLP(B) Aug 1917 - Feb 1918. Pluto Press. London. 1974.
4. Brandt, B., Schwartz, B. and Fairbank, J., *A Documentary History of Chinese Communism*, George Allen and Unwin Ltd, London, 1952
5. Bukharin, N., *Lenin as a Marxist*, in *In Defence of the Russian Revolution: A Selection of Bolshevik Writings 1917 - 1923.* Richardson. A. (Ed), Porcupine Press, London, 1995
6. Chester, R., (Ed) *Discussions on the Class Nature of the East European States.* SWP(USA), 1966
7. Chester, R., *Workers and Farmers Governments Since the Second World War.* Pathfinder Press, New York, 1978
8. Clark, S., (Ed) *Bolshevism and the Russian Revolution: a Debate.* Pathfinder Press, New York, 1985
9. Clark, S., (Ed) *The Rise and Fall of the Nicaraguan Revolution*, New International, No 9 (Special Edition devoted to the Nicaraguan revolution).Pathfinder Press, New York, 1994
10. Cliff, T., *Trotsky* in 3 Volumes, Bookmarks, London, 1991
11. Cliff, T., *Permanent Revolution*, International Socialism Reprint No. 5, 1981
12. Degras, J., (Ed) *The Communist International 1919 - 1943*, London, 1960.
13. Deutscher, I., *Stalin*, Penguin Books, 1966
14. Endicott, M.A., *Five Stars Over China*, Published by the Author, 1953
15. Hansen, J., *The Workers and Farmers Government*, Pathfinder Press, New York, 1974
16. Hansen, J., *The Communist International 1919-1943 Documents*, Book Review. International Socialist Review, Vol 19 No 3, Summer 1958, pp.107-108
17. Figes, O., *Peasant Russia, Civil War*, Phoenix Press, London, 2001
18. Frankel, E.R., (Ed) *Revolution in Russia, reassessment of 1917*, Cambridge University Press, 1992
19. Frankel, J., *Lenin's Doctrinal Revolution of April 1917*, Jnl of Contemporary History, 1969, $\underline{4}$(2) pp117-142

20. Hansen, J., *The Leninist Strategy of Party Building*, Pathfinder Press, New York 1979

21. Hansen, J., *Class, Party and State*, Pathfinder Press, New York, 2001.

22. Isaacs, H.R., *The Tragedy of the Chinese Revolution*, Stanford University Press, 1951

23. Johnson, G. and Feldman, F., *On the Nature of the Vietnamese Communist Party*, International Socialist Review, July-August 1973, pp 4-9 and 63-90

24. Koenker, D., *Moscow Workers and the 1917 Revolution*, Princeton University Press, 1981

25. Lazitch, B. and Drachkovitch, M., *Biographical Dictionary of the Comintern*, Hoover Institution Press, Stanford, 1973

26. Lenin, V.I., *Selected Works* in 12 Volumes, Lawrence and Wishart Ltd, London, 1936. (This is included for the editorial and explanatory comments and footnotes added by the soviet state bureaucracy.)

27. Mandel, E., *Trotsky, A Study in the Dynamic of His Thought*, NLB, London,1979

28. Medvedev, R., *The October Revolution*, Columbia University Press, 1979

29. Montefiore, S.S., *Young Stalin,* Weidenfield & Nicolson, London, 2007

30. Morrow, F., *Revolution and Counter-Revolution in Spain*, Pathfinder Press New York, 1974

31. Novak, G., *Democracy and Revolution*. Merit Books New York, 1971

32. Peng, S. and Peng, P., *The Chinese Revolution, Parts 1,2 and 3*, Education Department SWP(USA), New York, 1972

33. Pipes, R., *The Unknown Lenin, From the Secret Archive*, Yale University Press, New Haven, 1998

34. Plekhanov, G., *The Materialist Conception of History*, International Publishers, New York, 1940

35. Plekhanov, G., *The Role of the Individual in History*, International Publishers, New York, 1940

36. Radek, K., *The Paths of the Russian Revolution*, in *In Defence of the Russian Revolution: A Selection of Bolshevik Writings 1917 - 1923*. Richardson. A. (Ed), Porcupine Press, London, 1995

37. Reed., J., *Ten Days That Shook the World*, Penguin Modern Classics, 1974

38. Richardson, A., (Ed) *The Revolution Defamed, A Documentary History of Vietnamese Trotskyism*, Socialist Platform Ltd., London, 2003

39. Riddell, J., (Ed) *Founding of the Communist International, Proceedings and Documents of the First Congress, March 1919,* Anchor Foundation, New York, 1987

40. Rosmer, A. *Lenin's Moscow*, Pluto Press, London, 1971
41. Schapiro, L, and Reddaway, P. (eds), *Lenin, the Man, the Theorist, the Leader, a Reappraisal*, Pall Mall Press, London, 1967
42. Segal, R., *The Tragedy of Leon Trotsky*, Hutchinson, London, 1979
43. Serge, V., *From Lenin to Stalin*. Pathfinder Press New York, 1973
44. Shanin, T., *Russia 1905-07, Revolution as a Moment of Truth*, MacMillan, London, 1986
45. Schapiro, L., *The Communist Party of the Soviet Union*, Eyre and Spottiswoode, London, 1960
46. Shlyapnikov, A., *On the Eve of 1917, Reminiscences from the Revolutionary Underground*, Allison & Busby, London, 1982
47. Short, P., *Mao, a Life*. John Murray London, 1999
48. Schram, S., *Mao Tse-Tung*, Penguin Books, London, 1966
49. Shub, D., *Lenin*, Penguin Books, London, 1966
50. Smith, S.A., *Red Petrograd, Revolution in the Factories 1917-18*, Cambridge University Press, 1985
51. Strachey, S., *The Theory and Practice of Socialism*,   Victor Gollanz Ltd., London, 1936
52. Trotsky, L., *The Principles of Democracy and Proletarian Dictatorship* The Class Struggle [United States], Vol. III, No. 1, February, 1919. www.marxists.org
53. Trotsky, L., *The Platform of the Left Opposition (1923 - 25)* Pathfinder Press, New York, 1975
54. Trotsky, L., *The Challenge of the Left Opposition (1927)* New Park Publications. London, 1963
55. Trotsky, L., *The New Course*, New Park Publications, 1956
56. Trotsky, L., *The Russian Revolution* (the Copenhagen Speech (1932)), Revolutionary Communist Party, London, undated
57. Trotsky, L., *Problems of the Chinese Revolution*, New Park Publications, London, 1969.
58. Trotsky, L., *The Transitional Programme for Socialist Revolution*, Socialist Labour League, London, 1963
59. Trotsky, L., *The First Five Years of the Communist International*, Vol 1 and 2, Pioneer Publishers, New York, 1953
60. Trotsky, L., *The Class Nature of the Soviet Union*, WIR Publications, London, Undated.
61. Trotsky, L., *The Chinese Revolution, Problems and Perspectives*, Bulletin of Marxist Studies, Vol 1 No 1, Pioneer Publishers, Undated
62. Trotsky, L., *Social Democracy and the Wars of Intervention. Russia 1918-1921*. New Park Publications, London. 1975

453

932433222222222222

63. Trotsky, L., *The Defence of Terrorism, A Reply to Karl Kautsky*, George Allen & Unwin, 1922
64. Wang, F., *Memoirs of a Chinese Revolutionary*, Columbia University Press, 1991
65. Warde, W.F., *The Irregular Movement of History*, Spark Publishers Ltd, Colombo. (Undated, and authors' initials not given in the publication.)
66. Waters, M-A., *Proletarian Leadership in Power*, Pathfinder Press, New York, 1980
67. Waters, M-A., *1848 to Today, Communism and the Fight for a Popular Revolutionary Government*, New International, No 3 pp 14 - 100, 1989
68. Woods, A. *The Venezuelan Revolution*, Wellred Publications, London, 2005

Other titles from Wellred

▶ **In the Cause of Labour -
History of British Trade Unionism**
By Rob Sewell
Price: £ 14.99

Pub. Date: 2003
Format: Paperback
No. Pages: 480
ISBN: 1900007142

History of British Trotskyism ◀
By Ted Grant
Price: £ 9.99

Pub. Date: 2002
Format: Paperback
No. Pages: 310
ISBN: 190000710X

▶ **Lenin and Trotsky -
What they really stood for**
By Alan Woods and Ted Grant
Price: £ 8.95

Pub. Date: 2000
Format: Paperback
No. Pages: 221
ISBN: 8492183268

Bolshevism - The Road to Revolution ◀
By Alan Woods
Price: £ 15.00
Pub. Date: 1999
Format: Paperback
No. Pages: 636
ISBN: 1900007053

▸ History of the Russian Revolution
By Leon Trotsky

Pub. Date: 2007
Format: Paperback

Vol 1
No. Pages: 530
ISBN: 1 9000 07 26 6
Price £11.99

Vol2
No. Pages: 349
ISBN: 1 9000 07 27 4
Price £10.99

Vol3
No. Pages: 413
ISBN: 1 9000 07 28 2
Price £11.99

The Venezuelan Revolution - A Marxist Perspective ◂
By Alan Woods
Price: £ 7.99
Pub. Date: April 2005
Format: Paperback
No. Pages: 180
ISBN: 1 9000 0721 5

▸ Ireland - Republicanism and Revolution
By Alan Woods
Price: £ 6.99

Pub. Date: 2005
Format: Paperback
No. Pages: 137
ISBN: 1 9000 07 20 7

▶ Russia - From Revolution to Counter-Revolution
By Ted Grant
(out of print)

Pub. Date: 1999
Format: Paperback
No. Pages: 636
ISBN: 1900007053

My Life ◀
By Leon Trotsky
Price: £ 14.99
Pub. Date: 2004
Format: Paperback
No. Pages: 512

▶ The Permanent Revolution and Results and Prospects
By Leon Trotsky
Price: £ 9.99

Pub. Date: 2004
Format: Paperback
No. Pages: 277
ISBN: 8492183268

1905 ◀
By Leon Trotsky
Price £11.99
Publisher: Wellred Publications
Pub. Date: 2005
Format: Paperback
No. Pages: 350
ISBN: 1900007223

▶ Not Guilty -
Dewey Commission Report
Price £14.99

Pub. Date: January 2005
Format: Paperback
No. Pages: 432
ISBN: 1 9000 07 19 3

Marxism and the USA ◀
By Alan Woods
Price: £ 9.99
Pub. Date: 2006
Format: Paperback
No. Pages: 154
ISBN: 1 90000724 X

▶ Dialectics of Nature
By Frederick Engels
Price £14.99

Pub. Date: 2006
Format: Paperback
No. Pages: 410
ISBN: 1 9000 0723 1